Managerial Economics

A Problem Solving Approach

Luke M. Froeb
Vanderbilt University

Brian T. McCann
Purdue University

SOUTH-WESTERN
CENGAGE Learning™

Australia · Brazil · Canada · Mexico · Singapore · Spain · United Kingdom · United States

SOUTH-WESTERN
CENGAGE Learning™

Managerial Economics: A Problem-Solving Approach

Luke M. Froeb   Brian T. McCann

VP/Editorial Director:
Jack W. Calhoun

Editor-in-Chief:
Alex von Rosenberg

Sr. Acquisitions Editor:
Mike Worls

Sr. Content Project Manager:
Cliff Kallemeyn

Marketing Manager:
Jennifer Garamy

Marketing Coordinator:
Courtney Wolstoncroft

Technology Project Manager:
Dana Cowden

Cover and Internal Designer:
Beckymeyer Design
Cincinnati, Ohio

Art Director:
Michelle Kunkler

Sr. First Print Buyer:
Sandee Milewski

Printer:
West Group
Eagan, MN

Cover Image:
@Medioimages/Getty Images, INC.

Library of Congress Control
Number: 2007921344

For more information about our
products, contact us at:

Cengage Learning
Customer & Sales Support
1-800-354-9706

South-Western Cengage Learning
5191 Natorp Boulevard
Mason, OH 45040
USA

For Lisa, Halley, Jake, and Chris

BRIEF CONTENTS

TABLE OF CONTENTS

Preface

Teaching Students to Solve Problems
by Luke Froeb

When I began teaching at a business school, I taught economics as I had learned it, using formal models and public policy applications. My students could not see its relevance to business, and our late dean, Marty Geisel, threatened to fire me unless customer satisfaction increased.

So I abandoned the public policy applications and began teaching students to exploit inefficiency as a money-making opportunity. I changed from a model-based to a problem-based pedagogy by focusing on business mistakes. I used models sparingly and only to the extent that they helped students to solve business problems. I reduced the analysis to a single lesson[1] that tied the different applications together. These changes kept me from getting fired, but students still had trouble making the connection between what I taught and the kind of decisions they faced at work.

The missing link was provided by the so-called Rochester[2] approach to organizational design. Traditional economic tools teach students to identify profitable decisions, while organizational design shows students how to implement them. Teaching one without the other may explain why students have difficulty seeing the relevance of economics to business. Identifying profitable decisions without being able to implement them, or implementing decisions without knowing whether they are profitable, are both fruitless exercises.

Organizational design is particularly useful for teaching students the two components of problem solving. First, to figure out what is wrong, students learn to ask three questions:

- Who made the bad decision?
- Did the decision maker have enough information to make a good decision?
- Did he or she have the incentive to do so?

Answers to these three questions will suggest changes in the organizational design focused on

- letting someone else make the decision,

---

[1] The art of business is to find an asset in a lower-valued use and figure out how to profitably move it to higher-valued use.

[2] Michael Jensen and William Meckling, *A Theory of the Firm: Governance, Residual Claims and Organizational Forms* (Cambridge, MA: Harvard University Press, 2000); and James Brickley, Clifford Smith, and Jerold Zimmerman, *Managerial Economics and Organizational Architecture* (Chicago: Irwin, 1997).

- changing the information flow, or
- changing incentives.

I wrote this book only because there was no other that used these ideas to teach MBAs. It differs from traditional managerial economics textbooks in several respects. First, it's relatively short. I cover only the most important ideas because teaching a few ideas well is better than teaching many poorly. In addition, the short text lets professors customize courses with their own supplementary material, knowing that each student, regardless of his or her background, should be able to read the book cover to cover and walk away with a basic understanding of how to use the rational-actor paradigm to identify problems and ways to fix them.

Second, the book follows a problem-based pedagogy rather than the traditional model-based pedagogy. I pose a problem, like the *fixed-cost fallacy*, and then give students just enough analytic structure to compute the costs and the benefits of various solutions. I then ask them to solve similar problems. Teaching students to solve problems, rather than learn models, is a much better way to teach economics in a terminal MBA economics course. To see this, ask yourself which of the following ideas is more likely to stay with your students after the class is over: the fixed-cost fallacy or that the partial derivative of profit with respect to price is independent of fixed costs.

A problem-based pedagogy means that we spend less time on formal models. As mentioned earlier, students find it very difficult to relate to abstract models because they learn differently than we do.[3] Second, and more important, some models aren't very useful for solving real problems. For example, I think price-taking behavior and upward-sloping marginal costs are rare. In my 10 years of investigating mergers at the Federal Trade Commission and the Department of Justice, we always asked managers of nonmerging firms whether they could double output at the same marginal cost in the event of a postmerger price increase. They invariably answered yes. So, I think the scope of firms is limited *not* by upward-sloping marginal costs but rather by downward-sloping marginal revenue. Because of this, I give short shrift to the study of price-taking firm behavior. This means that I have to motivate the supply–demand model at the aggregate level by showing students that it is a good description of aggregate (industry-level) behavior even though it may not accurately describe individual firm or buyer behavior.

Third, the book does not devote much space to teaching the mechanical aspects of benefit–cost analysis. Because the only way to learn this material is by doing problems, it is better taught online using interactive programs, like the managerial economics module of South-Western Cengage Learning's MBAPrimer.com or Samuel Baker's *Economic Interactive Tutorials*.[4] These programs teach an idea, like

---

[3] Charles C. Schroeder, "New Students—New Learning Styles," *Change* 25, no. 5 (September 1993): 21.
[4] http://hadm.sph.sc.edu/Courses/Econ/Tutorials.html.

marginal analysis, and then immediately ask the student to apply the idea by filling in cells on a spreadsheet. At the end of each section, students take a quiz to test themselves. If they do not know the answer to a question, they can scroll back to the relevant material. Then, when students are confident that they understand the material, I give them an online closed-book quiz on the same material.

Using online material to teach the tools of benefit–cost analysis accomplishes two things. First, it allows students to learn them at their own pace. This allows a professor to teach students of varying backgrounds in the same class. Those with good analytic ability or economics training can cruise through the online material without much effort but still learn a lot from the in-class business applications, while students with less aptitude or training will devote more time to learning the tools. Second, it allows residential MBA programs to differentiate their classes from those in online programs by using scarce class time to teach students how to apply economic tools. For example, I begin each class with a problem and cold-call students until they figure out what is wrong and how to fix it. For those of you teaching in executive MBA programs, make sure to reserve some class time for group presentations built around the group homework problems. You will hear some great stories from your students, and they will see an immediate payoff from the class by applying the tools to their own companies. The group problems are less effective for students with less work experience, so I use them sparingly, or not at all, in the regular MBA program.

Finally, as mentioned, the book integrates organizational design into the traditional economic analysis. Identifying a problem using benefit–cost analysis is only the first step. Fixing it requires an understanding of how organizations behave.

This book is aimed at three different audiences. First, it's accessible to anyone who can read and think clearly. But because the pedagogy is built around business problems, the book is most effective for those with work experience. Second, the book is useful for executive education, in both degree and nondegree programs. Third, it works in a full-time MBA program. In the degree programs, I supplement the material in the book with online interactive exercises.

Anyone who has read *Economics in One Lesson* will recognize the book as an homage to Henry Hazlitt. As he does in his book, I try to impart the intuition of economics with problems and anecdotes. I try for the same directness, simplicity, and clarity but wrap the stories in a stronger analytic framework, more suited to a course in a degree program.

I wish to acknowledge 13 classes of MBA students, without whom none of this would have been possible—or necessary. Many of my former students will recognize their companies in the notes. The stories in the book are from students and are for teaching purposes only.

I owe a special debt to my coauthor Brian McCann not only for contributing significant amounts of new material to the book, but also for re-writing and editing all of the text, in addition to lecturing to my Vanderbilt MBA class while I was on leave as chief economist at the Federal Trade Commission.

Thanks to everyone who contributed, knowingly or not, to the book. I owe intellectual debts to former colleagues at the U.S. Department of Justice (among them, Cindy Alexander, Tim Brennan, Ken Heyer, Kevin James, Bruce Kobayahsi, and Greg Werden); to former colleagues at the Federal Trade Commission (among them Bill Blumenthal, Bob Brogan, Jerry Butters, Liz Callison, James Cooper, Susan Creighton, Pat DeGraba, Tim Deyak, Jeff Fischer, Mark Frankena, Hadeishi Hajime, Dan Hosken, David Hyman, Pauline Ippolito, Jim Lacko, Bill Kovacic, Tom Krattenmaker, Rob McMillan, Joe Mulholland, Tim Muris, Dan O'Brien, Maureen Ohlhausen, Jan Pappalardo, John Parisi, Lydia Parnes, Paul Pautler, Lee Peeler, Dave Schmidt, Joel Schrag, Lou Silvia, Chris Taylor, Steve Tenn, Randy Tritell, and Mike Vita); to colleagues at Vanderbilt (among them, Germain Boer, Jim Bradford, Bill Christie, Mark Cohen, Myeong Chang, Craig Lewis, Doug Meeks, Rick Oliver, David Rados, Steven Tschantz, David Scheffman, Mikhael Shor, and Bart Victor); and to numerous friends and colleagues who offered suggestions, problems, and anecdotes for the book, among them, Pat Bajari, Roger Brinner, the Honorable Jim Cooper, Matthew Dixon Cowles, Jeff and Jenny Hubbard, Dan Kessler, Jim Overdahl, Mike Saint, Bill Shughart, Whitney Tilson, and Susan Woodward. I owe intellectual and pedagogical debts to Armen Alchian and William Allen,[5] Henry Hazlitt,[6] Shlomo Maital,[7] John MacMillan,[8] Steven Landsburg,[9] Ivan Png,[10] Victor Tabbush,[11] Michael Jensen and William Meckling,[12] and James Brickley, Clifford Smith, and Jerold Zimmerman.[13] Thanks as well to everyone who helped guide us through the publishing process, including Alex von Rosenberg, Michael Worls, Jennifer Garamy, Cliff Kallemeyn, Trish Taylor, and Emily Thompson.

[5] Armen Alchian and William Allen, *Exchange and Production*, 3rd ed. (Belmont, CA: Wadsworth, 1983).

[6] Henry Hazlitt, *Economics in One Lesson* (New York: Crown, 1979).

[7] Shlomo Maital, *Executive Economics: Ten Essential Tools for Managers* (New York: Free Press, 1994).

[8] John McMillan, *Games, Strategies, and Managers* (Oxford: Oxford University Press, 1992).

[9] Steven Landsburg, *The Armchair Economist: Economics and Everyday Life* (New York: Free Press, 1993).

[10] Ivan Png, *Managerial Economics* (Malden, MA: Blackwell, 1998).

[11] http://www.mbaprimer.com.

[12] Michael Jensen and William Meckling, *A Theory of the Firm: Governance, Residual Claims and Organizational Forms* (Cambridge, MA: Harvard University Press, 2000).

[13] James Brickley, Clifford Smith, and Jerold Zimmerman, *Managerial Economics and Organizational Architecture* (Chicago: Irwin, 1997).

PROBLEM SOLVING AND DECISION MAKING

Chapter 1

Introduction: What This Book Is About

In 1992, a young geologist was preparing a bid recommendation for an oil tract on the outer continental shelf in the Gulf of Mexico. He suspected that this new tract of land contained a large accumulation of oil because the adjacent tract contained several productive wells—wells that his company, Oil Ventures International (OVI), already owned. The geologist estimated both the amount of oil the tract was likely to contain and what competitors were likely to bid; then, given these estimates, he recommended a bid of $5 million. No competitors had neighboring tracts, so none suspected a large accumulation of oil.

Surprisingly, OVI's senior management ignored the recommendation and submitted a bid of $20 million, and the company won the tract—over the next-highest bid of $750,000.

If the board of directors hired you as a management consultant to review the bidding procedures at OVI, how would you proceed? What questions would you ask? Where would you begin your investigation?

You'd find it difficult to gather information from those closest to the bidding. Senior management would be suspicious, if not openly hostile. No one likes to be singled out for bidding $19 million more than necessary to win. Likewise, our junior geologist would be reluctant to criticize his superiors. You might be able to rely on your experience—provided that you had ever run into a similar problem. But when you have no experience or when facing novel problems, you'd be lost.

Our goal in this book is to give you the tools you need to complete an assignment like this one.

PROBLEM SOLVING

To solve a problem like OVI's, you have to figure out what's wrong, and then you have to figure out how to fix it. Here, you'd begin by determining whether the $20 million bid was too high at the time it was made, not just in retrospect. Next, if the bid was too high at the time it was made, you'd have to figure out why the senior managers overbid and find ways to make sure they don't do it again.

Both steps require that you predict how people are likely to behave in different circumstances—this is where the economic content of the book comes in. The one thing that unites economists is their use of the **rational-actor paradigm** to predict behavior. Simply put, this paradigm says that people act rationally, optimally, and self-interestedly. The paradigm not only helps you figure out why people behave the way they do but also suggests how to motivate them to change. To change behavior, you have to change people's self-interests; you can do that by changing incentives.

Let's go back to OVI's story. After his company won the auction, our geologist increased the company's oil reserves by the amount of oil estimated to be in the tract. But then the company drilled a well that was essentially dry. Furthermore, the company could access what little oil there was in the new tract through existing wells, so the acquisition did nothing to increase the size of the company's oil reserves. Our geologist reevaluated the reservoir map and then reduced the reserve estimate by two-thirds. Senior management, however, rejected the revised estimate and directed the geologist to do what he could to increase the size of the estimated reserves. So he revised the reservoir map again and added ''additional'' reserves to the company's asset base. Several months later, OVI's senior managers resigned, collecting bonuses tied to the increase in oil reserves that had accumulated during their tenure.

The bonus plan is the key piece of evidence that ties all the evidence together. You can see that both the overbidding and the effort to inflate the reserve estimate were rational, self-interested responses to incentives. Even if you didn't know about the geologist's bid recommendation, you'd still suspect that the senior managers overbid because they had the incentive to do so. Senior managers' ability to manipulate the reserve estimate made it difficult for shareholders and their representatives on the board of directors to spot the mistake.

To fix this problem, you have to find a better way to align the managers' incentives with company goals.[1] You want to find a way to reward management for increasing profitability, not for acquiring reserves. This is not as easy as it sounds because it's difficult to measure a manager's contribution to company profitability. You can do this measurement subjectively, with annual performance reviews, or objectively, using company earnings or stock price appreciation as performance metrics. Each of these performance measures has problems, as we'll see in later chapters.

In general, rational, self-interested rational actors make mistakes for one of two reasons. Either they do not have enough information to make good decisions,

[1] James Brickley, Clifford Smith, and Jerold Zimmerman, "The Economics of Organizations," *Journal of Financial Economics* 8, no. 2 (Summer 1995): 19–31, for a fuller exposition of the basic principles of organizational design.

or they lack incentives to do so. Accordingly, when you're using the rational-actor paradigm to find the cause of a problem, you need ask only three questions:

- Who is making the bad decision?
- Does the decision maker have enough information to make a good decision?
- Does the decision maker have the incentives to make a good decision?

Answers to these three questions will immediately suggest ways to fix the problem by

- letting someone else make the decision,
- giving more information to the decision maker, or
- changing the decision makers' incentives.

In OVI's case, we see that (1) senior management made the bad decision to overbid; (2) they had enough information to make a good decision, but (3) they didn't have the incentive to do so. These answers suggest changing incentives as one potential way to fix the problem.

When reading about various business mistakes in this book, you should ask yourself these three questions to see if you can diagnose and fix the problems before reading the answers. By the time you finish the book, this kind of analysis should become second nature.

ETHICS AND ECONOMICS

Using the rational-actor paradigm in this way—to change behavior by changing incentives—makes some students uncomfortable because it seems to deny the altruism, affection, and personal ethics that most people use to guide their behavior. These students resist learning the paradigm because they think it implicitly endorses self-interested behavior, as if the primary purpose of economics were to teach students to behave rationally, optimally, and selfishly.

These students would probably agree with a *Washington Post* editorial, "When It Comes to Ethics, B-Schools Get an F,"[2] which blames business schools in general, and economists in particular, for the ethical lapses at Enron, WorldCom, and other companies.

> *A subtle but damaging factor in this is the dominance of economists at business schools. Although there is no evidence that economists are personally less ethical than members of other disciplines, approaching the world through the dollar sign does make people more cynical.*

What these students and the author, a former Harvard ethics professor, do not understand is that to control unethical behavior, you first have to understand

---

[2] Amitai Etzioni, "When It Comes to Ethics, B-Schools Get an F," *Washington Post*, August 4, 2002.

why it occurs. When we analyze problems like the one at OVI, we're *not* encouraging students to behave opportunistically. Rather, we're teaching them to anticipate opportunistic behavior and showing them how to design organizations that are less susceptible to it. Remember, the rational-actor paradigm is only a tool for analyzing behavior, not advice on how to live your life.

Economists generally share another common assumption: that the objective function of firms, and of their managers, is profit maximization for shareholders. Nobel laureate Milton Friedman stated this point succinctly: "There is one and only one social responsibility of business—to use its resources and engage in activities designed to increase its profit so long as it stays within the rules of the game, which is to say, engages in open and free competition without deception or fraud."[3] Economists believe that open and free competition between profit-maximizing firms results in more efficient allocation of a society's resources. We acknowledge, however, that opinions differ on this issue. Consider this recent story from *The Wall Street Journal* (*WSJ*).[4]

When Notre Dame entered the 2006 season as one of the top-ranked football teams in the country, demand for local hotels during home games rose dramatically. In response, local hotels nearest the school raised room rates. According to *The Wall Street Journal*, the Hampton Inn charged $400 a night on football weekends for a room that cost travelers only $129 a night on nonfootball dates. Rates climbed even higher for games against top-ranked foes. For the game against the University of Michigan, the South Bend Marriott charged $649 per night—$500 more than its normal weekend rate of $149.

On a campus founded by Jesuits where many students dedicate their year after graduation to working with the underprivileged, these high prices alarm some observers. *The Wall Street Journal* quotes one observer, Joe Holt, a former Jesuit priest who teaches ethics in the school's executive MBA program: "It is an 'act of moral abdication' for businesses to pretend they have no choice but to charge as much as they can based on supply and demand." The article further reports Mr. Holt's intention to use the example of rising hotel rates on football weekends for a case study in his class on the integration of business and values.

Versions of this debate—the one between those who take a moral or ethical approach to business and those who are simply trying to make money—have been going on in this country since its founding. Economists take a utilitarian, or consequentialist, approach to behavior by comparing it with the implied alternative of *not* raising prices. Economists would analyze the implied "constant

---

[3] Milton Friedman, *Capitalism and Freedom* (Chicago: University of Chicago Press, 1962).
[4] Ilan Brat, "Notre Dame Football Introduces Its Fans to Inflationary Spiral," *The Wall Street Journal*, September 7, 2006.

price" alternative, then show, using supply–demand analysis, that that if prices did not rise, the consequence would be excess demand for hotel rooms. Would-be guests would find their rooms rationed, perhaps on a first-come/first-served basis. Or, possibly, "arbitrageurs" could set up a black market, by making early reservations, then "selling" their rooms to customers willing to pay the market-clearing price. Also, without the ability to earn additional profit during times of scarcity, hotels would have smaller incentives to add new capacity to the market by building additional rooms.

Ethicists like Notre Dame's Joe Holt, on the other hand, might object to the practice of raising prices in times of shortage.[5] The first objection is a simple beneficence argument. Property rights might give a company the *option* of increasing prices, but possession of these rights does not relieve the company of its *obligations* to be concerned about the consequences of its choices. We might label this the *Spider Man principle*: With great power comes great responsibility. The laws of capitalist systems allow corporations to amass significant power; in turn, society should demand a high level of responsibility from corporations.

The second objection is related to the first, although it's often used in the context of enacting regulations that take away or limit individual property rights. When markets fail or when market adjustment costs are unfairly distributed, we may need to place restrictions on market mechanisms. In other words, markets need constraints to prevent harmful outcomes. The Great Potato Famine in Ireland is a frequently cited example of such a potential harmful outcome.

In this text, our perspective is consistent with Friedman's view. Firms serve consumers and society best by engaging in free and open competition within legal limits while attempting to maximize profit. This view is in no way a license to engage in illegal behavior—nor is it an attempt to deny that concerns exist about the ethical dimension of business, especially in today's society. Although a full treatment of the ethical dimensions of business is beyond the scope of this book, we should all acknowledge that reasonable people have disagreed for millennia on what constitutes "ethical" behavior, and they are likely to continue to do so, even after this book is long forgotten.

ECONOMICS IN JOB INTERVIEWS

If this well-reasoned introduction doesn't motivate you to learn economics, read the following interview questions—all from real interviews of my students. These questions should awaken interest in the material for those of you who think of economics as merely an obstacle between you and a six-figure salary.

---

[5] We thank Bart Victor for his enumeration of these objections.

-----Original Message-----

From: "Student A"
Sent: Tuesday, January 18, 2000 1:22 PM
Subject: Economics Interview Questions

I got a question from Compaq last year for a marketing internship position that partially dealt with sunk costs. It was a "true" case question where the interviewer asked the following, using the Internet to pull up the actual products as he asked the question.

I am the product manager for the new X type server with these great features. It is to be launched next month at a cost of $5,500. Dell launched their new Y type server last week; it has the same features (and even a few more) for a cost of $4,500. To date, Compaq has put over $2.5 million in the development process for this server, and as such my manager is expecting above normal returns for the investment.

My question to you is "what advice would you give to me on how to approach the launch of the product, i.e. do I go ahead with it at the current price, if at all, even though Dell has a better product out that is less expensive, not forgetting the fact that I have spent all the development money and my boss expects me to report a super return?"

I laughed at the question because it was the very first thing we spoke about in the interview, catching me off-guard a bit. He wanted to see if I got caught worrying about all the development costs in giving advice to scrap the launch or continue ahead as planned. (I'm not an idiot and could see that coming a mile away...thanks to economics, right?!!!)

```
-----Original Message-----

From: "Student B"
Sent: Tuesday, January 18, 2000 1:37 PM
Subject: Economics Interview Questions

I got questions regarding transfer price within entities of a
company. What prices could be used and why...

-----Original Message-----

From: "Student C"
Sent: Tuesday, January 18, 2000 1:28 PM
Subject: Economics Interview Questions

You are a basketball coach with five seconds on the clock, and
you are losing by two points. You have the ball and can take only
one more shot (there is no chance of a rebound). There is a 70%
chance of making a two-pointer, which would send the game into
overtime with each team having an equal chance of winning.
There is only a forty percent chance of making a three-pointer
(winning if made). Should you shoot the two- or the three-point
shot?
```

SUMMARY & HOMEWORK PROBLEMS

SUMMARY OF MAIN POINTS

- Problem solving requires two steps: First, you identify profitable decisions (figure out what's wrong); then you determine how to implement them (figure out how to fix it).
- The **rational-actor paradigm** assumes that people act rationally, optimally, and self-interestedly. To change behavior, you have to change people's view of what's in their own self-interests by changing incentives.
- A well-designed organization is one in which employee incentives are aligned with organizational goals.
- Good incentives are created by rewarding good performance.

- You can analyze any problem by asking three questions: Who is making the bad decision? Do the decision makers have enough information to make a good decision? Do the decision makers have incentives to make a good decision? Answers to these questions will suggest solutions centered on letting someone else make the decision, giving the decision maker more information, or changing incentives.

MULTIPLE-CHOICE QUESTIONS

See the end of the next chapter for multiple-choice questions.

INDIVIDUAL PROBLEMS

See the end of the next chapter for individual homework problems.

GROUP PROBLEMS

See the end of the next chapter for group homework problems.

Chapter 2

The One Lesson of Business

Recently, both Beth Israel Deaconess Medical Center (affiliated with Harvard Medical School) and New York University Hospital refused to perform kidney transplants for two seriously ill patients.[1] The reason? The kidneys were "directed donations" from strangers rather than anonymous donor organs or kidneys from close relatives. A number of hospitals refuse to support such directed donation programs. They hold this position despite the fact that more than 66,000 Americans are on the waiting list for kidney donations, and some 40,000 of those have been waiting for more than a year to receive a kidney. Unfortunately, "the most common way to get off the list is to die."[2] The problem afflicts rich and poor alike because it's illegal to buy or sell human kidneys in the United States.

Let's start this chapter by asking the following question: Why is buying or selling human kidneys in the United States illegal? Here are some common, and conflicting, views on the question. Choose the answer that best reflects your views.

- **A.** Trafficking in body parts is morally abhorrent and should be condemned as such. Only libertarians and investment bankers would trust markets to make such life-and-death decisions.
- **B.** Do-gooders and religious leaders don't understand that outlawing kidney sales reduces the quantity of kidneys available for transplant. I hold them responsible for the thousands of patients who die each year waiting for donated kidneys.
- **C.** Who cares why it's illegal? If I can borrow $100 million at 20% interest, I can buy a hospital ship, anchor it in international waters, and begin selling kidneys. I can set up a database to match donors to recipients, broker sales, and fly in experienced transplant teams. If I charge $200,000 and earn 10% on each transaction, the break-even quantity is just 1,000 transplants each year. This represents about 1% of the potential demand in the United States alone.

[1] See Virginia Postrel, "'Unfair' Kidney Donations," *Forbes*, June 5, 2006.
[2] Ibid.

If you're like most people, you answered A. If you paid attention during your economics class, you have the analytical tools to know that B is correct. But rather than wading into the ethical debate[3] between A and B, the purpose of this book is to show you how to solve the problem profitably (answer C). Those of you starting at B have a slight edge, but getting to C requires as much creativity and imagination as analytic ability.

Students who've had some economics training will find the material in this chapter especially useful because it shows how *managerial economics* differs from its public policy cousin, microeconomics, or equivalently, how business differs from economics.

CAPITALISM AND WEALTH

To identify money-making opportunities, we first have to understand how wealth is created and destroyed.

Wealth is created when assets are moved from lower- to higher-valued uses.

An individual's **value** for a good or service is the amount of money he or she is willing to pay for it.[4] This willingness requires both desire for the good and the ability to pay for it.[5] If we adopt the linguistic convention that buyers are male and the sellers, female, we say that a buyer's value for an item is how much he will pay

---

[3] Response from a Methodist theologian:

1. A principle derived from biblical and church traditions is that what is necessary for life should not be a commodity (or exhaustively a commodity).
2. Are you sure there is such a thing as a pure market that does not manipulate? Aren't most persons who would sell one of their own kidneys under the duress of poverty?
3. A second kidney—one of a pair—may be somewhat different from other vital organs, but the loss of a kidney does put one in greater jeopardy. We do our best to block other markets that decrease the health prospects of persons.
4. The tradition offers many reservations not only against selling a person (an embodied spirit) but also a part of this embodiedness.
5. Why has the mystery of giving one's life for the sake of another life become such an aporia for us?

[4] This definition of value as "willingness to pay" carries strong normative connotations, just as other definitions of value carry strong alternative normative connotations. For example, under Communism, a labor theory of value is used. Value depends on how much labor produced it. This value (how much labor is embodied in the good) has an independent "existence" even if no one wants to buy the good. This can lead to situations where goods are produced that nobody "wants."

The defining tenet of Communism is "from each according to his ability; to each according to his need." Communism is bad at creating wealth because it allocates goods according to "needs," not "wants," and because it's tough to gauge how much people "need" goods. Individuals have great incentive to claim they are "needier" than they really are. In the political arena, groups compete for government funds by claiming they are the "neediest."

Economists dislike the word *need* because it is so often used to manipulate others into giving away something. Listen to news reports about proposed government spending cuts. Most often those affected claim they "need" the programs targeted for elimination. That sounds better than saying they "want" the programs.

The definitions of value differ because Communism and Socialism are more concerned with the distribution of wealth than with the creation of wealth, which is capitalism's greatest concern. While capitalism is concerned with making the proverbial "pie" as large as possible, Socialism and Communism are concerned more about how to slice up that pie.

[5] It is the ability-to-pay component of value that is behind most critiques of capitalism. Unless you have enough money to purchase an item, then you do not value it.

for it, his "top dollar." Likewise, a seller won't accept less than her value, "cost," or "bottom line."

The biggest advantage of capitalism is that it creates wealth by letting people follow their self-interests.[6] A buyer willingly buys if the price is below his value, and a seller sells for the same selfish reason—because the price is above her value. Both buyer and seller gain; otherwise, they would not transact.

Voluntary transactions create wealth.

Suppose that a buyer values a house at $130,000 and a seller at $120,000. If they can agree on a price—say, $128,000—the seller receives $8,000 more for the house than she's willing to sell it for. The difference between the agreed-on price and the seller's value is called **seller surplus.** Likewise, the buyer receives an item worth $2,000 more than he is willing to pay for it; therefore, he has a **buyer surplus.** The total surplus or *gains from trade* created by the transaction is the sum of buyer and seller surplus ($10,000), the difference between the buyer's and the seller's values.

The following are examples of wealth-creating, voluntary transactions:

- Internet auctions, like those on eBay, have replaced traditional selling mechanisms (like garage sales and newspaper classified ads) because Internet auctions are much better at matching buyers and sellers. An enthusiastic collector in Boise can now buy an item that a Shreveport resident might have otherwise relegated to the trash heap for lack of local interest.[7]
- Corporate raiders buy up companies and sell off their component pieces. They earn money only if the value of the sum of the pieces is higher than the value of the company as a whole.
- When consumers purchase insurance, they pay an insurance company to assume risk for them. In this context, you can think of risk as a "bad," the opposite of a "good," moving from consumers willing to pay to get rid of it to insurance companies willing to assume it for a fee.
- Factory owners purchase labor from workers, borrow capital from investors, and sell manufactured products to consumers. In essence, factory owners are intermediaries who move labor and capital from lower-valued to higher-valued uses, determined by consumers' willingness to pay for the labor and capital embodied in manufactured products.

---

[6] This is the idea behind the French phrase *laissez-faire* (leave them alone).

[7] Because of Internet technology, auctions are being used to trade more and different types of goods than ever before. According to a *New York Times* article, less than 10% of the sellers are responsible for more than 80% of the sales. "Power sellers" sell items like collectible dolls, cards and coins, jewelry, and overstocked clothing. See, for example, Lisa Guernsey, "The Power behind the Auctions," *New York Times,* August 20, 2000, section 3, 1; David Lucking-Reiley, "Auctions on the Internet: What's Being Auctioned, and How?" *Journal of Industrial Economics* 48, no. 3 (September 2000): 227–252; and Miriam Herschlag and Rami Zwick, "Internet Auctions—A Popular and Professional Literature Review," *Quarterly Journal of Electronic Commerce* 1, no. 2 (2000): 161–186.

- AIDS patients will often sell their life insurance policies to investors at a discount of 50% or more. The transaction allows patients to collect money from investors, who must wait until the patient dies to collect from the insurance company. This transaction moves money across time, from investors who do not mind waiting, to those who do mind waiting.

I always ask my students to name the individual who has created the most wealth during their lifetimes. To answer this question, you might begin with the biggest and most valuable assets in our economy—corporations. Until the late 1970s, it was very difficult to move corporate assets to higher-valued uses. At that time, the invention of new financial instruments, like junk bonds, allowed investors to buy up underperforming companies, fire current management, and do something more productive with the corporate assets. Michael Milken was instrumental in the development of the "market for corporate control."

How do you create wealth? Which assets do you move to higher-valued uses?

DO MERGERS MOVE ASSETS TO HIGHER-VALUED USES?

In 2006, Dell purchased Alienware, a manufacturer of liquid-cooled, high-end gaming computers. Dell planned to leave the design, sales, marketing, and support of Alienware computers under the control of a separate division, run by the acquired firm's management team; but Dell planned to take control of their manufacture. By plugging Alienware into the Dell supply chain, Dell hoped to be able to manufacture Alienware computers much faster and at lower cost than Alienware did. For this reason, the acquired company was worth more to Dell than it was to Alienware's shareholders. In other words, the acquisition moved the assets of Alienware to a *higher-valued use*.

For most mergers, however, the value creation is not nearly so obvious. Following announcement of a merger, the stock price of the acquired firm typically increases, but the stock price of the acquiring firm simultaneously decreases. And more often than not, the fall in value of the acquiring firm is bigger than the increase in value of the acquired firm, so that the merger appears to be destroying value, or moving assets to *lower-valued uses*.

This observation corresponds to the experience of regulators who enforce the antitrust laws that prevent anticompetitive mergers. The internal documents of the merging firms rarely articulate the value-creating purpose of the merger. Instead, the internal merger memos say only that the acquired firm is unusually profitable or has a large market share.[8]

---

[8] Luke Froeb, "If Merger Is the Answer, What Is the Question?," *M&A Journal* (March 2006).

But profit or share is worth just as much to the acquired company's shareholders as it is to the acquiring firm, so this motivation is not a good reason to transact. Unless some synergy—like that between Dell and Alienware—makes the acquired firm more valuable to the buyer than it is to the seller, the assets are not necessarily moving to a higher-valued use.

The movement of assets to higher-valued uses is the wealth-creating engine of capitalism. Our biggest, and most valuable, assets are corporations. The fact that we cannot document for many mergers a good reason for the movement of assets is troublesome.

DOES THE GOVERNMENT CREATE WEALTH?

Governments play a critical role in the wealth-creating process by enforcing property rights and contracts—legal mechanisms that facilitate voluntary transactions.[9] Wealth-creating transactions are more likely to occur when sellers and buyers can keep the gains from trade. The U.S. legal system, with its protections for private property, is designed to secure the gains from trade and is responsible for our nation's enormous wealth-creating ability.[10]

Conversely, the absence of property rights contributes to poverty. People living in countries with little economic freedom had an average per-capita income of just $2,560 and an average *negative* economic growth rate of 0.9%.[11] Compare these figures to the per capita income of $23,450 and a growth rate of 2.6% in countries in which citizens enjoy more economic freedom.[12] The reasons are simple: Without private property protection and contract enforcement, wealth-creating transactions are less likely to occur,[13] and this stunts development. Ironically, many poor countries survive largely on the wealth created in the so-called underground or black market economy, where transactions are hidden from the government.

Interestingly, secure property rights are also associated with measures of environmental quality and human well-being. In nations where property rights are well protected, more people have access to safe drinking water and sewage treatment and people live about 20 years longer (to 70 instead of 50).[14] In other

---

[9] "The only proper functions of a government are: the police, to protect you from criminals; the army, to protect you from foreign invaders; and the courts, to protect your property and contracts from breach or fraud by others, to settle disputes by rational rules, according to objective law." Ayn Rand, *Atlas Shrugged* (New York: Random House, 1957), 977.

[10] Tom Bethell, *The Noblest Triumph: Property and Prosperity through the Ages* (New York: St. Martin's Press, 1995).

[11] Similar findings are in Lee Hoskins and Ana I. Eiras, "Property Rights: The Key to Economic Growth," in *2002 Index of Economic Freedom,* ed. Gerald P. O'Driscoll Jr., Kim R. Holmes, and Mary Anastasia O'Grady (Washington, D.C.: Heritage Foundation and Dow Jones, 2002).

[12] James Gwartney and Robert Lawson, *The Economic Freedom of the World: 2002 Annual Report* (Vancouver: Fraser Institute, 2002).

[13] "The inherent vice of capitalism is the unequal sharing of blessings; the inherent virtue of socialism is the equal sharing of miseries" (Winston Churchill).

[14] Seth Norton, "Property Rights, the Environment, and Economic Well-Being," in *Who Owns the Environment?* ed. Peter J. Hill and Roger E. Meiners (Lanham, Md.: Rowman and Littlefield, 1998).

words, if you give people ownership to their property, they take care of it, invest in it, and keep it clean.

Peruvian economist Hernando de Soto is trying hard to convince third world governments to try this approach to fighting poverty.

> *"Imagine a country," de Soto says, "where nobody can identify who owns what, addresses cannot be verified and the rules that govern property vary from neighborhood to neighborhood, or even from street to street." This is what life is like, he says, for 80% of the people in the developing world and the former communist countries.* [15]

Professor de Soto is particularly concerned that without legal protection for private property, it is difficult for people to borrow money because they have no collateral to use for loans.

> *In the United States, up to 70% of starting businesses need credit, and they get it on the basis of some kind of real-property collateral. If you have a situation in which 90% of Peruvians in a particular sector of the economy do not have title to their property, they cannot get credit.* [16]

Without title to the property, not only do you find it difficult to get credit, but you have to spend an enormous amount of time protecting your property—often from the government itself. All of this makes it much more difficult to rise out of poverty.

Professor de Soto has encouraged governments to fight poverty with legal systems that protect private property and encourage transactions. Fortunately, his ideas are gaining credence in the world community, if only because most other approaches to fighting poverty have failed.

ECONOMICS VERSUS BUSINESS

Economics is useful to business because it shows us how to spot money-making opportunities (assets in lower-valued uses). However, economics is not easy to learn given its very formal approach and high levels of abstraction. Fortunately, the most useful ideas in economics are not that difficult. In this section we teach the big ideas of economics that will help you spot money-making opportunities.

We begin with efficiency, the Holy Grail of economics.

> *An economy is **efficient** if all assets are employed in their highest-valued uses.*

Economists obsess about efficiency. They search for assets in lower-valued uses and then suggest public policies to move them to higher-valued ones. A good policy is one that increases efficiency by facilitating the movement of assets to

---

[15] Matthew Miller, "The Poor Man's Capitalist: Hernando de Soto," *New York Times Magazine,* July 1, 2001.
[16] Interview with Hernando de Soto by Dario Fernandez-Morera at *Reason Online,* http://reason.com/DeSoto.shtml.

higher-valued uses; a bad policy is one that prevents assets from moving to higher-valued uses or, worse, moves assets to lower-valued uses.

Determining whether an economic policy is good or bad requires analyzing all of its effects—the unintended as well as the intended effects. Henry Hazlitt, former editorial page editor of *The Wall Street Journal*, reduced all of economics into a single lesson:[17]

> *The art of economics consists in looking not merely at the immediate but at the longer effects of any act or policy; it consists of tracing the consequences of that policy not merely for one group but for all groups.*[18]

In our example of the illegality of kidney trade, well-intentioned legislators were probably trying to stop what they considered immoral trade in human flesh. The one lesson of economics tells them to consider that their policy also reduced incentives to donate kidneys, which meant fewer kidneys available to save people and, consequently, more deaths. The low number of available kidneys is inefficient because live patients in need of a transplant value kidneys more highly than current kidney owners, some of whom would willingly sell their organs, provided the price were high enough.

Having identified inefficient outcomes, economists will argue for changes in public policies. Economists see inefficiency as something to be eliminated through better public policy. This focus on changing public policy is mostly irrelevant for our purposes. Businesspeople, on the other hand, see inefficiency as something to be exploited—they realize that inefficiency (like that created by bad public policy) implies opportunity. If an asset is not employed in its highest-valued use, someone can make money by moving it. In this way, business can sometimes mitigate the harmful effects of bad government policy.

Making money is simple in principle—find an asset employed in lower-valued use, buy it, and then sell it to someone who puts a higher value on it. Each underemployed asset represents a potential wealth-creating transaction.

> **The one lesson of business**: *The art of business consists of identifying assets in low-valued uses and devising ways to profitably move them to higher-valued ones.*

In other words, inefficiency implies the existence of unconsummated wealth-creating transactions. The art of business is to identify these transactions and find ways to profitably consummate them.

---

[17] Henry Hazlitt, *Economics in One Lesson* (New York: Crown, 1979).

[18] For chilling examples of the unintended consequences of government policy, read Jagdesh Bhagwati's recent book, *In Defense of Globalization* (New York: Oxford University Press, 2004). In 1993, for example, the U.S. Congress seemed likely to pass Senator Tom Harkin's Child Labor Deterrence Act, which would have banned imports of textiles made by child workers. Anticipating its passage, the Bangladeshi textile industry dismissed 50,000 children from factories. Many of these children ended up as prostitutes. Ironically, the bill, which was designed to help children, had the opposite effect.

For example, once the government banned kidney sales, it simultaneously created an incentive to try to circumvent the ban. Buying a hospital ship and sailing to international waters is just one solution. Alternatively, businesspeople have convinced several countries, among them Israel, to quietly allow brokered kidney transplants to take place within their borders.

In the following examples, I want you to first apply the "one lesson of economics" to each government policy to identify which assets end up in lower-valued uses. Next, think about applying the "one lesson of business" to devise a way to profitably move the assets to higher-valued uses.

TAXES

The government collects taxes out of the surplus created by a transaction. If the tax is larger than the surplus, the transaction will not take place. In our housing example, if a sales tax is 10%, the tax has to be at least $12,000 because the price has to be above the seller's value ($120,000). If it is paid by the seller, this pushes the seller's bottom line to $132,000, which is above the buyer's top dollar. Since the tax is more than the $10,000 surplus created by the transaction, the buyer and seller can find no price that could consummate the transaction and still pay the tax.[19]

First apply the "one lesson of economics" to determine all of the consequences of the tax, both the intended and unintended ones. The intended effect of a tax is to raise revenue for the government, but the unintended consequence of a tax is that it stops some wealth-creating transactions. If too many transactions are deterred, then raising tax rates can actually reduce tax revenue. As John F. Kennedy said, "An economy hampered by restrictive tax rates will never produce enough revenues to balance our budget—just as it will never produce enough jobs or profits." To illustrate the transaction-deterring effect of sales taxes, we look back to 1980, when Marion Barry, mayor of the District of Columbia, raised the tax rate on gasoline sold in the district by 6%. Following the tax increase, motorists stopped buying gas inside the district, and tax revenue fell.

Next, apply the "one lesson of business." All of these unconsummated transactions represent money-making opportunities to a businessperson. To make money, figure out how they can be profitably consummated. Here's an example. In 1983, Sweden imposed a 1% "turnover" (sales) tax on stock sales on the Swedish Stock Exchange. Before the tax, large institutional investors paid

---

[19] With a 10% tax, the seller receives 90% of the sales price. If her bottom line is $120,000, then the transaction price must be at least $133,333 = $120,000/0.9. If the tax is levied on the seller, her bottom-line price increases to $132,000, which is above the buyer's top dollar of $130,000. If the tax is levied on the buyer, his top dollar decreases to $118,182, which is below the seller's bottom line. The buyer is willing to pay only $130,000 after paying the tax; that is, $X(1.1) = \$130,000$ or $X = \$118,182$.

commissions that averaged 25 basis points (0.25%). The turnover tax, by itself, was four times the size of the old trading costs, and it fell most heavily on frequent traders and institutional investors with big portfolios.

After the tax was imposed, institutional traders began trading shares on the London and New York stock exchanges, and the number of transactions on the Swedish Stock Exchange fell by 40%. Smart brokers recognized this opportunity and profited by moving their trades to London and New York. The Swedish government finally removed the turnover tax in 1990, but the Swedish Stock Exchange has never recovered its former vitality.

SUBSIDIES

The opposite of a tax is a subsidy. By encouraging low-value consumers to buy or high-value sellers to sell, subsidies destroy wealth by moving assets from higher- to lower-valued uses—in exactly the wrong direction.

For example, government-subsidized flood insurance creates an incentive to build houses in flood plains or in low coastal areas susceptible to flooding. Without the subsidy, only people who place a very high value on living in these areas will build houses there. They are the only ones willing to pay the high costs of flood insurance.

However, with subsidized insurance, more people build houses in the flood plain. Since these homeowners do not bear the full costs of their actions, they end up building houses whose value is less than their cost, when you include the cost of insurance.

Economists label these transactions as inefficient—we know that these transactions destroy wealth because without the subsidy, the houses would not have been built. Instead, the money would have been spent on different and higher-valued uses. To see this, we could offer each potential home buyer a payment equal to the amount of the subsidy. If they would rather spend the money on something besides flood insurance, then clearly the money could be channeled toward a higher-valued use.

The one lesson of business alerts us to the fact that the inefficiency created by a subsidy represents a potential money-making opportunity. To see this, let's turn to a simple example: health insurance that fully subsidizes visits to the doctor. If you get a cold, you go to the doctor, who charges the insurance company $200 for your care. Is this a wealth-creating transaction? (Hint: Would you rather self-medicate and keep the $200 or visit the doctor?) If employees would rather suffer at home and keep the $200, then this subsidy destroys wealth.

As an employer offering health insurance to your workers, how could you profit from stopping this wealth-destroying transaction? Employers could profit by offering workers insurance that requires a deductible or copayment. These fees would stop low-value doctor visits and dramatically reduce the cost of insurance. Employers could keep the money or simply raise workers' wages (by the amount they save on insurance) to attract better workers.

PRICE CONTROLS

*A **price control** is a regulation that allows trade only at certain prices.*

Two types of price controls exist: **price ceilings,** which outlaw trade at prices above the ceiling, and **price floors,** which outlaw trade at prices below the floor. The prohibition on buying and selling kidneys is a form of price ceiling. Americans are allowed to buy and sell kidneys—but only at a price of zero or less.

Price floors above the buyer's top dollar and price ceilings below a seller's bottom line deter wealth-creating transactions.[20] In our kidney example, potential kidney sellers are deterred from selling because they can do so only at a price of zero.

Rent control in New York City is another example of a price ceiling. Potential tenants who are willing to pay more than the price ceiling and potential landlords who are willing to rent at prices above the ceiling are deterred from transacting. The price control destroys wealth by preventing the movement of apartments to higher-valued uses.

Price controls also create money-making opportunities. For example, the Federal Reserve's Regulation Q (enforced until the mid-1970s) placed a 5.25% price ceiling on interest rates that U.S. banks paid to depositors. This price control deterred wealth-creating transactions between consumers willing to lend at a rate higher than 5.25% and borrowers willing to borrow at a higher rate. As intermediaries between lenders and borrowers, banks had a big incentive to try to circumvent the regulation. U.S. banks began to offer nonprice incentives, like toasters, to attract additional deposits. And foreign banks, not subject to U.S. regulation, offered dollar-denominated savings accounts to U.S. depositors at higher interest rates. The success of these dollar-denominated savings accounts, called *eurodollars,* in attracting U.S. deposits eventually forced the Federal Reserve to abandon Regulation Q.

Price controls on credit card interest rates create a similar profit opportunity. In the 1970s, credit card companies faced ceilings on the amount of interest they could charge for credit card debt. This led them to deny credit cards to all but the most credit-worthy borrowers.

High-risk borrowers and the bankers who wanted to lend to this particular clientele at higher interest rates were deterred from transacting. Since state

---

[20] Price floors below a seller's bottom line and price ceilings above a buyer's top dollar have no effect.

regulations imposed these price ceilings, some banks convinced the state of South Dakota to remove its interest rate ceiling. In return, banks moved their credit card operations to South Dakota. To avoid losing jobs to South Dakota, all states except Arkansas have raised interest rate ceilings on credit card debt.

WEALTH CREATION IN ORGANIZATIONS

Companies can be thought of as collections of transactions, from buying raw materials like capital and labor to selling finished goods and services. In a successful company, these transactions move assets to higher-valued uses and thus make money for the company.

As we saw from the story of the oil company in the introductory chapter, a firm's organizational design influences decision making within the firm. Some designs encourage profitable decision making; others do not. A poorly designed company will consummate unprofitable transactions or fail to consummate profitable ones.

Many factors affect a firm's failure to consummate wealth-creating transactions, and they are often analogous to the wealth-destroying effects of government policies. Organizations impose "taxes," "subsidies," and "price controls" that lead to unprofitable decisions. For example, overbidding at the oil company was caused by a "subsidy" paid to management for acquiring oil reserves. Senior management responded to the subsidy by acquiring reserves, regardless of the price. Our solution to the problem was to eliminate the subsidy.

SUMMARY & HOMEWORK PROBLEMS

SUMMARY OF MAIN POINTS

- Voluntary transactions create wealth by moving assets from lower- to higher-valued uses.
- Anything that impedes the movement of assets to higher-valued uses, like taxes, subsidies, or price controls, destroys wealth.
- Economic analysis is useful to business for identifying assets in lower-valued uses.
- The art of business consists of identifying assets in low-valued uses and devising ways to profitably move them to higher-valued ones.
- A company can be thought of as a series of transactions. A well-designed organization rewards employees who identify and consummate profitable transactions or who stop unprofitable ones.

MULTIPLE-CHOICE QUESTIONS

1. Which of the following is most likely to value a new pickup truck?
   a. A recent college graduate with a new child
   b. A financially comfortable construction manager
   c. A college student getting ready to move
   d. A wealthy Fortune 500 executive

2. Which of the following is not an example of the government's role in helping create wealth?
   a. Assessing property taxes
   b. Recording property transactions
   c. Providing federal courts to adjudicate contract disputes
   d. Assigning street addresses

3. When are parties likely to engage in transactions?
   a. If they both gain from the transaction
   b. If the sale price is above the seller's value and below the buyer's value
   c. When the total gains from trade are greater than zero
   d. All of the above

4. The existence of underemployed assets
   a. is inefficient because not all assets are being put to their highest use.
   b. implies the potential for money-making opportunities.
   c. provides the opportunity for wealth-creating transactions.
   d. All of the above

5. In a transaction for a good valued at $100,000 by a buyer and $95,000 by a seller, what amount of tax would result in an unconsummated transaction?
   a. Any tax amount would result in an unconsummated transaction.
   b. A tax of $1,500
   c. A tax of $5,500
   d. It depends on how much the parties are willing to pay (and accept) for the good.

INDIVIDUAL PROBLEMS

2-1. Property Rights
Why are property rights so important in creating wealth?

2-2. Goal Alignment at a Small Manufacturing Concern
The owners of a small manufacturing concern have hired a manager to run the company with the expectation that he will buy the company after five years. Compensation of the new vice president is a flat salary plus 75% of the first $150,000 of profit and then 10% of profit over $150,000. Purchase price for the company is set as 4½ times earnings (profit),

computed as average annual profitability over the next five years. Does this contract align the incentives of the new vice president with the goals of the owners?

2-3. Rent Control
Figure out how to profitably consummate the unconsummated wealth-creating transaction created by rent control.

2-4. Price Ceilings
Defenders of Communist economic systems may point out that consumers pay lower prices for certain goods because the government imposes a limit on what producers may charge. Cite at least two other ways that consumers may be "paying" for these goods.

2-5. Taxes
Consider a seller who values a car at $9,500 and a buyer who values the same car at $10,000. What total surplus will result from a transaction between the two when the seller is faced with the following sales tax rates: 0%, 2%, 4%, 6%, and 8%?

GROUP PROBLEMS

G2-1. Goal Alignment in Your Company
Are your incentives aligned with the goals of your company? If not, identify a problem caused by goal misalignment. Suggest a change that would address the problem. Compute the profit consequences of the change.

G2-2. One Lesson of Business
Identify an unconsummated wealth-creating transaction (or a wealth-destroying one) created by some tax, subsidy, price control, or other government policy, and then figure out how to profitably consummate it (or deter it). Estimate how much profit you would earn by consummating (or deterring) it.

G2-3. One Lesson of Business (within an Organization)
Identify an unconsummated wealth-creating transaction (or a wealth-destroying one) within your organization, and figure out how to profitably consummate it (or deter it). Estimate how much profit you would earn by consummating it (or deterring) it.

Chapter 3

Benefits, Costs, and Decisions

Prior to the 1990s, Cadbury India offered its managers free housing in company-owned flats to offset the high cost of living in Bombay. In 1991, when Cadbury added low-interest housing loans to its benefits package, managers took advantage of this incentive and purchased their own houses, leaving the company flats empty. The empty flats remained on the company's balance sheet for the next six years.

In 1997, Cadbury adopted Economic Value Added (EVA®) practices—a financial performance measure trademarked by management consulting firm Stern Stewart & Co. EVA charges each division within a firm for the amount of capital it uses and rewards management for increasing its division's economic value added, or EVA. EVA dictated that Cadbury India take on a capital charge of 15%, representing the return that Cadbury could have made had it invested the capital elsewhere.

After EVA adoption, Bombay's division saw a charge on its annual income statement equal to $600,000 (15% times $4,000,000—the value of the apartments).[1] To increase their division's EVA, senior managers decided to sell the unused apartments. By charging each division for the amount of capital it uses, the company gives managers incentives to abandon investments earning less than 15% and to undertake only those investments that would earn more than 15%.

By giving managers incentives to make decisions whose benefits were greater than their costs, the main point of this chapter, Cadbury increased its profitability.

BACKGROUND: VARIABLE, FIXED, AND TOTAL COSTS

As you consider decisions that affect output, knowing how costs vary with output will help you compute some of the costs associated with these decisions. Suppose you were a Cadbury manager and were responsible for opening a new factory. Among many other decisions, you would need to purchase a factory to produce

---

[1] We do not know the actual size of the charges—they should be viewed as illustrative.

your candy, hire employees to run the factory and sell your product, and purchase raw ingredients. Say your factory cost is $1 million, you need 10 employees at $50,000 total cost per employee for every 1,000 candy bars produced, and ingredients cost $0.50 per bar. If you decided to produce 1,000 candy bars, your costs would be $1,500,500—$1 million for the factory, $500,000 in employee costs, and $500 in ingredient costs. If you decided to produce 2,000 bars, your costs would be $2,001,000—$1 million for the factory, $1 million in employee costs, and $1,000 in ingredients.

Notice that some, but not all, of the costs change as you increase output. Total costs increase as you produce more candy bars, but your factory costs $1 million regardless of the amount you produce. Your factory is a **fixed cost,** as opposed to the labor or ingredients, whose costs vary with input. We call costs that change with output level **variable costs.** The distinction is a key lesson for this chapter:

> *Fixed costs do not vary with the amount of output. Variable costs change as output changes.*

Table 3-1 shows total, fixed, and variable costs for your new candy factory at various production levels. Notice that the fixed costs remain the same whether your factory produces nothing or 5,000 candy bars. Variable costs, on the other hand, rise and fall as output changes. Total costs show a similar pattern with the important exception that total costs are also greater than zero regardless of output.

To reinforce the relationships among these costs, we can also represent them graphically. Figure 3-1 shows the general relationship between output and total, fixed, and variable costs. Again, notice at output levels of zero, both fixed and total costs are greater than zero. Total and variable costs both

TABLE **3-1**	**CANDY FACTORY COSTS**		
	COSTS		
Output	**Fixed**	**Variable**	**Total**
0	1,000,000	0	1,000,000
1,000	1,000,000	500,500	1,500,500
2,000	1,000,000	1,001,000	2,001,000
3,000	1,000,000	1,501,500	2,501,500
4,000	1,000,000	2,002,000	3,002,000
5,000	1,000,000	2,502,500	3,502,500

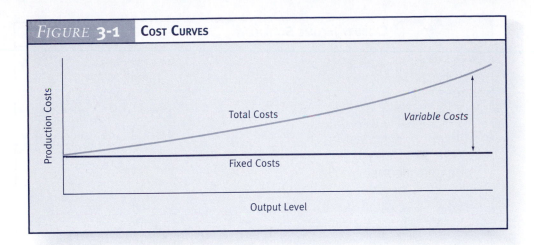

FIGURE 3-1 COST CURVES

Production Costs

Total Costs

Variable Costs

Fixed Costs

Output Level

increase with output, and variable costs appear as the difference between the total cost curve and the fixed cost line.[2] To test your understanding of the distinction between fixed and variable costs, consider which of the following costs would be variable costs for your candy factory:

- Payments to your accountants to prepare your tax returns   *fixed*
- Electricity to run the candy making machines   √
- Fees to design the packaging of your candy bar   *f*
- Costs of material for packaging[3]   √

BACKGROUND: ACCOUNTING VERSUS ECONOMIC PROFIT

The Bombay Cadbury managers likely had a very good sense of their factories' variable, fixed, and total costs. So why were they making bad decisions concerning the company-owned flats? To understand this problem, we must recognize another very important distinction: the difference between accounting and economic costs. Table 3-2 presents a recent annual income statement for Cadbury.[4] The firm sold over £6 billion in goods for the year; and after

---

[2] Note that the shape of the total cost curve is not a straight line as it would have been if we graphed the costs of the candy factory. The reason: Per unit variable costs often drop with increasing output—a topic we will discuss in later chapters.

[3] Electricity and packaging material are both variable costs. As you make more candy bars, the machines will consume more electricity, and packaging costs will increase. Your accounting fees and packaging design fees will not change as output changes, so they are fixed costs.

[4] Adapted from the Cadbury Schweppes PLC 2004 Annual Report. Note that this income statement is for worldwide Cadbury operations, not just the Bombay Division, and is presented for a general illustration of economic versus accounting costs.

TABLE 3-2 CADBURY INCOME STATEMENT		
NET SALES	£ 6,738	
Cost of Sales	3,020	
GROSS PROFIT		3,718
Operating Expenses:		
Selling, General and Administrative	2,654	
Depreciation and Amortization	215	
Total Operating Expenses		2,869
OPERATING INCOME		849
Other Income (Expense):		
Net Interest	(226)	
Other Income	(3)	
Total Other Income (Expense)		(229)
EARNINGS BEFORE PROVISION FOR INCOME TAXES		620
Provision for Income Taxes		(189)
NET EARNINGS		£ 431

amounts in millions of pounds

subtracting various expenses, it ended up with a profit of £431 million, or approximately 6.4%. Expense categories include items like these:

- Costs paid to its suppliers for product ingredients
- General operating expenses, like salaries to factory managers and marketing expenses
- Depreciation expenses related to investments in buildings and equipment
- Interest payments on borrowed funds

These types of expenses are the **accounting costs** of the business.

Economists, however, are also interested in **implicit costs,** costs that likely do not show up in the accounting statements. What's an example of an implicit cost? Look at the income statement again, and notice that it lists payments to one class of capital providers of the company (debt holders). *Interest* is the cost that creditors charge for use of their capital. But creditors are not the only capital providers to firms. Firms rely on equity providers (stockholders) as well, yet the income statement reflects no charge for the use of this capital. Suppose that Cadbury had received £4 billion in equity financing. If these equity holders expect an annual return of 10% on their money (or £400 million), we would subtract this amount from the £431 million in net earnings to get a better idea of the economic profit of the business. Similarly, if equity investors expected a 12% annual return (or £480 million), Cadbury would have an economic loss of £49 million (£431 million in net earnings less the £480 million expected return). The economic profit tells investors whether they should keep investing in the firm. Negative economic profit means that the firm is earning less than equity holders expect to make from their capital.

What does this mean in practical terms? It means that a firm may show an accounting profit while experiencing an economic loss. The two amounts are not equal because economic profit recognizes both the explicit and implicit costs of capital. A failure to consider these implicit costs is why the Cadbury India managers continued to maintain their flats. Once senior management calculated the implicit costs of capital and made them explicit to the local managers (by adopting EVA), the right decision was made. To be able to calculate these types of implicit costs, it is critical to understand the concept of opportunity costs.

COSTS ARE WHAT YOU GIVE UP

So how do we calculate implicit costs? The trick is recognizing how implicit or economic costs relate to the decisions that you are trying to make. When deciding between two alternatives, always choose the one that returns the highest profit. We define the costs of one as the forgone opportunity to earn profit from the other. With this definition, costs imply decision-making rules, and vice versa. If the benefits of the first alternative are larger than its costs—the profit of the second alternative—then choose the first. Otherwise, choose the second.

The **opportunity cost** of an alternative is what you give up to pursue it.

In what follows, when we use the term *cost*, we refer to opportunity cost. Costs depend on what you give up (your next-best alternative). Since these costs vary with the decision that you are trying to make, cost and decisions are inherently linked to one another.

To illustrate the link, consider the Cadbury managers' decision to hold onto the company-owned flats. Management could have sold them and used the capital to expand operations. In other words, the cost to the company of holding onto the apartments was the foregone opportunity to invest capital in the company's operations and earn a 15% return. Holding onto the flats cost the company $600,000 each year. Unless the benefits to the company of holding onto the apartments were at least $600,000, the capital was not employed in its highest-valued use.

Managers ignored the empty flats on the company's balance sheet because they had no incentive to do otherwise. To fix the problem, the company began rewarding managers for increasing EVA—which is more closely associated with the profit that matters to the shareholders. The company-instituted change in measuring costs motivated the managers of the Bombay operation to move the capital tied up in the apartments to a higher-valued use.

Does your company charge you for the capital that you use? If not, does this lead you to make bad decisions?

FIXED- OR SUNK-COST FALLACY

Opportunity costs are conceptually simple; the hard part is identifying the profit consequences of the associated decisions.

When making decisions, you should consider all costs and benefits that vary with the consequence of a decision and only costs and benefits that vary with the decision. These are the relevant costs and relevant benefits of a decision.

You can make only two mistakes as you make decisions: You can consider irrelevant costs, or you can ignore relevant ones. In this section and the next, we describe these two potential mistakes and how to avoid them.

The fixed-cost fallacy or sunk-cost fallacy means that you consider costs and benefits that do not vary with the consequences of your decision. In other words, you make decisions using irrelevant costs and benefits.

As a simple example, consider a football game. You pay $20 for a ticket, but by halftime your team is losing 56–0. You stay because you say to yourself, "I want to get my money's worth." Of course, you cannot get your money's worth, even if you stay. The ticket price does not vary with the decision to stay or leave. You should make the decision without considering the ticket price, which is a **sunk cost** and therefore irrelevant.

One of the most frequent causes of the fixed-cost fallacy in business is the "overhead" allocated to various activities within a company. Because overhead is a fixed or sunk cost, it should not influence most business decisions within a company. If managers make decisions based on their overhead allocations, they commit the fixed-cost fallacy. Look back at the Table 3-2 income statement. Overhead costs appear in the line item of Selling, General, and Administrative Expense. An example of such an overhead expense would be costs associated with the corporate headquarters staff or with the sales force. These costs are considered fixed because output can be increased without the need to increase the corporate staff, like the CFO or CEO. Because these costs will not vary with decisions about changing output, they should be ignored in the decision-making process.

For example, suppose that you, as head of a new products division, are considering launching a product that you will be able to distribute through your existing sales force without incurring extra expenses. However, if you launch the new product, your division will be forced to pay for a portion of the sales force. If this "overhead" charge is big enough to deter an otherwise profitable product launch, then you commit the fixed-cost fallacy. Overhead expenses are analogous to a "tax" on launching a new product. In this case, the tax deters a profitable product launch.

Depreciation[5] often becomes another case of the fixed-cost fallacy. For example, in 1996, a washing machine firm considered outsourcing its plastic agitator production, rather than making them internally as had been done for several years. The firm received a bid of $0.70 per unit from a trusted supplier and compared this bid with its internal production costs. Play along and make your decision on the basis of the Table 3-3.

The relevant comparison should neglect the costs of depreciation and overhead[6] because your firm incurs these costs regardless of whether you decide to outsource. The relevant cost of production is $0.80, and the relevant cost of outsourcing is $0.70. So outsourcing is cheaper.

In this example, identifying the right decision was easier than making it for the manager in charge of the manufacturing division. At the time, $400,000 worth of undepreciated capital still appeared on the company's balance sheet

TABLE 3-3   OUTSOURCING A WASHING MACHINE AGITATOR

INTERNAL PRODUCTION		OUTSOURCING	
Category	Cost	Category	Cost
Material	$0.60	Material	$0.50
Labor	$0.20	Labor	$0.10
Depreciation	$0.10	Tooling	$0.10
Other Overhead	$0.10		

Table Notes: Annual unit volume is 1,000,000. Depreciation refers to straight-line depreciation of the $1,000,000 initial tooling cost, equal to $100,000 per year for 10 years ($0.10 = $100,000/1,000,000).

---

[5] *Depreciation* is an accounting methodology to allocate the costs of capital equipment to the years over the lifetime of the capital equipment.
[6] Labor would not be considered a fixed cost unless the company would keep the workers on payroll regardless of whether the part was produced internally or externally.

related to the original tooling costs, incurred six years earlier. Accountants at his firm told the manager that if he decided to outsource the agitator, these "assets" would "become worthless," and the manager would be forced to take a charge[7] against his division's profitability. The $400,000 charge would prevent him from reaching his performance goal, and he would have to forgo his bonus. The manager rationally decided not to outsource even though outsourcing would have been a profitable move for the company.

The company's incentive compensation scheme that rewarded managers for increasing accounting profit rather than economic profit created this sunk-cost fallacy behavior. This leads to an important lesson:

Accounting profit does not necessarily correspond to real or economic profit.

Economic profit measures the true profitability of decisions. Rewarding employees for increasing accounting profit may lead to decisions that reduce economic profit. In the case of the washing machine agitator, the company should have rewarded its manager for increasing economic profit. This would have better aligned his incentives with the goals of the shareholders.

Companies find it difficult to avoid the sunk-cost fallacy because the person who decided to make the sunk-cost investment is often the only one who has enough information to know when the investment should be abandoned. If decision makers fear punishment for making what turns out to be a bad investment, then they may continue the investment to hide the mistake. We see this in the pharmaceutical industry, where drug development programs are very difficult to stop once they get started, and in companies that continue to develop computer software in-house, even after cheaper and better alternatives become available on the market. In each case, the person or division who made the decision to develop the drug or software fears punishment should the decision be exposed as a mistake. For this reason, drug and software development frequently continues long after it should stop.

HIDDEN-COST FALLACY

The second mistake you can make is to ignore hidden costs.

*The **hidden-cost fallacy** occurs when you ignore relevant costs—those costs that* do *vary with the consequences of your decision.*

As a simple example of this, consider another football game. You buy a ticket for $20, but at game time scalpers are selling tickets for $50 because your team is playing its cross-state rivals who have legions of fans willing to pay

---

[7] Taking a "charge" against profitability means that accounting profit would be reduced by the amount of the charge—in this case, $400,000.

over $50 to go to the game. Even though you do not value the tickets at $50, you go anyway because, you say, "These tickets cost me only $20."

But wait, the tickets really cost you $50. By going to the game, you give up the opportunity to scalp them. Unless you value going to the game as much as the rival fans, then yours is not the highest-valued use for the ticket. In other words, you are sitting on an unconsummated wealth-creating transaction. Scalp the tickets and stay home!

Consider another example: Suppose that you wish to fire an employee. You estimate that the employee contributes $2,500 per month to the company and that his compensation package costs the company $1,900 per month. Should you fire the employee? How does your answer change if you can sublet his office for $800 per month?

If you can rent the employee's office space for $800 per month, the hidden cost of the employee is $800. The total cost of the employee is $2,700 per month, which is higher than the benefit he contributes to the company. Fire him.

ECONOMIC VALUE ADDED

You may recall that the Cadbury India story discussed a way of measuring costs and profit called EVA. EVA charges each division within a firm for the amount of capital it uses and rewards management for increasing its division's economic value, or EVA. This method points out that just because a cost doesn't appear on an accounting statement doesn't mean that it isn't important. When making decisions that involve capital expenditures or savings, it is obviously important to explicitly consider what else you could do with the capital—lest you commit the hidden-cost fallacy. Typically, the cost of capital is computed as the risk-adjusted cost of equity, the cost of debt, or a weighted average of the two, sometimes called the *weighted average cost of capital,* or WACC.

EVA is the net operating profit after taxes minus the cost of capital times the amount of capital utilized. In equation form:

$$[EVA = NOPAT - (\text{Cost of Capital} \times \text{Capital Utilized})].$$

By adopting compensation schemes tied to EVA, firms are less likely to commit the hidden-cost fallacy. As the promotional material of Stern Stewart & Co. puts it:

> *The capital charge is the most distinctive and important aspect of EVA®.*
> *Under conventional accounting, most companies appear profitable but*
> *many in fact are not. As Peter Drucker put the matter in a* Harvard Business
> Review *article, "Until a business returns a profit that is greater than its cost*
> *of capital, it operates at a loss. Never mind that it pays taxes as if it had a*
> *genuine profit. The enterprise still returns less to the economy than it*
> *devours in resources. . . . Until then it does not create wealth; it destroys it."*

EVA corrects this error by explicitly recognizing that when managers employ capital they must pay for it, just as if it were a wage.

By taking all capital costs into account, including the cost of equity, EVA shows the dollar amount of wealth a business has created or destroyed in each reporting period. In other words, EVA is profit the way shareholders define it. If the shareholders expect, say, a 10% return on their investment, they "make money" only to the extent that their share of after-tax operating profit exceeds 10% of equity capital. Everything before that is just building up to the minimum acceptable compensation for investing in a risky enterprise.[8]

This is not to say that EVA is a cure-all method for managers. Implementing EVA to avoid the hidden-cost fallacy still requires managers to exert a considerable amount of judgment and analysis. Even though EVA is designed to make visible the hidden cost of capital, unless you can identify all hidden costs, you can still commit the hidden-cost fallacy. For example, if it is difficult to value the uncertain future benefits of an investment, you can commit the fallacy if you ignore the investment's future benefits while considering current costs. As economists nearly always answer, "it depends"—in this case, on being able to identify all the relevant costs and benefits of each decision. Stern Stewart & Co. can be credited for designing a system that makes visible the hidden cost of capital, but it is only a performance metric, not a substitute for careful analysis.

DOES EVA WORK?

By adopting EVA, or a similar economic profit plan[9] (EPP), and linking pay to performance, firms reward managers for making good decisions—those that increase economic profit. If managers begin making better decisions, firms that adopt such plans should experience improved operating performance. Stern Stewart & Co. claims that "more than 300 client companies worldwide now use EVA, and evidence shows that most of them significantly outperform other companies in their industries."

As expected, Professors Craig Lewis and Chris Hogan find that operating performance of companies adopting EPPs significantly improves following adoption.[10] For the companies that they examined, the median return on assets (ROA) increases from 3.5% in the year prior to adoption to 4.7% four years later. Median operating income-to-total assets rises to 16.7% from 15.8% in four years. It appears that firms adopting EPPs realize dramatic long-run improvements in operating performance.

[8] See http://www.sternstewart.com/evaabout/whatis.php.
[9] Other EPPs include earnings-based bonuses and stock ownership (including employee stock ownership plans, restricted stock, phantom stock, and stock options).
[10] Chris Hogan and Craig Lewis, "Long-Run Investment Decisions: Operating Performance and Shareholder Value Creation of Firms Adopting Compensation Plans Based on Economic Profits," *Journal of Financial and Quantitative Analysis,* forthcoming.

But before we can conclude that adopting an EPP is a good idea, we have to figure out what the firm would have done had it not adopted an EPP. We have to compare EPP adoption with the next-best alternative: That is, what else can firms do to increase profitability? This is the opportunity cost of EPP adoption. To answer this question, Lewis and Hogan set up "natural experiments" matching each adopting company with a comparable firm (same industry, similar operating performance, same size) that did *not* adopt an EPP. Surprisingly, they found that operating performance of nonadopting firms was statistically indistinguishable from that of adopting firms.[11]

Although bonus payments increase 39.1% in the adoption year for EPP firms, they also increase 37.4% for the nonadopters. Thus, well-managed firms respond to poor recent performance by strengthening the link between pay and performance, but the choice of performance evaluation metric, whether economic profit (including the hidden cost of capital) or earnings (accounting profit), does not seem to matter.

The bottom line is that new trends, fads, or analytical tools should be viewed skeptically. If a radical change is necessary to kick managers into action, the conclusion could well be that adoption of an economic performance plan is the necessary boot. However, Lewis and Hogan's research points out that change can also be accommodated within the structure of existing compensation schemes.

SUMMARY & HOMEWORK PROBLEMS

SUMMARY OF MAIN POINTS

- Costs are associated with decisions, *not* activities.
- The **opportunity cost** of an alternative is the profit you give up to pursue it.
- In computing costs and benefits, consider *all* costs and benefits that vary with the consequences of a decision and *only* those costs and benefits that vary with the consequences of the decision. These are the **relevant costs** and **benefits** of a decision.
- **Fixed costs** do not vary with the amount of output. **Variable costs** change as output changes. Decisions that change output will change only variable costs.

---

[11] For an alternative view of the "fairness" of Lewis and Hogan's selection methodology, check out the Stern Stewart & Co. Web site. Lewis and Hogan reply, "After reading the attack of our work, we feel reassured knowing that a number of alternative selection techniques have been tried and yielded similar results. Why do we choose the one we report in the paper? Because academics have shown that it has the best statistical properties."

- Accounting profit does not necessarily correspond to real or economic profit.
- The **fixed-cost fallacy** or **sunk-cost fallacy** means that you consider irrelevant costs. A common fixed-cost fallacy is to let overhead or depreciation costs influence short-run decisions.
- The **hidden-cost fallacy** occurs when you ignore relevant costs. A common hidden-cost fallacy is to ignore the opportunity cost of capital when making investment or shutdown decisions.
- EVA is a measure of financial performance that makes explicit the hidden cost of capital.
- Rewarding managers for increasing economic profit increases profitability, but evidence suggests that economic performance plans work no better than traditional incentive compensation schemes based on accounting measures.

MULTIPLE-CHOICE QUESTIONS

1. A manufacturing company is considering purchasing a new machine that doubles capacity from 500 to 1,000 units per week. The machine will occupy approximately 500 square feet of vacant (unused) space on the factory floor. Which of the following costs are irrelevant in the decision to purchase this machine?
   a. The additional cost of utilities necessary to run the machine
   b. Monthly rental expense associated with the 10,000-square-foot factory
   c. Additional machinists who will need to be hired to run the machine
   d. Maintenance costs for regular repair and cleaning of the machine

2. A company manufactures both pens and pencils in the same facility. The firm's production capacity is shared between these two products. Due to a federal ruling requiring all elementary school students to use only pencils, the overall demand for pencils has shifted outward leading to an increase in pencil prices. Surprisingly, this has had no effect on pen demand. The firm will find in the short term that
   a. the cost of producing pencils rises.
   b. the cost of producing pens falls.
   c. pencils are less profitable than pens.
   d. the cost of producing pens rises.

3. In comparing a firm's accounting costs with its economic costs, the accounting costs
   a. are the same, if the firm is earning a normal rate of return.
   b. are larger.
   c. take account of the implicit cost of owned resources.
   d. are smaller.

4. The average capital invested in Firm X during the year is $20,000. During that same year, Firm X produces after-tax income of $3,200. If the firm's cost of capital is 12%, what is the economic profit?

    a. $0

    b. $800

    c. $1,200

    d. $3,200

5. Which of the following costs always must be considered relevant in decision making?

    a. Variable costs

    b. Avoidable costs

    c. Fixed costs

    d. Sunk costs

INDIVIDUAL PROBLEMS

3-1. Production Opportunity Cost

A can manufacturing company produces and sells three different types of cans: Versions X, Y, and Z. A high-level, simplified profit/loss statement for the company is provided here. Corporate overhead (rent, general and administrative expense, etc.) is allocated equally among the three product versions. After reviewing the statement, company managers are concerned about the loss on Version Z and are considering ceasing production of that version. Should they do so? Why or why not?

	Version X	Version Y	Version Z	Total
Net Can Sales	$180,000	$240,000	$105,000	$525,000
Variable Costs	105,000	135,000	82,500	322,500
Corporate Overhead	60,000	60,000	60,000	180,000
Contribution to Profit	15,000	45,000	−37,500	22,500

3-2. Opportunity Cost of Renting

You currently pay $10,000 per year in rent to a landlord for a $100,000 house, which you are considering purchasing. You can qualify for a loan of $80,000 at 9% if you put $20,000 down on the house. To raise money for the down payment, you would have to liquidate stock earning a 15% return. Neglect other concerns, like closing costs, capital gains, and tax consequences of owning, and determine whether it is better to rent or own.

3-3. Opportunity Cost of Steel

Your firm usually uses about 200 to 300 tons of steel per year. Last year, you purchased 100 tons more steel than needed (at a price of $200 per ton). In the meantime, the price of steel jumped to $250 per ton delivered (which means that any firm selling the steel must pay any shipping costs), and the price has since stabilized at that price. The cost of shipping steel to the nearest buyer would be $20 per ton. In the meantime, a business next door just went bankrupt, and the bank is offering a special deal where you can buy another 100 tons of steel for $180 per ton. Assume that the interest rate is 0%. Which of the following are correct?

    a. Sell your 100 tons at the going market price of $250, and make a profit of $30 per ton ($50 less $20 cost of shipping).

    b. Buy the 100 tons next door at $180, and resell at a price of $250 less $20 shipping, for a net profit of $50 per ton.

    c. Hold onto your 100 tons, and wait until it is needed for production.

    d. Buy the 100 tons next door at $180, and hold onto it until it is needed in production.

3-4. Foreign Currency

You've completed your vacation in a foreign country. At the airport, you discover you have the equivalent of $20 local currency left over. The exchange control officer tells you that you can't convert the local money back to dollars. Nor can you take it out of the country. Because the gift shop was closed, you decided to spend the remaining money on refreshments—for complete strangers! What is the cost of the refreshments?

3-5. Evaluating Performance in a Small Business

A few years ago, a construction manager earning $70,000 per year working for a regional home builder decided to open his own home building company. He took $100,000 out of one of his investment accounts that had been earning around 6% a year and used that money to start up the business. He worked hard the first year, hiring one employee (his only salary cost for the business was the $40,000 paid to this employee), and generated total sales of $1,000,000. Total material and subcontracted labor costs for the year were $900,000. Calculate accounting profit. What are the opportunity costs for the manager of being in this business relative to returning to his old job? What is the economic profit of the business?

GROUP PROBLEMS

G3-1. Fixed-Cost Fallacy

Describe a decision made by your company that involved costs that should have been ignored. Why did your company make the decision? What should they have done? Compute the profit consequences of the decision.

G3-2. Hidden-Cost Fallacy

Describe a decision that you or your company made that involved opportunity costs that should have been considered. Why did your company make the decision? What should they have done? Compute the profit consequences of the decision.

G3-3. Hidden Cost of Capital

Does your company charge your division for the capital that it uses? If not, does this lead to bad decision making?

Chapter 4

Extent (How Much) Decisions

Memorial Hospital is a large community hospital licensed for over 600 beds. Its facilities cover over two million square feet and span an area of nearly 38 acres. The hospital offers a full line of services, including cardiac care, neurosurgery, orthopedics, oncology, and obstetrics. The obstetrics area has provided delivery services to area patients for over 80 years and recently underwent a multimillion-dollar renovation.

In 2005, Memorial Hospital's CEO conducted performance reviews of all of the hospital's departments, including the obstetrics area. As part of this review process, the chief of obstetrics proposed increasing the number of babies being delivered by the department. The CEO examined the department's financial statements from a recent month and noted that for 540 deliveries, costs totaled $3,132,000, while revenues totaled $2,754,000. Pointing out that the hospital was losing $700 per patient, the CEO asked why anyone would want to increase a service that was losing $700 every time the hospital delivered another baby.

As most of you will now recognize, the CEO's analysis was mistakenly based on total costs and revenues. As we learned in the last chapter, the relevant costs and benefits of a decision are only those that vary with the consequences of that decision. Had the CEO adopted this decision rule, he would have quickly realized that after excluding nonrelevant costs, the hospital was actually making over $3,000 per delivery. Increasing the number of deliveries would lead to an increase in hospital profit.

We call the decision facing the hospital an "extent" decision because the managers are trying to decide "how many" babies to deliver. In this chapter, we show you what the relevant costs and benefits of **extent decisions** are and how to make these decisions profitably.

BACKGROUND: AVERAGE AND MARGINAL COSTS

As managers make extent decisions, many mistakenly consider the average cost of each unit. **Average cost** is simply the total cost of production divided by the number of units produced. Say Memorial Hospital had fixed costs of $1 million and variable costs of $3,000 to deliver 500 babies. Total costs would be $2.5 million ($1,000,000 + [$3,000 × 500]), and average cost per delivery would be $5,000. Suppose that Memorial would incur no additional fixed costs to serve more patients, up to a limit of 600 patients. We would end up with the average cost curve depicted in Figure 4-1. Notice that the curve slopes downward due to fixed costs.[1] Recall that total costs are the sum of fixed and variable costs. Similarly, average total cost is the sum of average fixed cost and average variable cost. Average variable costs stay the same in our example ($3,000 per patient), but average fixed costs fall as output increases—the numerator (fixed cost) stays the same while the denominator (quantity) increases.

Using average costs in extent decision making can lead to unprofitable decisions of how much of a product to make or to sell. The lessons in this chapter will help you avoid this common error. Managers make profitable extent decisions when they consider marginal costs rather than average costs.

Average cost (AC) is irrelevant to an extent decision.

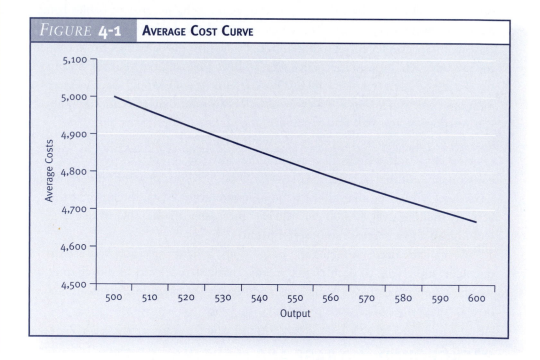

FIGURE 4-1   AVERAGE COST CURVE

[1] Average cost curves will generally not slope down indefinitely. At some point, average costs will begin to increase either through the need to add additional fixed costs or from rising per unit variable costs. We will examine the U-shaped average cost curve in a later chapter.

Marginal cost is the cost to make and sell one additional unit of output. Formally, Marginal Cost = Total Cost$_{Q+1}$ − Total Cost$_Q$. In our hypothetical baby delivery example, increasing output from 500 to 501 units raises costs from $2,500,000 to $2,503,000, so the marginal cost is $3,000. Fixed costs do not change as output increases, so they do not factor into marginal cost calculations. Compare Memorial's marginal cost for the 501st unit of $3,000 to its average cost ($2,503,000/501) of $4,960.78, and you will see that marginal and average costs can be very different.

Marginal costs are not always lower than average costs; it depends on the range of output we are considering. It is possible that increasing output will add expenses or decrease productivity for the firm. For example, consider a factory near capacity that tries to increase production. Workers may run out of space, leading to lower productivity and higher costs. The marginal cost of these additional units could rise above average cost.

MARGINAL ANALYSIS

To analyze extent decisions, we break down the decision into tiny steps and then examine the costs and benefits of taking another one of these tiny steps. You should take another step (e.g., deliver another baby) if the benefits of taking that step are greater than the costs of doing so. Stop when the costs of taking another step are greater than the benefits of doing so.

We call this approach *marginal analysis*. To illustrate, we analyze the common extent decision of how much to sell, where marginal analysis applies to both costs and revenues.

> *Marginal cost (MC) is the additional cost incurred by producing and selling one more unit.*

> *Marginal revenue (MR) is the additional revenue gained from selling one more unit.*

If the benefits of selling another unit (MR) are bigger than the costs (MC), then sell another unit.

> *Sell more if MR > MC; sell less if MR < MC. If MR = MC, you are selling the right amount (maximizing profit).*

Marginal analysis works for any extent decision, such as whether to change the level of advertising, the quality of service, the size of your staff, or the number of parking spaces to lease. The same principle applies to each decision— do more if MR > MC, and do less if MR < MC.

Returning to the introductory example of Memorial Hospital, after a more detailed analysis, managers calculated the *marginal* cost of delivery at approximately $1,800, while marginal revenue was around $5,000. The hospital was not delivering enough babies; that is, at the current output, MR > MC. Contrary to the CEO's initial view, Memorial could increase profit by delivering *more* babies, not by reducing the number of deliveries.

The main difficulty in applying marginal analysis is measuring the costs and benefits of additional steps. To illustrate, suppose you are working for a long-distance phone company trying to decide whether to adjust the amount you spend for TV advertising. If you recently increased your TV advertising budget by $50,000, and the ads yielded 1,000 new customers, the data can tell you something about marginal benefit of *additional* TV advertising expenditures.

In this example, we have data on a big jump ($50,000) but not on the little steps ($1) that make up the jump. The only available data correspond to the bigger change, so we do the best that we can. We estimate the marginal effect of another dollar of advertising by dividing the $50,000 by 1,000 customers to get $50 per customer, sometimes called the *acquisition cost* of a customer. This means that the marginal cost of acquiring another customer is $50.[2] If the marginal benefit of another customer is bigger than $50, then increase advertising. Otherwise, do not.

Note that marginal analysis points you in the right direction, but it cannot tell you how far to go. After taking a step, recompute marginal costs and benefits to see whether further steps are warranted. When the marginal benefit equals the marginal cost, stop then because you are maximizing profit (i.e., further steps are unprofitable).

We can also use marginal analysis to compare the relative effectiveness of two different advertising media. For example, suppose that you are trying to decide how to adjust your promotional budget, currently allocated between TV advertising and telephone solicitation. How much should you spend on advertising for each medium?

In this case, the *opportunity cost* of spending *one more* dollar on TV advertising is the forgone opportunity to spend *that* dollar on telephone solicitation. Increase spending on whichever medium has a higher marginal effect, and pay for the increase by reducing spending on the other medium.

If you recently decreased your telephone solicitation budget and this saved $10,000, but you lost 100 customers, the marginal effectiveness of phone solicitation is one customer for $100 (alternatively, the marginal customer acquisition cost is $100). Note that we are implicitly assuming that you could get the customers back by restoring your telephone solicitation budget.

---

[2] Or that the marginal benefit of $1 worth of advertising is 1/50 of a customer.

Since it is cheaper to gain *another* customer using TV advertising, increase TV advertising and spend less on telephone solicitation. Note that marginal analysis doesn't even require you to measure the marginal benefit of acquiring a customer. All it requires is that you measure the *marginal* effectiveness of each activity. If one activity has higher marginal effectiveness than the other, then increase that activity and reduce expenditures on the other. Then remeasure and decide whether to make further changes.

When you adjust your advertising expenditures, make the changes one at a time. Do not increase telephone solicitation at the same time you decrease TV advertising because you lose valuable information about the marginal impact of each change when you change both at the same time. Only by changing them separately can you measure the marginal effectiveness of each expenditure to see whether further changes are profitable.

It is essential that you not confuse marginal cost with average cost. Recall that to calculate the average cost, divide total cost by the number of units produced. In our current example, the average per-customer cost for TV would be computed by dividing the total spent on TV advertising by the total number of customers gained. Remember that average costs do not provide the information you need to make extent decisions. In some instances, they might lead to poor decisions. To compute marginal cost, look only at the *additional* cost of producing one more unit. The two cost figures may be very different. For example, some psychological models of advertising say that any fewer than four exposures to an advertisement has no effect on purchase decisions. The *marginal* effectiveness of that fourth exposure is thus very large, but the *average* effectiveness of the entire advertising budget would be much lower.

Now that you understand the differences between marginal and average analysis, let's try to use it to help reduce costs at a Fortune 50 company that produces textile products at various manufacturing facilities in Latin America. The manufacturing facilities operate as **cost centers,** meaning that plant managers are rewarded for reducing costs. To evaluate the cost centers, the firm measures production using standard absorbed hours (SAH). For each garment produced, the firm computes the time required to complete each step in the manufacturing process. Complex garments like overalls require more time and thus are assigned a higher SAH (15 minutes) than simple garments like T-shirts (two minutes). The output of a factory is thus measured in SAH, and each factory is evaluated based on how much it costs to get one hour's worth of production in terms of cost per SAH.

Obviously, measuring output in this way allows managers to identify lower cost factories. Suppose that a factory in the Yucatán operates at $20/SAH, and a factory in the Dominican Republic operates at $30/SAH. As a manager, do you think you could save $10/SAH by shifting production from the Dominican Republic to the Yucatán? Remember, this is an extent decision about how much to produce at each factory, so you want to measure the marginal production costs at each plant. The extent decision here is similar to our hospital's decision of how many babies to deliver.

The first thing to remember is the fixed-cost fallacy. If the cost figures used to compute cost per SAH include overhead that cannot be avoided, then you won't save these costs as you shift production—the charges will remain regardless of amount produced. So, first you must adjust the cost per SAH to remove the influence of any fixed costs.

Second, make sure that cost per SAH is a good proxy for marginal costs. To check whether this is so, make sure that when you reduce output in the Dominican Republic, you really are avoiding close to $30/SAH for each SAH of output reduction in the Dominican Republic facility, and make sure that you are incurring only about $20/SAH for each SAH of output increase in the Yucatán. If this is not correct, then cost per SAH is a poor proxy for marginal cost.

If you are convinced that $10 cost per SAH is a reasonable proxy for difference in marginal costs between the two factories, then you can lower costs by moving production from the Dominican Republic to the Yucatán. Finally, remember that marginal analysis tells you what direction to go (shift production), but it doesn't tell you *how far* to go. Decide how far to go by taking a step and then remeasuring marginal costs to determine whether to take another step.

In this example, the Fortune 50 company shifted some production, but not as much as the managers wanted because they had to maintain good working relationships with politicians in the Dominican Republic who would have been upset if too many local workers lost jobs.

INCENTIVE PAY

A person's decision of how hard to work is an extent decision, so marginal analysis can be used to design incentives to encourage hard work. To illustrate, suppose you are a landowner evaluating two different bids for harvesting a tract of timber containing 100 trees. One bid is for $150 per tree, and the other bid is for $15,000 for the right to harvest all the trees. Which bid should you accept?

Although both bids have the same face value, they have dramatically different effects on the logger's incentives. If you charge a fixed fee of $15,000 for the right to harvest all the trees, the logger treats the price paid to the landowner as a fixed or sunk cost—and should, by our reasoning in Chapter 3, ignore that cost. He has an incentive to cut down trees as long as each tree's value is greater than the cost of harvesting it, and he will likely end up cutting down all the trees.

On the other hand, if you charge the logger a royalty rate of $150 per tree, the logger will cut down only those trees with a value greater than $150. If the forest is a mix of pine worth $200 per tree and fir worth $100 per tree, the logger will harvest only the pine and leave the fir.[3] Consequently, the landowner will receive less money under a royalty contract because the logger will harvest only the pine trees. The royalty rate is analogous to a sales tax because it deters some wealth-creating transactions (i.e., the fir trees are not harvested).[4]

The same idea can be applied to the problem of motivating salespeople. For example, suppose you want to evaluate the incentive effects of two different incentive compensation schemes. One is based on a 10% commission rate, where the salesperson is paid 10% of all sales. The other compensation plan pays a 5% commission rate plus a $50,000 per year flat salary. Each year, you expect salespeople to sell 100 units at a price of $10,000 per unit. Which incentive compensation scheme should you use?

As in our earlier example, the contracts have the same face value but different effects on the behavior of the salesperson. If you pay a 10% commission, then the marginal benefit to the salesperson of making a sale is $1,000. If you pay a 5% commission, the marginal benefit is only $500. If some sales are relatively easy to make (i.e., the salesperson gives up less than $500 worth of time and effort to make them), and some sales are relatively difficult to make (i.e., they require at least $800 worth of effort), then only the easy sales will be made under the 5% commission rate.

In essence, the sales force responds to the smaller marginal benefit of selling with less effort, which we call *shirking*. This kind of shirking is analogous to the decision of the logger to harvest only the high-value, low-cost trees when he pays a royalty rate for each tree harvested. The logger responds negatively to the high marginal costs of logging just as the salesperson responds negatively to the low marginal benefit of selling. To induce higher effort, use incentives that reduce marginal costs or increase marginal benefits. Fixed costs or benefits do not change effort.[5]

TIE PAY TO PERFORMANCE MEASURES THAT REFLECT EFFORT

The method of tying pay to performance is an important decision in the design of any organization, as the following story illustrates. In 1997, a 50-year-old chief operating officer (COO) with a bachelor's degree in journalism and a law degree

---

[3] Alternatively, if the trees differ in their harvesting costs (some are near a logging road, and some are not), the logger will cut down only those trees that yield a profit of at least $150.

[4] Recall that we noted in Chapter 2 that when a sales tax is larger than the surplus of a transaction, it deters that transaction. Similarly, when the royalty rate is larger than the surplus here, it deters the wealth-creating transaction (the harvesting of the fir tree).

[5] The point of discussing these different compensation schemes is not to argue that one or the other is the optimal design but rather to simply note that incentives will affect behavior.

managed a consulting firm with 10 account executives. The COO was in charge of keeping clients happy and ensuring that the account executives were working in the best interests of the company. The COO earned a flat salary of $75,000.

After taking classes in human resources, economics, and accounting, the CEO of the company became convinced of the merits of incentive pay. He sat down with his COO, and together they set profit goals for the year. All revenues counted toward the COO's profit goal. But only the expenses that the COO controlled directly—like compensation and office expenses—were "charged" against his profit. All overhead items, like rent, were placed under another budget because the COO could not control them; that is, they were "fixed" with respect to his effort.

By creating this new budget, the CEO implicitly recognized that the usual accounting statements were inadequate for evaluating the COO's performance. The CEO and the COO both agreed that without much effort, the COO could earn[6] $150,000 each quarter. But earning an amount over $150,000 would take more effort. To reward the COO for exerting extra effort, they agreed on an incentive compensation scheme that allowed the COO to keep one-third of each dollar the company earned above $150,000.

After making the change, the COO's compensation jumped to $177,000—an increase of 136%—while the firm's revenues jumped from $720,000 to $1,251,000—an increase of 74%. A good economy certainly contributed to the increase in revenues, but the compensation plan also helped. Revenue increased because the COO pushed hard to make and exceed earnings goals, and, for the first time, he worried about expenses. For example, he attempted to contain costs by asking why phone bills were so high.

Along with changing the COO's compensation scheme, the CEO also moved to a system of incentive pay for the account representatives. This had equally dramatic effects on the account representatives—except for one employee who was going through a divorce. The incentive pay scheme did little to increase his marginal incentives because half of everything he earned went to his estranged wife.

IF INCENTIVE PAY IS SO GOOD, WHY DON'T MORE COMPANIES USE IT?

Although the benefits of incentive pay seem clear, it is not a panacea—especially in cases where it is difficult to measure performance. Later on, as we develop more tools to analyze incentives, we will see that there are situations where

---

[6] *Earnings* refers to company profit.

incentive pay can be counterproductive. Its successful application "depends" on a number of factors.

Also, trying to implement incentive pay in an organization can be more difficult than turning a Communist country toward capitalism. Consider this 1998 reaction from a "faculty" member in the "corporate learning center" of a Fortune 50 company to a suggestion that the company adopt an incentive compensation plan:

> Forfeiting our most recently espoused values of equal ownership in Firm X's success is not the answer. I fear that we will be attempting to compete for employees interested in a class-oriented system of compensation. From where I sit, this is the last thing a corporation needing vast, systemic, team-oriented change should be trying to do to compete in the global marketplace. Many folks know I am a staunch opponent of incentive plans, and I often quote Alfie Kohn (1993), whose research shows that rewards punish. Saying "If you do this, you'll get that" differs little from saying "Do this or this will happen to you." Incentives are controlling.

> However, another aspect of the punishment is much more evident in this change of policy: "Not receiving a reward one expects to receive is also indistinguishable from being punished." Just ask all those who don't receive the bonuses they were previously entitled to how they feel about it. The incentive pay policy is overt in its support of class separation over collective team participation. It ignores the premises of modern systems thinking and reverts to the mechanistic theories of Descartes and Newton for justification. A typical business school text from the 1950s would have suggested instituting such an aristocratic policy.

If you want to short the stock of this company, call me and I will tell you which one it is.

SUMMARY & HOMEWORK PROBLEMS

SUMMARY OF MAIN POINTS

- Do not confuse average and marginal costs.
- **Average cost** (AC) is total cost (fixed and variable) divided by total units produced.
- Average cost is irrelevant to an extent decision.
- **Marginal cost** (MC) is the additional cost incurred by producing and selling one more unit.

- **Marginal revenue** (MR) is the additional revenue gained from selling one more unit.
- Sell more if MR > MC; sell less if MR < MC. If MR = MC, you are selling the right amount (maximizing profit).
- The relevant costs and benefits of an extent decision are marginal costs and marginal revenue. If the marginal revenue of an activity is larger than the marginal cost, then do more of it.
- An incentive compensation scheme that increases marginal revenue or reduces marginal cost will increase effort. Fixed fees have no effects on effort.
- A good incentive compensation scheme links pay to performance measures that reflect effort.

MULTIPLE-CHOICE QUESTIONS

1. A company is producing 1,000 units. At this output level, price is $1.50, and marginal revenue is $1.25. Average total cost is $1.10, and marginal cost is $1.40. What can we conclude from this information?

   a. The company is producing too much.
   b. The company should produce more.
   c. The company is maximizing profit at this output.
   d. Not possible to determine.

2. Sal's Pizza Shop has a unique recipe for pizza, and currently its optimal price is $20 per pizza at a quantity of 200 pizzas per week. Its marginal cost is $12 per pizza when it produces fewer than 180 pizzas per week. The marginal cost is $15 per pizza when it produces 180 to 210 pizzas per week. The marginal cost is $18 per pizza when it produces between 211 and 300 pizzas per week. The staff cannot produce more than 300 pizzas per week. Assuming that fixed costs are $300 per week, its marginal revenue from the 200th pizza sold this week is

   a. $20.
   b. $12.
   c. $15.
   d. $17.57.

3. A sofa manufacturer can produce 10 sofas for $2,500 and 12 sofas for $2,760. What is the difference between the average cost per sofa for 12 sofas and the marginal cost of the 12th sofa?

   a. $100
   b. $130
   c. $230
   d. $260

4. A firm can hire 10 workers at a wage of $10 but has to pay a wage of $12 to get 11 workers. What is the marginal cost of the 11th worker?

  a. $12

  b. $32

  c. $100

  d. $132

5. Which of the following choices represents an extent decision?

  a. A firm is considering whether to enter a business.

  b. A firm is considering whether to leave a business.

  c. A firm is considering whether to sell a division.

  d. The human resources director is deciding how many employees to lay off.

INDIVIDUAL PROBLEMS

4-1. Zero Defects

Amazon's "autobot" recently recommended a book to one of us titled *Quality Maintenance: Zero Defects through Equipment Management*. The book's description is "Achieve zero-defect product quality by eliminating the root causes of your equipment defects. An easy-to-read case study of TPM, TQC, and JIT at a world-class manufacturing plant." Without reading this book, we know that its advice is wrong. How do we know?

4-2. Shoe Company

A domestic shoe company distributes running shoes and tennis shoes for $95 per pair. The marginal cost of producing a pair of running shoes is $60, and the marginal cost of producing a pair of tennis shoes is $45. A Chinese retailer offers to purchase running shoes for $55 per pair and tennis shoes for $55 per pair for distribution in China. Should the shoe company sell any shoes to the Chinese retailer? (Ignore any potential issues of bundling the two types of shoes together as part of the sale and any competitive effects that international sales might have on current domestic sales.)

4-3. In-Sourcing Sales Force

Five years ago, to respond to cost-cutting pressure during a weak economy, your company decided to close five sales offices employing five people each. Currently your company employs independent sales agents who earn a 2.5% commission on all sales. The economy has recently turned around, and one of your colleagues suggests that you could hire 25 people for $50,000 per employee to do the sales job as independent agents at a cost of goods sold (COGS) of only 0.5%. What concerns might you have about such an approach?

4-4. Copier Company

A copy company wants to expand production. It currently has 20 workers who share eight copiers. Two months ago, the firm added two copiers, and output increased by 100,000 pages per day. One month ago, they added five workers, and productivity also increased by 50,000 pages per day. Copiers cost about twice as much as workers. Would you recommend they hire another employee or buy another copier?

4-5. Incentive Pay

A company recently raised the pay of workers by 20%. Yet workers' productivity did not improve (i.e., they produced the same amount and quality as before). Why?

GROUP PROBLEMS

G4-1. Extent Decision

Describe an extent decision made by your company. Compute the marginal cost and marginal benefit of the decision. Was the right decision reached? If not, what would you do differently? Compute the profit consequences of the decision.

G4-2. Contracts

Does your firm use royalty rate contracts or fixed-fee contracts? Describe the incentive effects of the contracts. Should you change the contract from one to the other? Compute the profit consequences of changing the contract.

Chapter 5

Investment Decisions: Look Ahead and Reason Back

By 2000, Mobil Oil (now ExxonMobil) was the leading supplier of industrial lubricants[1] in the United States. It achieved that position—a 13% market share—by bundling engineering services with its high-quality lubricants. With twice as many field engineers as its next-largest competitor, Mobil was able to offer custom-designed lubrication programs to complement sales of their lubricants.

One of its largest customers was a regional producer of electric power (let's call this company CBA) whose annual consumption of lubricants exceeded one million gallons. Early in 2000, Mobil conducted a three-month engineering audit of CBA. This audit included employee training, equipment inspections, and, for each piece of CBA equipment, repair, service, and lubricant recommendations.

CBA made the recommended repairs, but then it gave the lubricant recommendation list to a Mobil competitor that offered lubricants at lower prices. When Mobil failed to match the lower prices, they lost the contract and their three-month investment.

Mobil and its managers forgot a basic business maxim: *Look ahead and reason back*. By failing to anticipate self-interested behavior, they were victimized by it. In this section, we study investment decisions, like Mobil's, that involve costs that cannot be recovered.

BACKGROUND: BREAK-EVEN QUANTITY

To analyze investment decisions, it helps to distinguish between marginal costs (MC), which vary with quantity, and fixed costs (F), which don't. You'll be able to analyze over 95% of your investment decisions with this very simple cost structure: You incur a fixed cost to enter an industry and a constant[2] per-unit marginal cost when you begin production. Why distinguish between fixed and marginal costs? The answer is simple: Fixed costs do not vary with production, so you should ignore them when setting price or production levels—otherwise, you commit the *fixed-cost fallacy*.

---

[1] Industrial lubricants are very costly to produce. One 55-gallon barrel of oil yields just two quarts of lubricant.
[2] In later chapters we will analyze situations in which marginal costs are not constant.

This does *not* mean you should ignore them altogether. You need to consider fixed costs *before* you incur them. To determine whether it's profitable to incur fixed costs, we ask the equivalent (but easier-to-answer) question: "Can I sell enough to break even?"

The break-even quantity (Q) is

$$Q = F/(P - MC),$$

where F *is fixed costs,* P *is price, and* MC *is marginal costs.*

To compute the break-even quantity (where profit equals zero), assume that you can sell as much as you want at a given price and that marginal costs are constant. The derivation of the break-even quantity formula is computed here as the quantity that will lead to zero profit:

$$
\begin{aligned}
0 &= \text{Profit} \\
0 &= \text{Revenue} - \text{Total Costs} \\
0 &= \text{Revenue} - \text{Variable Costs} - \text{Fixed Costs} \\
0 &= (P \times Q) - (MC \times Q) - F \\
0 &= Q(P - MC) - F \\
F &= Q(P - MC) \\
F/(P - MC) &= Q \\
Q &= F/(P - MC)
\end{aligned}
$$

The logic behind this calculation is simple. Each unit sold earns the *contribution margin* (P − MC) because this is the amount that one sale contributes toward covering fixed costs. So you have to sell at least the break-even quantity to earn enough to cover fixed costs. To see this, multiply the break-even quantity by the contribution margin to see that it equals the amount of the fixed costs. If you sell more than the break-even quantity, you have earned more than enough to cover your fixed costs, or to earn a profit.

For example, consider a university contemplating a new football stadium that costs $200 million. If it can borrow the money at a 10% interest rate, the annual capital cost is $20 million. These are the fixed costs.

If the contribution margin is $10 on each ticket sold, then the university has to sell two million tickets in a season to break even (2,000,000 = 20,000,000/10). If it doesn't expect to sell two million tickets, then the stadium investment is not profitable.

ENTRY DECISIONS

We can use a variant of break-even analysis to choose between different manufacturing technologies. In 1986, John Deere was building a capital-intensive factory to produce large, four-wheel-drive farm tractors. Then the price of wheat dropped dramatically, reducing demand for such tractors because they're used exclusively for harvesting wheat. John Deere stopped construction of its own factory and attempted to purchase Versatile, a Canadian company that assembled tractors in a garage using off-the-shelf components.

We can characterize John Deere's decision as a choice between two different technologies: its planned capital-intensive factory, characterized by big fixed costs but small marginal costs, or Versatile's technology, characterized by small fixed costs but big marginal costs. Did John Deere make the right decision?

As you should now begin to realize, the right answer is always "It depends." In this case, it depends on how much John Deere expected to sell. Suppose that the capital-intensive technology had fixed costs of $100 and marginal costs of $10, while the Versatile technology had fixed costs of $50 but marginal costs of $20. (Note: We're deliberately choosing easy-to-work-with numbers so that we can illustrate the general point.)

To determine the quantity at which John Deere is indifferent between the two technologies—the break-even quantity—solve for the quantity that equates the two costs. At a quantity of five units, total costs are $150 for both technologies.[3] If you expect to sell more than five units, choose the low-marginal-cost technology; otherwise, choose the low-fixed-cost technology.

John Deere would have been better off if it had abandoned the construction project and acquired Versatile because projected demand for tractors was low. However, the Antitrust Division of the U.S. Department of Justice challenged the acquisition as anticompetitive.[4] John Deere and Versatile were two of just four firms that sold large four-wheel-drive tractors in North America.

We end this section with a warning to avoid a very common business mistake:

Do not invoke break-even analysis to justify higher prices or greater output.

Managers often reason, for example, that they must raise prices so that price can cover fixed costs. This is wrong if fixed costs do not vary with the pricing decision. Similarly, managers sometimes reason that since *average* fixed costs decline with quantity, they must sell as much as they can to reduce average cost. Both lines of reasoning are incorrect because, as you know, pricing and

---

[3] We can represent the different technologies by the following two cost functions:

$Cost_1 = 100 + 10Q$
$Cost_2 = 50 + 20Q$

And solve for the break-even point by equating costs:

$Cost_1 = Cost_2$
$100 + 10Q = 50 + 20Q$
$50 = 10Q$
$Q = 5$

[4] This was the first big case for one naive but enthusiastic young economist.

production are *extent* decisions that require *marginal analysis,* not *break-even analysis.*

Remember, the relevant costs depend on which question you are asking. We've just seen that fixed costs are relevant before you incur them. In the next section, we show that they can also be relevant when you decide to shut down operations.

SHUTDOWN DECISIONS AND BREAK-EVEN PRICES

To study shutdown decisions, we work with break-even prices rather than quantities. If you shut down, you lose your revenue, but you get back your **avoidable costs.** If revenue is less than avoidable cost, or equivalently, if price is less than average avoidable cost,[5] then shut down.

The break-even price is the average avoidable cost per unit.

The only hard part in applying break-even analysis is deciding which costs are avoidable. For that, we use the Cost Taxonomy shown in Figure 5-1.[6]

To understand how to use the taxonomy, consider the following problem. Fixed costs are $100, marginal costs are $5, and you're producing 100 units per year. How low can price go before it is profitable to shut down?

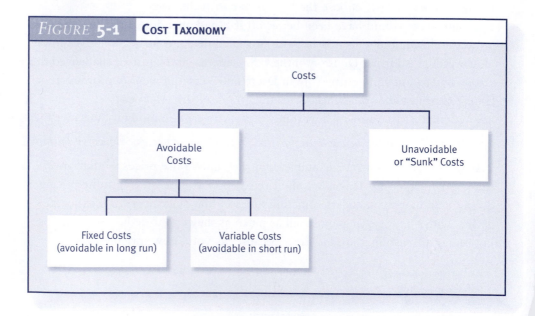

FIGURE 5-1   COST TAXONOMY

---

[5] Profit = Revenue − Cost

= $(P \times Q) - (AC \times Q)$, where AC = Average Cost = (Total Cost)/Q

= $(P - AC)Q$

Note that if price is less than average cost, profit will be negative.

[6] Ivan Png, *Managerial Economics* (Malden, MA: Blackwell, 1998).

Again, the answer is "It depends." In this case it depends on which costs are avoidable. In the short run, only marginal cost is avoidable, so the shutdown price is $5. In the long run, fixed costs become avoidable, so they become relevant. In the long run, the shutdown price goes up to $6.[7]

To make this concrete, think of the fixed costs as a one-year renewable lease. When the lease comes up for renewal, it is relevant to the shutdown decision because it is avoidable. However, until the lease comes up for renewal—during the period that economists call the *short run*—it is unavoidable, so you should ignore it when deciding whether to shut down.

SUNK COSTS AND POSTINVESTMENT HOLD-UP

Economics is often called the "dismal science," partly because of its dark view of human nature. We have already seen the utility of using this perspective to look ahead and reason back to worst-case scenarios. Nowhere is this more important than in analyzing sunk-cost investments. Sunk costs are unavoidable, even in the long run, so if you make sunk-cost investments, you are vulnerable to **postinvestment hold-up.** Let's look at the problem of postinvestment hold-up by working again with break-even prices.

Consider the case of a magazine, like *National Geographic,* trying to negotiate with a regional commercial printer to print its magazine. For the magazine, using a regional printer saves on shipping costs. But to print a high-quality magazine, the printer must buy a $2 million rotogravure printing press. If the marginal cost of printing the magazine is $1 and the printer expects to print about one million copies per year over a two-year period, the average cost of printing the magazine over two years is $2.[8] This is the break-even price for the printer and represents the bottom line in negotiations with the magazine. Before they are incurred, sunk costs are relevant to the negotiation.

However, once the printer purchases the printing press, the profit calculus changes. If the printer cannot recover any of the press's value by reselling it, then the cost of the press is *sunk.* Once sunk costs have been incurred, the magazine can renegotiate terms of the deal; that is, the printer is subject to *hold-up.* Since the cost of the press is unavoidable, the printer's break-even price falls to the marginal cost of printing the magazine ($1).

If the managers of the commercial printer foresee that they are vulnerable to hold-up, they will be reluctant to deal with the magazine. The one lesson of

---

[7] Average Avoidable Cost = (Fixed Cost + Average Variable Cost $\times$ Q)/Q = ($100 + $5 $\times$ 100)/100 = $6 per unit.
[8] AC = ($2,000,000 + $2,000,000)/(2,000,000) = $2.

business is to figure out how to profitably consummate the transaction between the magazine and the printer.

If possible, the printer's negotiators will insist on a contract that penalizes the magazine should it decide to hold them up. With the assurance of a contract, the printer may feel confident enough to incur sunk costs. But contracts are often difficult and costly to enforce. A better solution is to make the magazine purchase the press and then lease it to the printer. The magazine no longer poses a hold-up threat to the printer because the printer has incurred no sunk costs.[9]

Note that if the cost of the printing press is *fixed,* meaning that it can be recovered by selling the machine, then the magazine cannot hold up the printer. If the magazine tries to renegotiate a price less than average cost, the printer will rationally refuse the business, sell the press, and recover his entire investment. Hold-up can occur only if costs are sunk, like those of Mobil's engineering services in our introductory story to the chapter.

VERTICAL INTEGRATION SOLVES THE HOLD-UP PROBLEM

Certain types of investments, known as **specific investments,** are specific to a relationship because they are sunk or lack value outside the relationship. Unless each party is confident that it will not be held up, it is unlikely that either will make relationship-specific investments.

In this case, it might be advantageous to write strong long-term contracts— those that impose heavy penalties for hold-up. Or it might be even better to remove the transaction from the marketplace and put it under the organizational umbrella of a single firm. If the same parent company owns both parties, it is less likely that either will hold the other up.

> *Vertical integration refers to the common ownership of two firms in separate stages of the vertical supply chain that connects raw materials to finished goods.*

Consider bauxite (aluminum ore) from mines in South America. The refining process used to produce alumina from bauxite is tailored to the specific qualities of the ore. In addition, transporting bauxite is costly, so it's advantageous to locate the refinery near the mine. Both the specificity of the refining process and the high transport costs make the investment in a refinery specific to the relationship between the mine and the refinery.

In this case, the enormous investment required to build a refinery is very vulnerable to postinvestment hold-up—the bauxite mine could raise the price of ore once the refinery is built. So, we rarely see refineries built without vertical

---

[9] However, now the magazine can be held up by the printer and may be reluctant to buy the machine unless the printer can reassure the magazine that it will not be held up.

integration or strong long-term requirements[10] contracts between the mine and refinery. These types of organizational forms "solve" the hold-up problem by reassuring the refiner that it will not be held up once its relationship-specific investment is made.

Marriages are vulnerable to the same type of postinvestment opportunism that plagues commercial relationships. Parties invest time, energy, and money in a marriage, the kinds of investments that differentiate marriages from more casual relationships, just as in spot market transactions. These investments are valuable to the marriage parties but are largely sunk, in that they have a much lower value outside the relationship. The marriage contract penalizes postinvestment hold-up (i.e., divorce) and thus makes couples willing to invest more in the marriage.[11]

Consider an apocryphal story of an economist and his fiancée. The two were receiving premarital counseling from a priest. The priest's first question to them was "Why do you want to get married?" The economist's fiancée answered, "Because I love him and want to spend the rest of my life with him." The economist had a somewhat different answer: "Because long-term contracts induce higher levels of relationship-specific investment." A year later, trying hard to find the right words to express how he felt about his wife, he wrote an anniversary e-mail—using a nice cursive font—declaring that his "relationship-specific investment was earning an abnormally high rate of return."

HOW TO DETERMINE WHETHER INVESTMENTS ARE PROFITABLE

All investment decisions involve a trade-off between current sacrifice and future gain. If you're willing to invest in projects with relatively low rates of return, say 5%, then you're willing to trade current dollars for future ones at a relatively even rate; for example, $1.05 next year is worth $1.00 today. Equivalently, we say that you have a low **discount rate** or that the future is worth almost as much to you as the present. Discounting (present value) = (future value)/(1 + r) is the opposite of compounding (present value)(1 + r) = (future value), where r is the discount rate.

Individuals with low discount rates invest in more projects because more investments meet their return criteria. These individuals are more likely to go to

---

[10] Requirements contracts "require" that one party purchase a certain percentage of its materials from the other party.

[11] The weakening of the marriage contract in the United States, dramatically reducing penalties for postinvestment hold-up, allows a test of this contractual view of marriage. Following the change, we would expect less relationship-specific investment, like the investment in children. Corresponding to the weakening of the contract, we have seen a decline in fertility rates. Couples are having fewer children and having them later in life, when it is easier to drop in and out of the labor market.

college and graduate school, own stocks, and exercise. The common thread in these activities is that they have current costs and future payoffs, just like investments.

Individuals who require bigger returns, say 20%, place a much lower value on the future. They invest only in projects with much higher rates of return, or, if none is available, they borrow money. These individuals are more likely to smoke, shun exercise, abuse drugs, and commit crime. The common thread in all of these activities is that they have current payoffs and future costs.

One reason for identifying individuals with different discount rates (other than to keep those with high discount rates out of your study group) is to recognize the possibility of trade between them. In the current example, there is an unconsummated wealth-creating transaction—at any interest rate above 5% and below 20%, the high-discount-rate individual would willingly borrow from the low-discount-rate individual.

Companies, like individuals, possess discount rates of their own, determined by their costs of capital.[12] Companies with a high cost of capital invest only in high-return projects, while companies with a lower cost of capital invest in a wider range of projects. And, as with individuals, there is the possibility of trade. Companies with high discount rates willingly borrow from those with low discount rates.

As you might imagine, time is a critical variable in investment decisions, whether companies have high or low costs of capital. Intuitively, this makes sense. Consider a company that can invest $1,000,000 in either of two projects. The first returns $1,200,000 at the end of year 1 and the second returns $1,200,000 at the end of year 2. The company would obviously prefer to get its profit more quickly and so would prefer the first project to the second.

This intuition can be formalized into a general rule that involves discounting a project's cash flows at the company's cost of capital. All net project cash flows are projected (outflows like project costs are subtracted from inflows like project revenues) and discounted back to their present value.

If the present value of the net cash flows is larger than zero, the project is profitable.

The use of net present value (NPV) leads to the rule's name—the **NPV rule.**

Consider the two projects shown in Table 5-1, both of which require an initial investment of $100. Project 1 pays off $115 at the end of the first year, while Project 2 pays off $60 at the end of the first year and $60 at the end of the second. The company's cost of capital is 14%. To determine whether the

---

[12] Calculating a company's cost of capital is not a simple matter. Proper methods are the subject of much debate in the field of finance. Many companies satisfy themselves with rough estimates.

TABLE 5-1	NPV EXAMPLE			
	Outflow	**Inflow 1**	**Inflow 2**	**Total**
Project 1	−$100	$115	N/A	$15
Project 2	−$100	$60	$60	$20
Present Values				
Project 1	−$100	$100.88	N/A	$0.88
Project 2	−$100	$52.63	$46.17	−$1.20

investments are profitable, we discount all future inflows and outflows to the present so we can compare them with the initial investment.

Inflow 1 is divided by (1.14); Inflow 2 is divided by $(1.14)^2$. From the bottom two lines of Table 5-1, it's clear that Project 1 earns profit while Project 2 does not.

The NPV rule has a clear link to our discussion of the concept of economic profit in Chapter 3. Projects with positive NPV create economic profit. Stated another way, only positive NPV projects earn a return higher than the company's cost of capital. If we were to calculate the returns of Projects 1 and 2, we would find that Project 1's return is higher than 14%, and Project 2's is lower than 14%. Projects with negative NPV may create accounting profit but not economic profit. In making investment decisions, choose only projects with a positive NPV.

SUMMARY & HOMEWORK PROBLEMS

SUMMARY OF MAIN POINTS

- **Break-even quantity** is equal to fixed cost divided by the contribution margin. If you expect to sell more than the break-even quantity, then incur the fixed costs to enter the industry.
- **Avoidable costs** can be recovered by shutting down. If the benefits of shutting down (you recover your avoidable costs) are larger than the costs (you forgo revenue), then shut down. The **break-even price** is average avoidable cost.
- If you incur **sunk costs,** you are vulnerable to **postinvestment hold-up.** Unless the parties are convinced they won't be held up, they will be reluctant to make sunk-cost investments.

- **Specific investments** are largely sunk. Once relationship-specific investments are made, parties are locked into a bargaining relationship with each other. If transactions are frequent and transaction costs are high, then organizational forms like **vertical integration** or long-term contracts reduce transactions costs and encourage relationship-specific investments.
- Investments imply willingness to trade dollars in the present for dollars in the future. Wealth-creating transactions occur when individuals with low discount rates lend to those with high discount rates.
- Companies, like individuals, have different discount rates. Invest only in projects with a positive NPV because they earn a return higher than the company's cost of capital.
- The **NPV rule** states that if the present value of the net cash flows of a project is larger than zero, the project is profitable.
- Projects with positive NPV create economic profit.

MULTIPLE-CHOICE QUESTIONS

1. As manager of a company that is trying to maximize long-run profit, which of the following is a rational profit-maximizing business decision?
   a. In the long run, shut down the business if price falls below long-run average costs.
   b. In the long run, shut down the business if price falls below short-run average variable costs.
   c. In the short run, shut down the business if price falls below average costs.
   d. In the short run, shut down the business if price is not high enough to cover fixed costs.

2. You are considering opening a new business to sell golf clubs. You estimate that your manufacturing equipment will cost $100,000, facility updates will cost $250,000, and on average it will cost you $80 (in labor and material) to produce a club. If you can sell clubs for $100 each, what is your break-even quantity?
   a. 1,000
   b. 3,500
   c. 4,375
   d. 17,500

3. You are the manager of a small production facility. Your annual fixed costs are $50,000, marginal costs are $10 per unit, and you are producing 50,000 units per year. In the short run, what is the minimum acceptable price level before it makes economic sense to shut down?
   a. $9.00
   b. $10.00
   c. $11.00
   d. $12.50

4. If production of a certain type of product requires a large specific investment, which of the following production setups would you *least* expect to see?

    a. Short-term outsourcing.

    b. Vertical integration.

    c. Long-term relationship with external supplier.

    d. All production met through internal sources.

5. Your new yo-yo has fixed costs of $2 per unit and marginal costs of $3 per unit, and you plan to sell the yo-yos for $9.50 each. What is the product's contribution margin?

    a. $3.00

    b. $4.50

    c. $6.50

    d. $9.50

INDIVIDUAL PROBLEMS

5-1. Printer Hold-Up

Suppose that in our *National Geographic* example, half of the original cost of the rotogravure printing press is fixed and half is sunk. How low can the offered price go before the printer will rationally refuse to print magazines?

5-2. OEM Hold-Up

Suppose you work for an original equipment manufacturer (OEM) who makes component pieces for a telecommunications company. The telecom company asks you for a price quote for 2,000,000 units that will require a $1,000,000 investment with marginal costs of $1. What is your bottom line in negotiations with the telecom? Suppose you agree on a price slightly above your bottom line. Immediately after quoting this price to the telecom company, you receive a faxed purchase order for one million units. What should you do?

5-3. Bagel Company Break-Even Analysis

You are considering opening a bagel restaurant aimed primarily at the breakfast trade. You'll sell bagels, coffee, and other items in relatively fixed proportions to one another. For each bagel sold, you expect the company to sell two cups of coffee and $2 of other items. You'll earn $0.50 on each bagel, $0.50 on each cup of coffee, and $1.00 on the other items. Salaries, equipment, and rent cost about $100,000 per year. What is the break-even quantity of bagels?

5-4. Pet Store—Part 1

A local pet store, Roscoe's Rascals, which has concentrated in selling puppies, is considering adding a line of pet food. A contractor estimates that it will cost $10,000 to convert some storage space into a retail area for the food. Roscoe's Rascals will purchase the specialty food for $15 and sell it for $30. Marketing research indicates that the store will sell 900 bags. Should Roscoe's Rascals add pet food to its products?

5-5. Pet Store—Part 2

Assume that Roscoe's Rascals decided to add the pet food line. Two months after it began selling the food, its pet food sales declined dramatically because a competitor across the street started selling the identical food for $22 per bag. Should Roscoe's Rascals match the price offered by the competitor?

GROUP PROBLEMS

G5-1. Shutdown Decision

Describe a shutdown decision your company has made. Compute the opportunity costs and benefits of the decision (using break-even analysis if appropriate). Did your company make the right decision? If not, what would you do differently? Compute the profit consequences of the decision.

G5-2. Investment Decision

Describe an investment decision your company has made. Compute the opportunity costs and benefits of the decision. Did your company make the right decision? If not, what would you do differently? Compute the NPV of the investment.

G5-3. Postinvestment Hold-Up

Describe an investment or potential investment your company (or one of your suppliers or customers) has made that is subject to postinvestment hold-up. What could your company do to solve the hold-up problem and ensure the investment gets made? Compute the profit consequences of the solution.

PRICING, COSTS, AND PROFITS

Chapter 6

Simple Pricing

Between December 20, 1994, and February 1, 1995, the Mexican peso fell by 40% against the dollar. Coincidentally, interest rates rose sharply, slowing business activity and increasing unemployment dramatically. Consumer income declined so precipitously that Mexican consumption of Sara Lee hot dogs fell by 35%. This was surprising to Sara Lee's management because they considered hot dogs to be consumer staples—the consumption of which would hold steady, or perhaps even rise, as income fell.

Sara Lee did a survey and found that many customers had turned to a cheaper source of protein—cat food mixed with eggs, rolled up in a tortilla. Further analysis showed that the decline in demand for hot dogs was limited to Sara Lee's premium brands. As many consumer products firms do, Sara Lee produced several brands of hot dogs, differentiated by ingredients, brand names, and, perhaps most important, price. Sales of Sara Lee's lower-priced brands took off, with double-digit volume increases. Unfortunately, Sara Lee had priced the lower-end brands too low and lost money.

Sara Lee would have profited from a better understanding of demand for its products and how to set prices, the topic of this chapter.

BACKGROUND: CONSUMER SURPLUS AND DEMAND CURVES

Let's consider a simplified relationship between price and quantity purchased by a single hot dog consumer in Mexico. Table 6-1 shows the number of hot dogs the consumer will purchase at various prices.

It's easy to see from the table that, as price falls, the consumer purchases more hot dogs, reflecting the **First Law of Demand:** Consumers demand (purchase) more as price falls, assuming other factors are held constant. This makes intuitive sense. Consider the value you, a hungry consumer, receive from the first hot dog you purchase and consume—it's likely to be substantial. The additional value you get from consuming the second hot dog is a bit less, and by the time you're chowing down on your fifth hot dog, the additional value is fairly small.

TABLE 6-1	HOT DOG DEMAND SCHEDULE
Hot Dog Price	**Hot Dogs Purchased**
$5	1
$4	2
$3	3
$2	4
$1	5

The marginal, or additional, value of consuming each subsequent hot dog diminishes the more you consume.

Suppose the consumer values that first hot dog at $5, the second at $4, the third at $3, and so on. Knowing the value our consumer places on each subsequent hot dog allows us to construct Table 6-2 showing total and marginal value for the various quantities, where total value is simply the sum of the preceding marginal values.

As always, *thinking in marginal terms is critical*. Say you just looked at the fact that five hot dogs have a total value of $15. You might be tempted to conclude that if hot dogs were priced at $3, the consumer would purchase five hot dogs since 5 × $3 = $15. Thinking in marginal terms, however, shows us that the marginal value of the fourth hot dog is only $2, so at a price of $3, the consumer will purchase just three. This insight leads to another important idea: consumer surplus. **Consumer surplus** is the difference between the price a buyer is willing to pay and what the buyer has to pay (the actual price). Purchasing

TABLE 6-2	HOT DOG VALUE TABLE	
Hot Dogs Purchased	**Marginal Value**	**Total Value**
1	$5	$5
2	$4	$9
3	$3	$12
4	$2	$14
5	$1	$15

three hot dogs at $3 each leads to consumer surplus of $3 (total value of $12 less total price of $9). Purchasing five hot dogs at $5 each would lead to consumer surplus of zero. Consumers attempt to maximize their surplus—they use marginal analysis and purchase only three hot dogs rather than five.

We can link our two tables to get a measure of how much our consumer is gaining from eating hot dogs. If the consumer pays less than the total value of the hot dogs, he or she has consumer surplus. Table 6-3 shows the amount of consumer surplus for different hot dog purchase levels.

To describe how consumers respond to price, economists use **demand curves**, which are simply plots of the information contained in demand schedules. Recall from the Law of Demand that we should expect demand curves to slope downward, as consumers purchase more as prices fall.

Demand curves describe buyer behavior and tell you how much consumers will buy at a given price.

To describe the buying behavior of a group of consumers, we add up all the individual demand curves to get an **aggregate demand curve.** Assume, for instance, that each consumer wants a single item (i.e., the marginal value of a second unit is zero). Now suppose that seven buyers each want to buy a single unit of a good. To construct a demand curve, simply arrange the buyers by what they are willing to pay, say $7, $6, $5, $4, $3, $2, and $1. At a price of $7, one buyer will purchase[1]; at a price of $6, two buyers will purchase; at $5, three buyers; and so on. At a price of $1, all seven buyers will purchase the good. An *aggregate* or *market demand curve*

TABLE 6-3	HOT DOG CONSUMER SURPLUS			
Hot Dog Price	**Hot Dogs Purchased**	**Total Price Paid**	**Total Value**	**Surplus**
$5	1	$5	$5	$0
$4	2	$8	$9	$1
$3	3	$9	$12	$3
$2	4	$8	$14	$6
$1	5	$5	$15	$10

[1] Don't get distracted by the fact that at a price of $6, the buyer is being charged a price exactly equal to his or her value and is thus earning no surplus. At a price of $6, the buyer is exactly indifferent between buying and not buying. This is a result of using whole numbers to describe prices and values. For convenience, imagine that the value is a fraction above the price, so that the buyer will purchase.

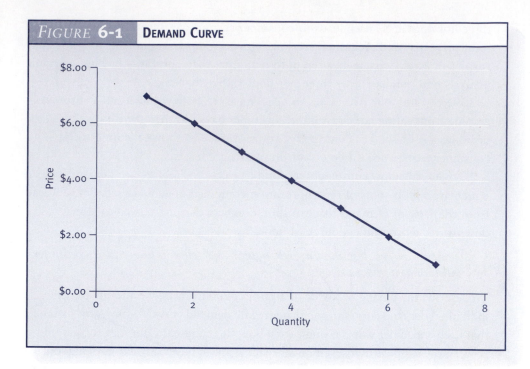

FIGURE **6-1**   DEMAND CURVE

is the relationship between the price and the number of purchases made by this group of consumers. In Figure 6-1, we illustrate this demand curve.

To determine the quantity demanded at each price, look for the quantity on the horizontal axis corresponding to a price on the vertical axis. At a price of $6, buyers demand two units; at a price of $5, three units; and so on. As price falls, quantity demanded increases. Note that we do not say that as price falls, demand increases. An increase in demand occurs when the whole curve shifts to the right such that consumers purchase greater quantities at the same prices. We'll discuss factors that shift demand in a later chapter.

MARGINAL ANALYSIS OF PRICING

Demand curves present sellers with a dilemma. Sellers can raise price and sell fewer units, but earn more on each unit sold. Or they can reduce price and sell more, but earn less on each unit sold. This fundamental trade-off is at the heart of pricing decisions, a trade-off we can resolve by using marginal analysis. If marginal revenue (MR) is greater than marginal cost (MC),[2] you can increase profit by selling another unit.

Reduce price (sell more) if MR > MC. Increase price (sell less) if MR < MC.

---

[2] Marginal profit = MR − MC and is the extra profit from selling one more unit.

it appears that an increase in quantity would increase profit.[3] However, this reasoning is incorrect because it doesn't recognize the dependence of Q on P—you cannot sell more without decreasing price. Put another way, you can say that to sell more, you have to reduce price for *all* customers, not just the additional customers who would be attracted by the reduced price.

Tell your boss that you are already making all profitable sales—those for which marginal revenue exceeds marginal cost. Marginal analysis, not average analysis, tells you where to price or, equivalently, how many to sell.

PRICE ELASTICITY AND MARGINAL REVENUE

Let's go back to Sara Lee's problem of selling hot dogs in Mexico. If the managers of Sara Lee had known what the Mexican demand curve for their hot dogs looked like, they could have easily computed the optimal price, just as we did in Table 6-4.

Unfortunately, you're never going to see a demand curve like the one in Figure 6-1. In general, it is very difficult to get information about demand at prices above or below the current price. In fact, if a consultant ever tries to show you a complete demand curve, don't trust it—the consultant has only a very rough guess as to what demand looks like away from current prices.

At this point (unless it's past the drop/add period), some students quit the class, shaking their heads and wondering why they have to learn about things they'll never see. The point of Figure 6-1 and the associated analysis is that you don't need the entire demand curve to know how to price—all you need is information on MR and MC. If MR > MC, reduce price; if MR < MC, increase price. As we saw earlier, marginal analysis points you in the right direction, but it doesn't tell you how far to go. You get to the best price by taking steps and then recomputing MR and MC to see whether you should take another step.

So how do we estimate marginal revenue? The answer involves measuring quantity responses to past price changes, "experimenting" with price changes, or running market surveys to see how quantity would change in response to a price change. If you do get useful information about demand, it's likely to come in the form of information about **price elasticity (e) of demand.**

Price elasticity of demand (e) = (% change in quantity demanded) ÷ (% change in price)

Price elasticity measures the sensitivity of quantity demanded to price changes. A demand curve on which quantity changes more than price is said to be **elastic,**

---

[3] Profit = Revenue − Cost = Q*(P − AC), where AC is average cost.

Recall that consumers and sellers are both using marginal analysis. But consumers are using marginal analysis to maximize consumer surplus (make all purchases so that marginal value exceeds price), while sellers use it to maximize profit.

To see how to use marginal analysis to maximize profit, examine Table 6-4. The columns list the Price, Quantity, Revenue, MR, MC, and total Profit for our demand curve. Suppose that the product costs $1.50 to make. At a price of $7, one consumer would purchase, so revenue would be $7. Cost would be $1.50, so profit on the first sale would be $5.50.

If we reduce price to $6, two consumers purchase, so revenue goes up to $12, an increase of $5. We say that the MR of the second unit is $5. If we reduce price further to $4, revenue increases to $15, so that the MR of the third unit is $3.

So far, all of these changes have been profitable because the increase in revenue (MR) has been greater than the increase in cost (MC). We earned $5.50 on the first unit, $3.50 on the second unit, and $1.50 on the third unit. These marginal profits sum to a total profit of $10.50, as indicated in the last column of Table 6-4.

However, if we sell a fourth unit, total profit would go down because the marginal revenue from selling the fourth unit is $1, which is less than the $1.50 marginal cost. So we don't sell the fourth unit. The optimal quantity is three; and to sell this amount, we look at the demand curve to tell us how much to charge to sell three units: $5.

After going through your analysis to compute the optimal price, suppose your boss looks at you and says, "This is the stupidest thing I've ever seen! Since the price is $5, and the cost of producing another good is only $1.50, we're leaving money on the table." What do you tell her?

Your boss has confused *average* revenue or price with *marginal* revenue. They're easy to confuse. Here's why. As long as price is greater than average cost,

TABLE **6-4**	**OPTIMAL PRICE**				
Price	**Quantity**	**Revenue**	**MR**	**MC**	**Profit**
$7.00	1	$7.00	$7.00	$1.50	$5.50
$6.00	2	$12.00	$5.00	$1.50	$9.00
$5.00	3	$15.00	$3.00	$1.50	$10.50
$4.00	4	$16.00	$1.00	$1.50	$10.00
$3.00	5	$15.00	−$1.00	$1.50	$7.50
$2.00	6	$12.00	−$3.00	$1.50	$3.00
$1.00	7	$7.00	−$5.00	$1.50	−$3.50

or sensitive to price; and a demand on which quantity changes less than price is said to be **inelastic,** or insensitive to price.

If |e| > 1, demand is elastic; if |e| < 1, demand is inelastic.

Since price and quantity move in opposite directions—as price goes up, quantity goes down, and vice versa—price elasticity is negative; that is, e < 0. However, people often refer to elasticity without the minus sign, resulting in confusion. To keep things clear, whenever we use price elasticity, as we do here, we will refer to its absolute value, represented by |e|.

To show how you might be able to estimate elasticity, consider this 1999 "natural experiment" at MidSouth, a medium-sized retail grocery store. The store's managers decreased the price of three-liter Coke (diet, caffeine-free, and Classic) from $1.79 to $1.50 because they wanted to match the price offered at a nearby Wal-Mart. In response to the price drop, the quantity sold doubled, from 210 to 420 units per week.

To compute elasticity, simply take the percentage quantity increase and divide by the percentage price decrease. Some confusion inevitably occurs because we can compute percentage changes several ways, depending on whether we divide the price or quantity change by initial or final prices or quantities. Divide by the midpoint of price $(P_1 + P_2)/2$ and the midpoint of quantity $(Q_1 + Q_2)/2$ to get a more accurate estimate of elasticity:

Price Elasticity Estimator[4] $= [(Q_1 - Q_2)/(Q_1 + Q_2)] \div [(P_1 - P_2)/(P_1 + P_2)]$

In the three-liter Coke example, the calculation works like this:

$$[(210 - 420)/(210 + 420)] \div [(1.79 - 1.50)/(1.79 + 1.50)]$$

In this case, the estimated price elasticity is -3.8, indicating that a 1% decrease in price of three-liter Coke leads to a 3.8% increase in quantity.[5] The change in revenue associated with the change is

$$(\$1.50 \times 420) - (\$1.79 \times 210) = \$630 - \$375.90 = \$254.10.$$

The relationship between revenue and elasticity can be derived from the following formula:

$$\%\Delta\text{Revenue} \approx \%\Delta\text{Price} + \%\Delta\text{Quantity}^{[6]}$$

---

[4] In computing the midpoints, we use the formulas $(Q_1 + Q_2)/2$ and $(P_1 + P_2)/2$. Since 2 divides both denominator and numerator, the formula simplifies, as here.

[5] Note that if we used the initial price and quantity to compute the percentage changes, the calculation would be $[(420 - 210)/210]/[(\$1.50 - \$1.79)/\$1.79$ or $100\%/-16.2\%$—that is, -6.17.

[6] This is a first-order approximation and will work well for small changes. The approximation does not work well for large changes.

The symbol %Δ means "percentage change in." All this says is that whichever change is bigger (price vs. quantity) determines whether revenue goes up or down. And elasticity tells you this.

For example, if demand is elastic, then a price decrease will be smaller than the corresponding quantity increase, so revenue will rise following a price decrease. Likewise, a price increase will be smaller than the corresponding quantity decrease, so revenue will fall following a price increase. This relationship is illustrated in the bottom row of Table 6-5.

On the other hand, if you try to increase price when demand is elastic, then revenue goes down (top row of Table 6-5). To see this, let's look at the story of Marion Barry's 6% tax rate increase on gasoline sales in the District of Columbia. Before the tax was put into law, gas station owners in the district argued against it, predicting that it would reduce quantity by 40%. Since the increase in price (6%) was smaller than the projected decrease in quantity (40%), the gas station owners predicted that gasoline revenue, and the taxes collected out of revenue, would decline.

Ultimately, the elasticity of demand for gasoline in the district of Columbia would determine whether quantity would decrease by more than price would increase. Since D.C. has many commuters who could buy gasoline in Maryland and Virginia instead of D.C., a reasonable guess would be that demand for gasoline sold in D.C. was very elastic. In fact, the actual reduction in quantity was 38%, very close to what the gas station owners had predicted, indicating that demand for gasoline sold in the District of Columbia was indeed very elastic. This scenario predicted by the gas station owners is illustrated in the top row of Table 6-5.

When demand is *inelastic,* this relationship is reversed; that is, price increases raise revenue because the price increase is bigger than the corresponding quantity decrease. Conversely, price decreases reduce revenue because the price reduction is bigger than the quantity increase (see Table 6-6).

TABLE **6-5**   **ELASTIC DEMAND ($|e| > 1$)**
Price increase ➡ Revenue decrease (decrease in Q is bigger than increase in P)
Price decrease ➡ Revenue increase (increase in Q is bigger than decrease in P)

TABLE 6-6   INELASTIC DEMAND (|e| < 1)
Price increase ➜ Revenue increase (decrease in Q is smaller than increase in P)
Price decrease ➜ Revenue decrease (increase in Q is smaller than decrease in P)

Let's test our understanding of the relationship between price changes, elasticity, and revenue by deriving the relationships in Table 6-5 and Table 6-6 using the approximation

$\%\Delta Revenue \approx \%\Delta Price + \%\Delta Quantity.$

The exact numerical relationship between marginal revenue (change in revenue) and elasticity is MR $= P(1 - 1/|e|)$.[7] We can use this formula to express the marginal analysis rule—reduce price if MR > MC, and raise price otherwise—using price elasticity in place of marginal revenue:

MR > MC means that $(P - MC)/P > 1/|e|$.

This expression has an intuitive interpretation. The left side of the expression is the *current markup* of price over marginal cost, $(P - MC)/P$, while the right side is the *desired markup*, which is the inverse elasticity, $1/|e|$. If the current markup is greater than the desired markup, reduce price because MR > MC, and vice versa. Intuitively, as demand becomes more elastic, the less you can mark up price over marginal cost because you lose too many customers.

For example, after MidSouth Grocery reduced the price of three-liter Coke to $1.50, its actual markup over marginal cost was 2.7%, which is much less than the desired markup of $1/|3.78| = 26\%$, so the price was much too low. Ordinarily, a profit-maximizing store manager would raise the price in such a situation. In this case, however, the managers were using three-liter Coke as a *loss leader,* deliberately pricing it too low as a way to attract customers to the store. Why? Because they hoped that customers would spend money on other items once they got there. We'll discuss these and other more complex pricing strategies in later chapters.

WHAT MAKES DEMAND MORE ELASTIC?

Given the importance of elasticity (price elasticity of demand) to pricing—the more elastic demand is, the lower the profit-maximizing price is—it's worthwhile to sharpen our intuitive feel for what would make demand more or less

[7] MR $= \Delta Revenue/\Delta Q = \Delta(PQ)/\Delta Q = (\Delta PQ + \Delta QP)/\Delta Q = P(1 - 1/|e|)$. The symbol Δ means "change in."

elastic. In this section, we list four factors that affect demand elasticity and optimal pricing.

Products with close substitutes have elastic demand.

Consumers respond to a price increase by switching to their next-best alternative. If their next-best alternative is a very close substitute, then it doesn't take much of a price increase to induce them to switch. For example, when District of Columbia mayor Barry raised the price of gasoline by 6%, many consumers began purchasing gasoline in nearby Virginia and Maryland.

In a similar vein, we see that individual brands have closer substitutes (other brands) than do aggregate product categories that include the brands. This leads to our next maxim.

Demand for an individual brand is more elastic than industry aggregate demand.

As a rough rule of thumb, we can say that brand price elasticity is approximately equal to industry price elasticity divided by the brand share. For example, if the elasticity of demand for all running shoes is -0.4, and the market share of Nike running shoes is 20%, price elasticity of demand for Nike running shoes is $(-0.4/.20) = -2$. Using our optimal pricing formula, we can see that Nike has a markup of about 50%.

If you search the Internet, you'll easily find industry price elasticity estimates that you can combine with market share estimates to get an estimate of brand elasticity. And you can use this estimate to gain a general idea of whether your brand price is too high or low.

Products with many complements have less elastic demand.

Products that are consumed as part of a larger bundle of complementary goods—say, shoelaces and shoes—have less elastic demand. If the price of shoelaces increases, you're not likely to stop buying shoelaces; if you don't have shoelaces, you don't have your favorite shoes. Conversely, products that are *not* part of a bundle of complementary goods have more elastic demand. As their price changes, consumers find it easier to stop consuming the good.

Another factor affecting elasticity is time. Given more time, consumers are more responsive to price changes. They have more time to find more substitutes when price goes up and more time to find novel uses for a good when price goes down. This leads to our third maxim:

In the long run, demand curves become more elastic: $|e|$ increases.

This phenomenon could also be explained by the speed at which price information is disseminated. As time passes, information about a new price becomes more widely known, so more consumers react to the change.

As an example, consider automatic teller machine (ATM) fees. In 1997, a bank in Evanston, Indiana, ran an experiment to determine elasticity of demand for ATMs with respect to ATM fees. At a selected number of ATMs, these bankers raised user fees from $1.50 to $2.00. When informed of the fee increase, users typically completed the current transaction but avoided the higher-priced ATMs in the future. If we define the short run as the current transaction and the long run as future transactions, then the maxim holds.

Our final maxim relates elasticity to the price level. As price increases, consumers find more alternatives to the good whose price has gone up. And with more substitutes, demand becomes more elastic.

As price increases, demand becomes more elastic: |e| increases.

For example, high-fructose corn syrup (HFCS) is a caloric sweetener used in soft drinks. For this application, sugar is a perfect substitute for HFCS. However, import quotas and sugar price supports have raised the U.S. domestic price of sugar to about twice that of HFCS. All soft drink bottlers now use HFCS instead of sugar. And because bottlers have no close substitutes for *low-priced* HFCS, its demand is relatively inelastic. But if the price of HFCS were to rise to that of sugar, sugar would become a good substitute for HFCS. In other words, demand for *high-priced* HFCS would become very elastic.

FORECASTING DEMAND USING ELASTICITY

We also use elasticity as a forecasting tool. With an elasticity and a percentage change in price, you can predict the corresponding change in quantity:

%ΔQuantity $\approx$ e(%ΔPrice)[8]

For example, if the price elasticity of demand is -2, and price goes up by 10%, then quantity is expected to go down by 20%.

Remember that price is only one of many factors that affect demand. Income, prices of substitutes and complements, advertising, and tastes all affect demand. To measure the effects of these other variables on demand, we define a factor elasticity of demand:

Factor elasticity of demand = (% change in quantity) ÷ (% change in factor)

---

[8] This is a first-order approximation and will work well for small changes. The approximation does not work well for large changes.

For example, demand for bottled water, iced tea, and carbonated soft drinks is strongly influenced by temperature. If the temperature elasticity of demand for beverages is 0.25, then a 1% increase in temperature will lead to a one quarter of 1% increase in quantity demanded.

Income elasticity of demand measures the change in demand arising from changes in income. Positive income elasticity means that the good is **normal**; that is, as income increases, demand increases. Negative income elasticity means that the good is **inferior**; that is, as income increases, demand declines. Sara Lee thought that demand for its hot dogs was inferior; but in Mexico, consumers regarded premium hot dogs as something of a luxury, so demand went down when income went down.

Cross-price elasticity of demand for Good A with respect to the price of Good B measures the change in demand of A owing to a change in the price of B. Positive cross-price elasticity means that Good B is a **substitute** for Good A: As the price of a substitute increases, demand increases. Negative cross-price elasticity means that Good B is a **complement** to Good A: As the price of a complement increases, demand decreases. Computers, for example, are complements to operating systems that run on them. We can trace part of Microsoft's success to its strategy of licensing its operating system to competing computer manufacturers. That strategy helped keep the price of computers low but stimulated demand for Microsoft's operating system.

We can estimate factor elasticities by using a formula analogous to the estimated price elasticity formula, and we can use factor elasticities to forecast or predict changes over time or even changes from one geographic area to another. Suppose you're trying to compare the year-to-year performance of one of your regional salespeople over a period in which income grew by 3%. If demand for your products has an income elasticity of 2, you would expect quantity to increase by 6%. You don't want to reward the manager for increases in quantity that are largely unrelated to her effort. A performance measure more closely related to effort would subtract 6% from the actual growth because that is the growth related to income.

Alternatively, suppose you're trying to decide whether to begin home delivery of the *New York Times* in Nashville, knowing demand for the product has an income elasticity of 2. To compute the break-even quantity, you need to know whether enough Nashvillians will choose home delivery to justify the investment in this service. If the *New York Times* recently began home delivery in Charlotte, and the income in Nashville is 5% higher than in Charlotte, you would expect a 10% higher per-capita consumption of the newspaper in Nashville than in Charlotte. If the forecast quantity would allow you to break even, then begin home delivery in Nashville.

STAY-EVEN ANALYSIS, PRICING, AND ELASTICITY[9]

Stay-even analysis is a simple but powerful tool that allows you to determine the volume required to offset a change in costs, price, or other revenue factor. For example, you know from the Law of Demand that raising price will result in selling fewer units. Stay-even analysis tells you how many unit sales you can lose before the price increase becomes unprofitable. When combined with information about elasticity of demand, the analysis will give you a quick answer to the question of whether changing price makes sense.

Let's start with a simple profit formula where profit equals revenue (price times quantity) less variable and fixed costs:

$$\text{Profit}_0 = P_0 Q_0 - VC_0 Q_0 - FC_0$$

If we change price, thus affecting quantity sold, our new profit equation is (assuming that fixed and variable costs do not change)

$$\text{Profit}_1 = P_1 Q_1 - VC_0 Q_1 - FC_0$$

Given a new proposed P_1, we want to find the Q_1 that makes these two profit equations equal. Through a bit of algebraic manipulation (setting the two equations equal to each other and solving for Q_1), we know that

$$Q_1 = Q_0 (P_0 - VC_0)/(P_1 - VC_0).$$

Say we're currently selling 600 units per week priced at $20 per unit with variable costs of $12 per unit. If we reduced price by 10%, how many more units would we need to sell to stay even on profit? Plugging the values into the formula results in a required new quantity of 800 units per week, or an increase of 33%.[10] As mentioned earlier, if we knew elasticity of demand, we could tell how quantity would respond to the price change and decide whether the price change would be a good idea. Suppose elasticity is −2.0, meaning we expect a quantity increase of 20% for a 10% price decrease. In this case, our price decrease wouldn't be a good idea because quantity wouldn't increase sufficiently.[11] Elasticity would need to be approximately −3.3 for the price drop to make sense.

To see the effect of a variety of potential price changes, we can draw a stay-even curve that shows the required quantities at each new price level. Calculate and then plot the required quantities for a series of price changes. As shown in Figure 6-2, this results in a smooth, downward-sloping curve showing the quantity changes necessary to maintain current profit levels as price changes.

---

[9] This section was inspired by material from Mike Shor's pricing class at Vanderbilt University.
[10] Verify the calculation using contribution margins. We originally sell 600 units at a margin of $8 for profit of $4,800. Our new margin after reducing price $2 (10%) is $6, and we sell 800 units for a profit of $4,800.
[11] For simplicity, these calculations use the simple formula for elasticity, not the arc price version.

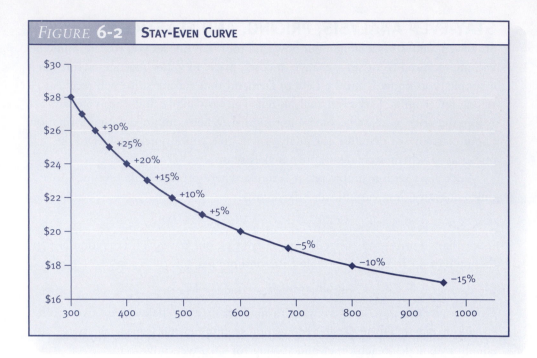

FIGURE **6-2**   STAY-EVEN CURVE

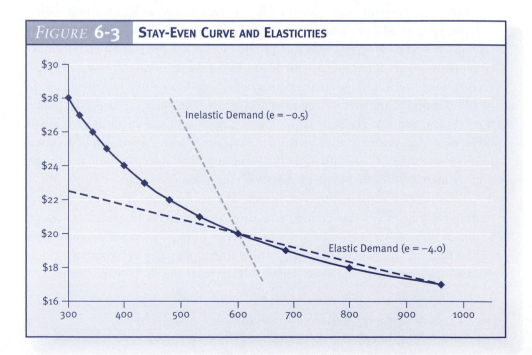

FIGURE **6-3**   STAY-EVEN CURVE AND ELASTICITIES

Starting at a price of $20, if we raise price, demand would have to be *less* elastic than the stay-even curve to make the price increase profitable; if we reduce price, demand would have to be *more* elastic than the stay-even curve to make the price increase profitable.

In Figure 6-3, we overlay two demand curves on top of the stay-even curve to illustrate this idea. Increasing price is profitable, provided demand is steeper (less elastic) than the stay-even curve; decreasing price is profitable provided that demand is flatter (more elastic) than the stay-even curve.[12]

SUMMARY & HOMEWORK PROBLEMS

SUMMARY OF MAIN POINTS

- **Aggregate demand** or market demand is the total number of units that will be purchased by a group of consumers at a given price.
- Pricing is an extent decision. Reduce price (increase quantity) if MR > MC. Increase price (reduce quantity) if MR < MC. The optimal price is where MR = MC.
- **Price elasticity of demand,** e = (% change in quantity demanded) ÷ (% change in price)
  - Estimated price elasticity = $[(Q_1 - Q_2)/(Q_1 + Q_2)] \div [(P_1 - P_2)/(P_1 + P_2)]$ is used to estimate demand from a price and quantity change.
  - If $|e| > 1$, demand is **elastic;** if $|e| < 1$, demand is **inelastic.**
- %ΔRevenue ≈ %ΔPrice + %ΔQuantity

Elastic Demand ($|e| > 1$): Quantity changes more than price.

	ΔRevenue
Price ↑	−
Price ↓	+

[12] As shown in Figure 6-3, the points along the elastic demand line e = −4.0 that are to the right of the current price and quantity of $20 and 600 units lie *above* the quantities of the stay-even curve (i.e., you'll sell more than necessary just to stay even). The points to the left lie below the stay-even curve—you won't sell enough to maintain current profitability levels. For the inelastic demand line, the points to the left are those that lie above the stay-even curve—in this case, raising price will yield higher profit.

Inelastic Demand ($|e| < 1$): Quantity changes less than price.

	ΔRevenue
Price ↑	+
Price ↓	−

- MR > MC implies that $(P - MC)/P > 1/|e|$; that is, the more elastic demand is, the lower the price.
- Four factors make demand more elastic:
  - Products with close **substitutes** (or distant **complements**) have more elastic demand.
  - Demand for brands is more elastic than industry demand.
  - In the long run, demand becomes more elastic.
  - As price increases, demand becomes more elastic.
- **Income elasticity, cross-price elasticity,** and advertising elasticity are measures of how changes in these other factors affect demand.
- It is possible to use elasticity to forecast changes in demand:
  %Δ Quantity $\approx$ (factor elasticity)(%Δ Factor).
- **Stay-even analysis** can be used to determine the volume required to offset a change in costs or prices.

MULTIPLE-CHOICE QUESTIONS

1. A company currently sells 60,000 units a month at $10 per unit. The marginal cost per unit is $6. The company is considering raising the price by 10% to $11. If the price elasticity of demand is _____ in that price range, then profit would increase if the company decided to raise the price by 10%.
- **a.** equal to −3
- **b.** greater than +1
- **c.** less than −2.5
- **d.** greater than or equal to −2

2. The price elasticity of demand for bread is −0.5. If the price falls by 5%, the quantity demanded will change by
- **a.** −2.5%.
- **b.** +2.5%.
- **c.** −1.0%.
- **d.** +10%.

3. Actions a firm can take to change a product's demand curve include
   a. reducing the price of a substitute product the firm also produces.
   b. reducing the price of a complementary product the firm also produces.
   c. differentiating its product from competitors by offering an extended warrantee.
   d. All of the above will change a product's demand curve.

4. A product can be classified as a normal good if an increase in the income of buyers causes
   a. a decrease in quantity demanded.
   b. a decrease in demand.
   c. an increase in demand.
   d. an increase in quantity demanded.

5. Assume that beer and pretzels are complements in consumption; if the price of beer increases, we would expect to see
   a. an increase in the demand for pretzels.
   b. a decrease in the demand for pretzels.
   c. an increase in the quantity of pretzels demanded.
   d. a decrease in the quantity of potatoes demanded.

Individual Problems

6-1. Optimal Pricing for an Aggregate Demand Curve
Suppose you have 10 individuals with values {$1, $2, $3, $4, $5, $6, $7, $8, $9, $10}. Your marginal cost of production is $2.50. What is the profit-maximizing price?

6-2. But What about Fixed Cost?
Using information from Question 6-1, your boss tells you that price cannot drop below $9 because you cannot earn enough profit to cover your fixed cost. What should you tell her?

6-3. Pricing ATM Machines
A bank in a medium-sized midwestern city, Firm X, currently charges $1 per transaction at its ATMs. To determine whether to raise price, the bank managers experimented with a number of higher prices (in 25-cent increments) at selected ATMs. The marginal cost of an ATM transaction is $0.50.

ATM Fee	Usage
$2.00	1,000
$1.75	1,500
$1.50	2,000
$1.25	2,500
$1.00	3,000

What ATM fee should the bank charge?

6-4. Kentucky Racetracks

There are five horseracing tracks in Kentucky. The Kentucky legislature allows only one track to be open at a time. How does this restriction affect the price the track can charge for its product?

6-5. Optimal Markup

If elasticity is −2, price is $10, and marginal cost is $8, should you raise or lower price?

GROUP PROBLEM

G6-1. Pricing

Describe a pricing decision your company has made. Was it optimal? If not, why not? How would you adjust price? Compute the profit consequences of the change.

*The **law of diminishing marginal returns** states that as you try to expand output, your marginal productivity (the extra output associated with extra inputs) eventually declines.*

We can identify several causes for diminishing marginal returns, among them the difficulty of monitoring and motivating larger workforces, the increasing complexity of larger systems, or, as in our example, the "fixity" of some factor, like testing capacity. The same problem occurs more generally when more workers, or any variable input, must share a fixed amount of capital or other fixed input.

Diminishing marginal returns imply increasing marginal costs.

If it requires more inputs to produce each extra unit of output, then the cost of producing these extra units—the marginal cost—must increase.

Increasing marginal costs eventually lead to increasing average costs.

If marginal cost is rising, it will eventually rise above average cost. And this will cause average cost to rise. Just as a baseball player's season batting average will rise if his game batting average is above his season batting average, so, too, will average cost rise if marginal cost is above average cost. In Figure 7-3, the rising average cost of production implies that marginal cost is above average cost.

In the presence of fixed costs, and marginal cost that eventually increases, you get a U-shaped average cost curve as shown in Figure 7-4.

The curve initially falls due to the presence of fixed costs, but then it rises due to rising marginal costs.

It's important to know what your average cost curve looks like when submitting bids or when making investment or shutdown decisions. Consider

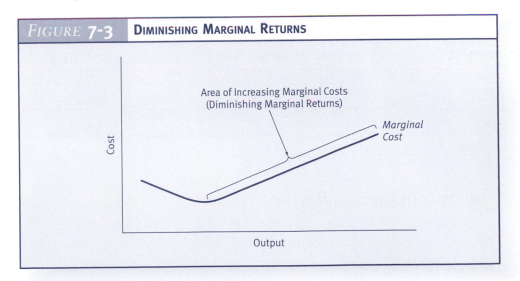

FIGURE 7-3   DIMINISHING MARGINAL RETURNS

Area of Increasing Marginal Costs
(Diminishing Marginal Returns)

Marginal Cost

Cost

Output

Chapter 7

Economies of Scale and Scope

ECONOMIES OF SCALE

In 2004, managers at Zimmerman, Adams, and Plover (ZAP), Inc., an electrical equipment manufacturer, thought the firm was having a banner year. Sales (revenue) had risen to nearly $40 million from $30 million the previous year. But total costs had risen together with revenues. As a consequence, *profit*—the difference between revenue and cost—had not changed. We can see ZAP's monthly sales, costs, and profit for 2003 and 2004 in Figure 7-1.

Costs as a percentage of revenue rose from 64% in 2003 to 76% in 2004. Raw materials costs remained constant, so labor costs accounted for almost all of the 12% increase.

Further investigation revealed that longer production times created most of the increase in labor cost. Each unit produced had to be tested, and the company employed only two testers, each of whom had a capacity of just 600 units per year. Thus, when 2004 production rose above 1,200 units, the testers began holding up the rest of the production line because quality control (QC) took a constant amount of time per unit. The result was idle production workers, who were being paid to wait for the testers.

When a private equity group bought ZAP, the new owners brought in new management, who immediately identified the problem. They hired another tester for $125,000. This simple action removed the production bottleneck, reducing production time per worker and decreasing costs by more than $3 million.

In many production processes, especially those involving large fixed assets, average costs fall as production increases. These types of processes exhibit economies of scale. In contrast, our electrical equipment manufacturer's process exhibited diseconomies of scale, in which average costs increased with output, until the QC bottleneck was resolved.

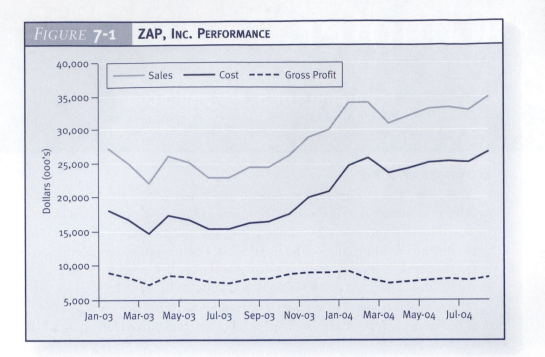

FIGURE 7-1 ZAP, INC. PERFORMANCE

DISECONOMIES OF SCOPE

A manufacturer, AnimalSnax, Inc., makes pet food on extruder lines in 23 plants. This manufacturer has a variety of customers, from large retailers like Wal-Mart to small mom-and-pop pet stores. Currently, the firm produces 2,500 different products, or stock-keeping units (SKUs), using 200 different formulas. All customers pay about the same price per ton. Recently, however, some of the large customers have demanded price concessions.

These requests worry the firm because of the so-called *80-20 rule*: According to this rule of thumb, 80% of a firm's sales come from 20% of its customers. Because big customers (the 20%) order in bulk, the manufacturer can set up its extruders for long production runs. These big orders are much more profitable than smaller orders because all orders require the same setup time regardless of the amount produced and packaged.

To reduce the costs associated with smaller orders, AnimalSnax recently reduced the variety of its product offerings to 70 SKUs, using only 13 different formulas. The firm also began offering price discounts for larger orders. Although some smaller customers were upset about being forced to use new formulas, most were willing to switch. This allowed the company to consolidate small orders into large ones to reduce setup costs. As a consequence, variable costs decreased by $3 million per year.

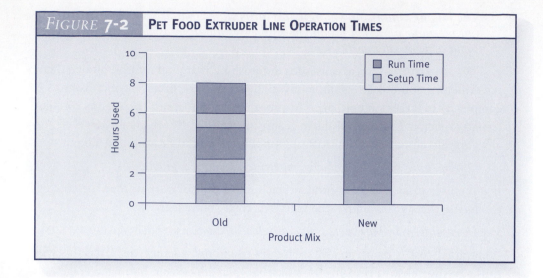

FIGURE 7-2 PET FOOD EXTRUDER LINE OPERATION TIMES

Typical savings for one extruder line are illustrated in Figure 7-2. Under the new regime, the same amount of pet food that had been produced in one eight-hour shift could now be produced in just six hours. This dramatic increase in productivity (25%) also allowed the company to close several of its 23 plants.

The product line consolidation allowed AnimalSnax to increase the length of its production runs, thereby dramatically reducing its production costs. In this case, we say that there are diseconomies of scope associated with producing too many different formulas of pet food.

Both of these stories illustrate the importance of recognizing ways to reduce costs. This chapter provides tools that show you how to do this. These tools are especially important for firms following a cost reduction strategy. However, managers should always be looking for ways to cut costs, whether they are explicitly following a cost reduction strategy or not. A reduction in average cost translates to an immediate increase in profit, and if MC goes down as well, you also get an "extra" increase in profit from the increase in output (recall that if MC falls below MR, you should increase quantity).

INCREASING MARGINAL COST

As they try to increase output, most firms eventually face increasing average costs like those ZAP, Inc. encountered. The firm eventually finds that each extra unit of input is less productive than the previous units. This phenomenon arises from a variety of factors collectively called the *law of diminishing marginal returns*.

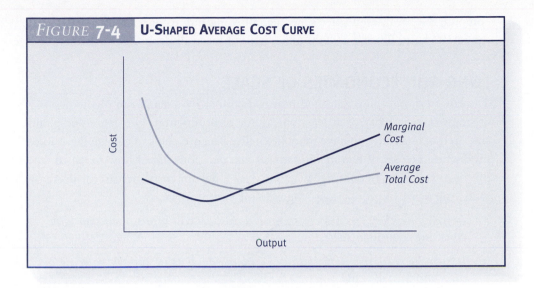

FIGURE 7-4 | **U-SHAPED AVERAGE COST CURVE**

Sony's growth from a bombed-out radio repair shack in Tokyo to a worldwide electronics powerhouse. One of the crucial steps in that impressive growth was Akio Morita's knowledge of what his cost curve looked like. For example, when Morita received an order for 100,000 transistor radios from a retail chain, he turned it down. Because the order was 10 times more than his factory was currently making, he knew that increasing output would significantly increase average costs. Increasing production would require hiring and training more workers, thus raising the average cost or break-even price.

> *I was inexperienced and still a little naive, but I had my wits about me. I considered all the consequences I could think of, and then I sat down and drew a curve that looked something like a lopsided letter U. The price for 5,000 would be our regular price. That would be the beginning of the curve. For 10,000 there would be a discount, and that was at the bottom of the curve. For 30,000 the price would begin to climb. For 50,000 the price per unit would be higher than for 5,000, and for 100,000 units the price would have to be much more per unit than for the first 5,000.*[1]

The retail chain decided to buy 10,000 units at the lower unit price, and the rest is history. The Sony brand radios became very popular, and the company evolved into the giant electronics firm it is today. The moral of the story: Know what your costs look like—otherwise, you could sell product at unprofitable prices. In this case, using a more realistic cost function, Morita was able to

---

[1] Akio Morita with Edwin M. Reingold and Mitsuko Shimomura, *Made in Japan: Akio Morita and Sony* (New York: Penguin, 1988).

compute the break-even price schedule, allowing him to bargain effectively with the retail chain. Beyond 10,000 units, Morita faced diseconomies of scale.

LONG-RUN ECONOMIES OF SCALE

The law of diminishing marginal returns is primarily a short-run phenomenon arising from the fixity of at least one factor of production, like capital or plant size. In the long run, you have more flexibility because you can change these fixed production factors. When making longer-run decisions about how much to produce, you have to consider whether your long-run costs increase or decrease with your scale of production—the amount you produce.

If your average costs are constant with respect to output, then you have **constant returns to scale.**

If average costs rise with output, you have **decreasing returns to scale** *or* **diseconomies of scale.**

If average costs fall with output, you have **increasing returns to scale** *or* **economies of scale.**

You can change more production factors in the long run, so you have more opportunities to reduce costs. However, the same factors (e.g., the fixity of some input) that cause diminishing marginal returns in the short run also cause decreasing returns to scale in the long run. Often the managerial structure of the company does not scale well. Management is an important input into the production processes; and as the company grows, so do the problems of coordination, control, and monitoring. Managers often behave as if they have a fixed amount of decision-making capability, so giving them more decisions often leads to managerial bottlenecks that raise price in the same way that the testers raised price for ZAP, Inc.

In contrast, if a firm's average costs decline with output, then we say they enjoy increasing returns to scale. Knowing whether your long-run costs exhibit constant, decreasing, or increasing returns to scale can help you make better long-run decisions. If your long-run costs exhibit increasing returns to scale, securing big orders allows you to reduce average costs.

One of the reasons the "big box" retail stores, like Staples and Office Depot, are so successful is that they sell so many units that their suppliers enjoy scale economies. Competition among the suppliers for the right to supply these office superstores allows the superstores to capture most of these scale economies for themselves in the form of lower input prices. Big box retailers are able to offer the supplier all of its demand (e.g., in an exclusive arrangement) that in turn allows the supplier to realize economies of scale. The big box retailer and the supplier share in these scale economies.

LEARNING CURVES

Learning curves are characteristic of many processes. That is, when you produce more, you learn from the experience; then, in the future, you are able to produce at a lower cost. Learning curves mean that current production lowers future costs, suggesting implications for strategy. Here the maxim "Look ahead and reason back" is particularly important.

For example, every time an airplane manufacturer doubles production, marginal costs decrease by 20%. If the first plane costs $100 million, then the second will cost $80 million, the fourth will cost $64 million, the eighth will cost $51.2 million, and so on. In Table 7-1, we illustrate such a learning curve.

To see how learning curves affect decision making, put yourself in American Airlines' place, where managers are contemplating placing a big order with Boeing for planes. From Boeing's point of view, a big order from the world's largest airline would allow it to "walk down its learning curve," as shown in Figure 7-5, and lower the costs of future production. And knowing how Boeing will benefit would allow American to bargain for some of these future savings.

If American Airlines knew exactly how many planes it was going to purchase, the airline could compute Boeing's cost of producing that quantity and offer to pay for the average cost of the planes. For example, if American were to order eight planes, it could offer $66.8 million per plane, and Boeing would break even on the order. However, American also knows that such an order would lower the cost of planes that Boeing will produce for (other) future customers. To capture some of the savings, American should ask for a price that reflects the average cost of the total estimated lifetime production for all customers. As another option, American could ask for "kickbacks" on sales of future Boeing planes to rivals;

TABLE 7-1	AIRPLANE MANUFACTURING COSTS		
Quantity	**Marginal Cost ($M)**	**Total Cost ($M)**	**Average Cost ($M)**
1	100.0	100.0	100.0
2	80.0	180.0	90.0
3	70.2	250.2	83.4
4	64.0	314.2	78.6
5	59.6	373.8	74.8
6	56.2	429.9	71.7
7	53.4	483.4	69.1
8	51.2	534.6	66.8
9	49.3	583.9	64.9
10	47.7	631.5	63.2

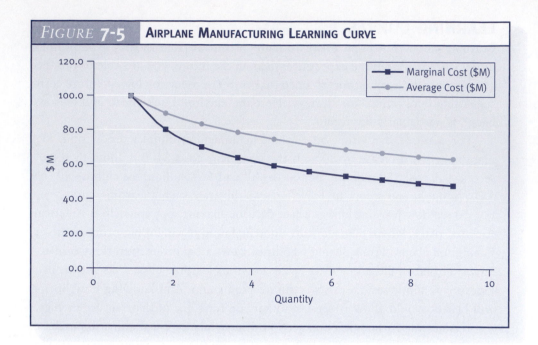

FIGURE **7-5** **AIRPLANE MANUFACTURING LEARNING CURVE**

however, this request would probably violate European and U.S. antitrust laws. Alternatively, American could ask for a percentage of the increase in Boeing's stock market value following announcement of the deal; such a request would be equivalent to buying (call) options to purchase Boeing stock before beginning negotiations. When Boeing's stock value increased because of the order, the value of the call options would also increase. These strategies may also violate securities laws on insider trading, so be sure to get legal advice before trying anything like this.

Probably because American's managers didn't know exactly how many planes they wanted, they offered to purchase planes *exclusively* from Boeing over the next 30 years in exchange for a very favorable price. Boeing accepted because the exclusivity guaranteed Boeing a stream of future orders that would lower costs on orders from other customers. Boeing was willing to give American a very good deal in exchange for such a guarantee.

Later, in 1998, Boeing tried to purchase rival McDonnell-Douglas. However, the European Commission antitrust authority objected because Boeing's only large competitor, Airbus, a consortium of European companies, objected to the long-term exclusive contracts as anticompetitive. Airbus claimed Boeing's exclusive contracts prevented it from competing for American's business. To complete its purchase of McDonnell-Douglas, Boeing agreed not to enforce its exclusive contracts with American, leaving American free to purchase from Airbus if it so chose.

ECONOMIES OF SCOPE

Traditionally, a guitar manufacturer has used rosewood to construct fingerboards on its budget guitars and has reserved ebony for high-end instruments. Both rosewood and ebony are excellent tone woods, but ebony is preferred for its distinct sound and pure black appearance. A significant number of ebony fingerboard blanks are rejected from high-end instrument production because carving of the fingerboard reveals brown streaks in the otherwise black wood. The percentage of fingerboards rejected has increased steadily over the past 10 years as the world supply of streak-free ebony wood has shrunk.

The guitar manufacturer recently began installing these streaked blanks on its budget instruments. Many buyers of budget instruments perceive the streaked ebony fingerboard as an upgrade over rosewood. The ability to use discarded ebony in its budget instruments gives this manufacturer both a cost and quality advantage over rivals that produce only high-end or only low-end instruments. In this case, we say there are *economies of scope* between production of high-end and low-end guitars.

We can make many business decisions, like break-even analysis, by using very simple characterizations of cost (like a fixed cost plus a constant per-unit cost). With economies of scale or scope, however, some kinds of decisions must be based on more complex (and realistic) cost functions.

In this section, we'll examine the analytic tools to understand how to make decisions when you face economies of scale and scope. Economies of scope and scale are especially important for firms trying to pursue the cost-leader strategy.

If the cost of producing two products jointly is less than the cost of producing those two products separately—that is,

$$Cost(Q_1, Q_2) < Cost(Q_1) + Cost(Q_2)$$

*—then there are **economies of scope** between the two products.*

Obviously, you want to exploit economies of scope by producing both Q_1 and Q_2. This is a major cause of mergers. For example, we are currently witnessing a consolidation in the food distribution business. Companies like Kraft, Sara Lee, and ConAgra sell a variety of meat products, hot dogs, sausage, and lunchmeats because they can derive economies of scope by distributing these products together. Once you set up a distribution network, you can easily pump more products through the network without incurring additional costs.

Consider the case of a regional breakfast sausage manufacturer in 1997. The firm used 18 trucks and a single distribution center serving retail customers located in 21 southern and midwestern states. Unfortunately, the demand for breakfast sausage is seasonal, with peaks in November and December and troughs in the eight months from March to September. During the heavy winter months, the firm must pay outside carriers a premium to handle excess product, but for the eight trough months, it must idle half of its trucking fleet.

The company finds itself at a competitive disadvantage with respect to Kraft, Sara Lee, and ConAgra, which ship full truckloads of a wide variety of meats, thus smoothing out the seasonal consumption peaks, at significantly lower cost. In addition, overall consumption of breakfast sausage is declining by 2% per year, and the company's strategy of expansion into new geographic areas is costly because of the low volumes associated with new product penetration.

Because the firm sells only a single product—breakfast sausage—it cannot exploit the scope economies associated with distributing a fuller product line. The firm has two choices. It could sell out to one of the larger, full-line companies, like ConAgra. Such a company could exploit the scope economies associated with distribution, thus placing a higher value on the firm. Or it could outsource its distribution function. Several regional and nationwide distribution companies distribute a variety of food products, and these companies could realize scope economies by distributing a full line of meat products.

Our sausage maker eventually decided to outsource its distribution, but after it sold its trucking fleet, it was held up by the distributor. It was a good idea, but poorly executed.

SUMMARY & HOMEWORK PROBLEMS

SUMMARY OF MAIN POINTS

- The **law of diminishing marginal returns** states that as you try to expand output, your marginal productivity (the extra output associated with extra inputs) eventually declines.
- Increasing marginal costs eventually cause increasing average costs and make it difficult to compute break-even prices. When negotiating contracts, it is important to know what your costs curves look like; otherwise, you could sell product at unprofitable prices.
- If average cost falls with output, then you have **increasing returns to scale.** In this case you want to focus strategy on securing sales that enable you to realize lower costs. Alternatively, if you offer suppliers big orders that

allow them to realize **economies of scale**, try to share in their profit by demanding lower prices.

- If your average costs are constant with respect to output, then you have **constant returns to scale.** If average costs rise with output, you have **decreasing returns to scale** or **diseconomies of scale.**
- **Learning curves** mean that current production lowers future costs. It's important to look over the life cycle of a product when working with products characterized by learning curves.
- If the cost of producing two outputs jointly is less than the cost of producing them separately—that is, $Cost(Q_1,Q_2) < Cost(Q_1) + Cost(Q_2)$—then there are economies of scope between the two products. This can be an important source of competitive advantage and can shape acquisition strategy.

MULTIPLE-CHOICE QUESTIONS

1. As a golf club production company produces more clubs, the average total cost of each club produced decreases. This is because
   a. total fixed costs are decreasing as more clubs are produced.
   b. average variable cost is decreasing as more clubs are produced.
   c. there are scale economies.
   d. total variable cost is decreasing as more clubs are produced.

2. What might you reasonably expect of an industry in which firms tend to have economies of scale?
   a. Exceptional competition among firms
   b. A large number of firms
   c. Highly diversified firms
   d. A small number of firms

3. Following are the costs to produce Product A, Product B, and Products A and B together. Which of the following exhibits economies of scope?
   a. 50, 75, 120
   b. 50, 75, 125
   c. 50, 75, 130
   d. All of the above

4. According to the law of diminishing marginal returns, marginal returns
   a. diminish always prior to increasing.
   b. diminish always.
   c. diminish sometimes.
   d. diminish eventually.

5. A company faces the following costs at the respective production level in addition to its fixed costs of $50,000:

Quantity	Marginal Cost	Sale Price	Marginal Return
1	$10,000	$20,000	$10,000
2	$11,000	$20,000	$9,000
3	$12,000	$20,000	$8,000
4	$13,000	$20,000	$7,000
5	$14,000	$20,000	$6,000

How would you describe the returns to scale for this company?
   a. Increasing
   b. Decreasing
   c. Constant
   d. Marginal

INDIVIDUAL PROBLEMS

7-1. Scale and Scope
What is the difference between economies of scale and economies of scope?

7-2. Brand Extensions
Suppose Nike's managers were considering expanding into producing sports beverages. Why might the company decide to do this under the Nike brand name?

7-3. Average and Marginal Costs
Describe the change in average costs and the relationship between marginal and average costs under the following three conditions as quantities produced increase:

	Average Cost	Marginal Cost versus Average Cost
Constant returns to scale	Rising Falling Flat	Higher Lower Equal
Decreasing returns to scale	Rising Falling Flat	Higher Lower Equal
Increasing returns to scale	Rising Falling Flat	Higher Lower Equal

7-4. Learning Curves
Suppose you have a production technology that can be characterized by a learning curve. Every time you increase production by one unit, your costs decrease by $6. The first unit costs you $64 to produce. If you receive a request for proposal (RFP) on a project for four units, what is your break-even price? Suppose that if you get the contract, you estimate that

you can win another project for two more units. Now what is your break-even price for those two units?

7-5. Multiconcept Restaurants Are a Growing Trend

A multiconcept restaurant incorporates two or more restaurants, typically chains, under one roof. Sharing facilities reduces costs of both real estate and labor. The multiconcept restaurants typically offer a limited menu, compared with full-sized, stand-alone restaurants. For example, KMAC operates a combination Kentucky Fried Chicken (KFC)/Taco Bell restaurant. The food preparation areas are separate, while orders are taken at shared point-of-sale (POS) stations. If Taco Bell and KFC share facilities, they reduce fixed costs by 30%; however, sales in joint facilities are 20% lower than sales in two separate facilities. What do these numbers imply for the decision of when to open a shared facility versus two separate facilities?

GROUP PROBLEMS

G7-1. Economies of Scale

Describe an activity or process or product of your company that exhibits economies or diseconomies of scale. Describe the source of the scale economy. How could your organization exploit the scale economy or diseconomy? Compute the profit consequences of the advice.

G7-2. Learning Curves

Describe an activity or process or product of your company characterized by learning curves. Describe the source of the learning curve. How could your organization exploit the learning curve? Compute the profit consequences of the advice.

G7-3. Economies of Scope

Describe two activities inside your organization, or one inside and one outside your organization, that exhibit economies (or diseconomies) of scope. Describe the source of the scope economies. How could your organization exploit the scope economy or diseconomy? Compute the profit consequences of the advice.

Chapter 8

Understanding Markets and Industry Changes

Throughout the 1990s, consumption of portable electric generators was very stable, exhibiting an average annual growth rate of 2%. In 1997, anticipating increased demand to ensure against power outages associated with the new millennium, managers from Walters, Rosenberg, and Matthews (WRM) implemented a Y2K (year 2000) strategy designed to double production capacity by 1999. Vertical integration[1] into alternator head production allowed the company to increase production capacity and to reduce materials costs. Other firms in the industry made similar investments.

In 1999, generator industry shipments increased by 87%. Prices also increased by an average 21%. Following the boom year in 1999, however, 2000 turned out to be a bust. Demand fell to 1998 levels, and prices tumbled to below-1998 levels. Industry profit declined dramatically, along with capacity utilization rates. The firm's investment to increase production capacity turned out to be unprofitable.

Undoubtedly, WRM's managers would have benefited from a better understanding of the changes that occurred in their industry. In particular, they should have been able to anticipate price and quantity changes, which would have allowed them to make more profitable investment decisions. Being able to forecast and interpret industry-level changes requires an understanding both of aggregate consumer behavior (demand) and of aggregate seller behavior (supply). Forecasting and interpreting these changes are the topic of this chapter.

WHICH INDUSTRY OR MARKET?

Each industry or market has a product, geographic, and time dimension. So before you begin analyzing an industry, you must carefully consider what information or understanding you want to gain from the analysis. Perhaps you want to forecast future changes or to understand past ones. For example, "Why did the price for portable generators in the United States increase in 1999 and

---

[1] *Vertical integration* refers to common ownership of adjacent stages in the vertical supply chain from raw materials down to finished product. In this case, alternators that had previously been purchased from outside suppliers were now being made by the generator company.

decrease in 2000?" Usually the question will suggest a particular market on which to focus. The questions raised in the introduction suggest that you will examine the annual market for portable generators in the United States. Notice that this market has a time (annual), product (portable generators), and geographic (the United States) dimension. Different questions suggest different markets to study.

Although this point may seem self-evident, people often overlook it. In many cases, you can sharpen your analysis and avoid confusion by first defining your market or industry. This is especially true when analyzing markets with imports and exports, as we'll see.

SHIFTS IN DEMAND

As we've seen, changes in price induce changes in consumer behavior that lead to quantity changes. For example, the demand curve that we saw in Chapter 6 shows that when we increase price from $6 to $7, one fewer consumer decides to purchase, so quantity demanded decreases from two units to one unit. This change is called a **movement along the demand curve**.

But price is only one factor that affects demand—we can identify a host of others. In general it helps to catalog these factors into controllable and uncontrollable factors.

> A **controllable factor** is something that affects demand that a company can change.

Price, advertising, warranties, product quality, distribution speed, service quality, and prices of substitute or complementary products also owned by the company—all of these are controllable factors.

To see how to use these controllable factors to your advantage, consider the example of Microsoft. In the late 1970s, Microsoft developed the DOS operating system to control IBM personal computers. Demand for the DOS operating system did not depend solely on the price of the operating system: it also depended on the price and availability of the computers that ran it, as well as on the applications that ran under it, like spreadsheets and word processors.

To increase demand for its DOS operating system, Microsoft manipulated the following controllable factors:

- Microsoft licensed its operating system to other computer manufacturers. The resulting competition between IBM and these new licensees lowered the price of computers—a complementary product.
- Microsoft developed its own versions of word processing and spreadsheet software—Word and Excel—two important complementary products in almost any office.

Chapter 7

Economies of Scale and Scope

ECONOMIES OF SCALE

In 2004, managers at Zimmerman, Adams, and Plover (ZAP), Inc., an electrical equipment manufacturer, thought the firm was having a banner year. Sales (revenue) had risen to nearly $40 million from $30 million the previous year. But total costs had risen together with revenues. As a consequence, *profit*—the difference between revenue and cost—had not changed. We can see ZAP's monthly sales, costs, and profit for 2003 and 2004 in Figure 7-1.

Costs as a percentage of revenue rose from 64% in 2003 to 76% in 2004. Raw materials costs remained constant, so labor costs accounted for almost all of the 12% increase.

Further investigation revealed that longer production times created most of the increase in labor cost. Each unit produced had to be tested, and the company employed only two testers, each of whom had a capacity of just 600 units per year. Thus, when 2004 production rose above 1,200 units, the testers began holding up the rest of the production line because quality control (QC) took a constant amount of time per unit. The result was idle production workers, who were being paid to wait for the testers.

When a private equity group bought ZAP, the new owners brought in new management, who immediately identified the problem. They hired another tester for $125,000. This simple action removed the production bottleneck, reducing production time per worker and decreasing costs by more than $3 million.

In many production processes, especially those involving large fixed assets, average costs fall as production increases. These types of processes exhibit economies of scale. In contrast, our electrical equipment manufacturer's process exhibited diseconomies of scale, in which average costs increased with output, until the QC bottleneck was resolved.

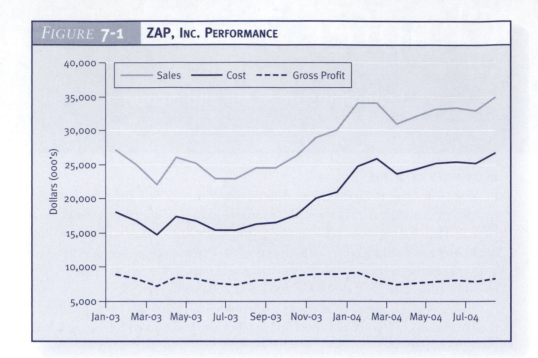

FIGURE **7-1**   ZAP, INC. PERFORMANCE

DISECONOMIES OF SCOPE

A manufacturer, AnimalSnax, Inc., makes pet food on extruder lines in 23 plants. This manufacturer has a variety of customers, from large retailers like Wal-Mart to small mom-and-pop pet stores. Currently, the firm produces 2,500 different products, or stock-keeping units (SKUs), using 200 different formulas. All customers pay about the same price per ton. Recently, however, some of the large customers have demanded price concessions.

These requests worry the firm because of the so-called *80-20 rule*: According to this rule of thumb, 80% of a firm's sales come from 20% of its customers. Because big customers (the 20%) order in bulk, the manufacturer can set up its extruders for long production runs. These big orders are much more profitable than smaller orders because all orders require the same setup time regardless of the amount produced and packaged.

To reduce the costs associated with smaller orders, AnimalSnax recently reduced the variety of its product offerings to 70 SKUs, using only 13 different formulas. The firm also began offering price discounts for larger orders. Although some smaller customers were upset about being forced to use new formulas, most were willing to switch. This allowed the company to consolidate small orders into large ones to reduce setup costs. As a consequence, variable costs decreased by $3 million per year.

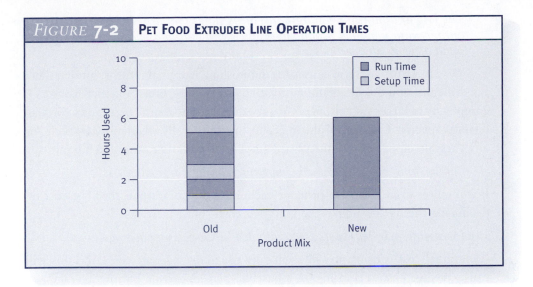

FIGURE 7-2   PET FOOD EXTRUDER LINE OPERATION TIMES

Typical savings for one extruder line are illustrated in Figure 7-2. Under the new regime, the same amount of pet food that had been produced in one eight-hour shift could now be produced in just six hours. This dramatic increase in productivity (25%) also allowed the company to close several of its 23 plants.

The product line consolidation allowed AnimalSnax to increase the length of its production runs, thereby dramatically reducing its production costs. In this case, we say that there are diseconomies of scope associated with producing too many different formulas of pet food.

Both of these stories illustrate the importance of recognizing ways to reduce costs. This chapter provides tools that show you how to do this. These tools are especially important for firms following a cost reduction strategy. However, managers should always be looking for ways to cut costs, whether they are explicitly following a cost reduction strategy or not. A reduction in average cost translates to an immediate increase in profit, and if MC goes down as well, you also get an "extra" increase in profit from the increase in output (recall that if MC falls below MR, you should increase quantity).

INCREASING MARGINAL COST

As they try to increase output, most firms eventually face increasing average costs like those ZAP, Inc. encountered. The firm eventually finds that each extra unit of input is less productive than the previous units. This phenomenon arises from a variety of factors collectively called the *law of diminishing marginal returns*.

*The **law of diminishing marginal returns** states that as you try to expand output, your marginal productivity (the extra output associated with extra inputs) eventually declines.*

We can identify several causes for diminishing marginal returns, among them the difficulty of monitoring and motivating larger workforces, the increasing complexity of larger systems, or, as in our example, the "fixity" of some factor, like testing capacity. The same problem occurs more generally when more workers, or any variable input, must share a fixed amount of capital or other fixed input.

Diminishing marginal returns imply increasing marginal costs.

If it requires more inputs to produce each extra unit of output, then the cost of producing these extra units—the marginal cost—must increase.

Increasing marginal costs eventually lead to increasing average costs.

If marginal cost is rising, it will eventually rise above average cost. And this will cause average cost to rise. Just as a baseball player's season batting average will rise if his game batting average is above his season batting average, so, too, will average cost rise if marginal cost is above average cost. In Figure 7-3, the rising average cost of production implies that marginal cost is above average cost.

In the presence of fixed costs, and marginal cost that eventually increases, you get a U-shaped average cost curve as shown in Figure 7-4.

The curve initially falls due to the presence of fixed costs, but then it rises due to rising marginal costs.

It's important to know what your average cost curve looks like when submitting bids or when making investment or shutdown decisions. Consider

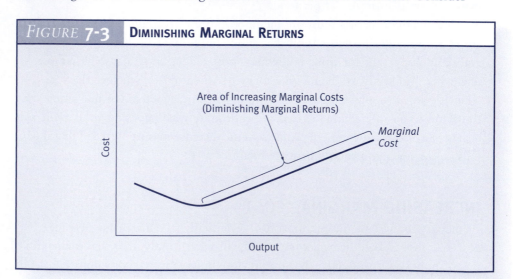

FIGURE 7-3   DIMINISHING MARGINAL RETURNS

Area of Increasing Marginal Costs
(Diminishing Marginal Returns)

Marginal Cost

Cost

Output

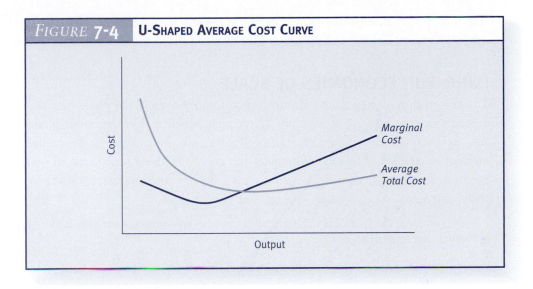

FIGURE 7-4   **U-SHAPED AVERAGE COST CURVE**

Sony's growth from a bombed-out radio repair shack in Tokyo to a worldwide electronics powerhouse. One of the crucial steps in that impressive growth was Akio Morita's knowledge of what his cost curve looked like. For example, when Morita received an order for 100,000 transistor radios from a retail chain, he turned it down. Because the order was 10 times more than his factory was currently making, he knew that increasing output would significantly increase average costs. Increasing production would require hiring and training more workers, thus raising the average cost or break-even price.

> *I was inexperienced and still a little naive, but I had my wits about me. I considered all the consequences I could think of, and then I sat down and drew a curve that looked something like a lopsided letter U. The price for 5,000 would be our regular price. That would be the beginning of the curve. For 10,000 there would be a discount, and that was at the bottom of the curve. For 30,000 the price would begin to climb. For 50,000 the price per unit would be higher than for 5,000, and for 100,000 units the price would have to be much more per unit than for the first 5,000.*[1]

The retail chain decided to buy 10,000 units at the lower unit price, and the rest is history. The Sony brand radios became very popular, and the company evolved into the giant electronics firm it is today. The moral of the story: Know what your costs look like—otherwise, you could sell product at unprofitable prices. In this case, using a more realistic cost function, Morita was able to

---

[1] Akio Morita with Edwin M. Reingold and Mitsuko Shimomura, *Made in Japan: Akio Morita and Sony* (New York: Penguin, 1988).

compute the break-even price schedule, allowing him to bargain effectively with the retail chain. Beyond 10,000 units, Morita faced diseconomies of scale.

LONG-RUN ECONOMIES OF SCALE

The law of diminishing marginal returns is primarily a short-run phenomenon arising from the fixity of at least one factor of production, like capital or plant size. In the long run, you have more flexibility because you can change these fixed production factors. When making longer-run decisions about how much to produce, you have to consider whether your long-run costs increase or decrease with your scale of production—the amount you produce.

If your average costs are constant with respect to output, then you have **constant returns to scale.**

If average costs rise with output, you have **decreasing returns to scale** *or* **diseconomies of scale.**

If average costs fall with output, you have **increasing returns to scale** *or* **economies of scale.**

You can change more production factors in the long run, so you have more opportunities to reduce costs. However, the same factors (e.g., the fixity of some input) that cause diminishing marginal returns in the short run also cause decreasing returns to scale in the long run. Often the managerial structure of the company does not scale well. Management is an important input into the production processes; and as the company grows, so do the problems of coordination, control, and monitoring. Managers often behave as if they have a fixed amount of decision-making capability, so giving them more decisions often leads to managerial bottlenecks that raise price in the same way that the testers raised price for ZAP, Inc.

In contrast, if a firm's average costs decline with output, then we say they enjoy increasing returns to scale. Knowing whether your long-run costs exhibit constant, decreasing, or increasing returns to scale can help you make better long-run decisions. If your long-run costs exhibit increasing returns to scale, securing big orders allows you to reduce average costs.

One of the reasons the "big box" retail stores, like Staples and Office Depot, are so successful is that they sell so many units that their suppliers enjoy scale economies. Competition among the suppliers for the right to supply these office superstores allows the superstores to capture most of these scale economies for themselves in the form of lower input prices. Big box retailers are able to offer the supplier all of its demand (e.g., in an exclusive arrangement) that in turn allows the supplier to realize economies of scale. The big box retailer and the supplier share in these scale economies.

LEARNING CURVES

Learning curves are characteristic of many processes. That is, when you produce more, you learn from the experience; then, in the future, you are able to produce at a lower cost. Learning curves mean that current production lowers future costs, suggesting implications for strategy. Here the maxim "Look ahead and reason back" is particularly important.

For example, every time an airplane manufacturer doubles production, marginal costs decrease by 20%. If the first plane costs $100 million, then the second will cost $80 million, the fourth will cost $64 million, the eighth will cost $51.2 million, and so on. In Table 7-1, we illustrate such a learning curve.

To see how learning curves affect decision making, put yourself in American Airlines' place, where managers are contemplating placing a big order with Boeing for planes. From Boeing's point of view, a big order from the world's largest airline would allow it to "walk down its learning curve," as shown in Figure 7-5, and lower the costs of future production. And knowing how Boeing will benefit would allow American to bargain for some of these future savings.

If American Airlines knew exactly how many planes it was going to purchase, the airline could compute Boeing's cost of producing that quantity and offer to pay for the average cost of the planes. For example, if American were to order eight planes, it could offer $66.8 million per plane, and Boeing would break even on the order. However, American also knows that such an order would lower the cost of planes that Boeing will produce for (other) future customers. To capture some of the savings, American should ask for a price that reflects the average cost of the total estimated lifetime production for all customers. As another option, American could ask for "kickbacks" on sales of future Boeing planes to rivals;

TABLE 7-1	AIRPLANE MANUFACTURING COSTS		
Quantity	**Marginal Cost ($M)**	**Total Cost ($M)**	**Average Cost ($M)**
1	100.0	100.0	100.0
2	80.0	180.0	90.0
3	70.2	250.2	83.4
4	64.0	314.2	78.6
5	59.6	373.8	74.8
6	56.2	429.9	71.7
7	53.4	483.4	69.1
8	51.2	534.6	66.8
9	49.3	583.9	64.9
10	47.7	631.5	63.2

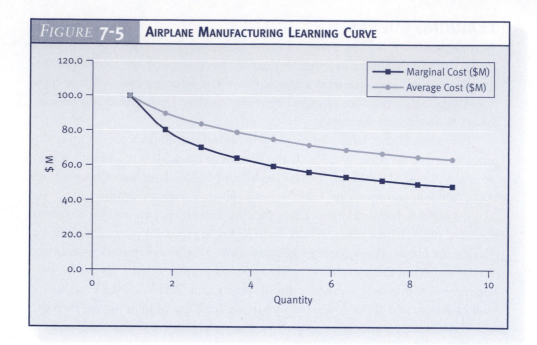

FIGURE **7-5**   **AIRPLANE MANUFACTURING LEARNING CURVE**

however, this request would probably violate European and U.S. antitrust laws. Alternatively, American could ask for a percentage of the increase in Boeing's stock market value following announcement of the deal; such a request would be equivalent to buying (call) options to purchase Boeing stock before beginning negotiations. When Boeing's stock value increased because of the order, the value of the call options would also increase. These strategies may also violate securities laws on insider trading, so be sure to get legal advice before trying anything like this.

Probably because American's managers didn't know exactly how many planes they wanted, they offered to purchase planes *exclusively* from Boeing over the next 30 years in exchange for a very favorable price. Boeing accepted because the exclusivity guaranteed Boeing a stream of future orders that would lower costs on orders from other customers. Boeing was willing to give American a very good deal in exchange for such a guarantee.

Later, in 1998, Boeing tried to purchase rival McDonnell-Douglas. However, the European Commission antitrust authority objected because Boeing's only large competitor, Airbus, a consortium of European companies, objected to the long-term exclusive contracts as anticompetitive. Airbus claimed Boeing's exclusive contracts prevented it from competing for American's business. To complete its purchase of McDonnell-Douglas, Boeing agreed not to enforce its exclusive contracts with American, leaving American free to purchase from Airbus if it so chose.

ECONOMIES OF SCOPE

Traditionally, a guitar manufacturer has used rosewood to construct fingerboards on its budget guitars and has reserved ebony for high-end instruments. Both rosewood and ebony are excellent tone woods, but ebony is preferred for its distinct sound and pure black appearance. A significant number of ebony fingerboard blanks are rejected from high-end instrument production because carving of the fingerboard reveals brown streaks in the otherwise black wood. The percentage of fingerboards rejected has increased steadily over the past 10 years as the world supply of streak-free ebony wood has shrunk.

The guitar manufacturer recently began installing these streaked blanks on its budget instruments. Many buyers of budget instruments perceive the streaked ebony fingerboard as an upgrade over rosewood. The ability to use discarded ebony in its budget instruments gives this manufacturer both a cost and quality advantage over rivals that produce only high-end or only low-end instruments. In this case, we say there are *economies of scope* between production of high-end and low-end guitars.

We can make many business decisions, like break-even analysis, by using very simple characterizations of cost (like a fixed cost plus a constant per-unit cost). With economies of scale or scope, however, some kinds of decisions must be based on more complex (and realistic) cost functions.

In this section, we'll examine the analytic tools to understand how to make decisions when you face economies of scale and scope. Economies of scope and scale are especially important for firms trying to pursue the cost-leader strategy.

If the cost of producing two products jointly is less than the cost of producing those two products separately—that is,

$$\text{Cost}(Q_1, Q_2) < \text{Cost}(Q_1) + \text{Cost}(Q_2)$$

—then there are **economies of scope** *between the two products.*

Obviously, you want to exploit economies of scope by producing both Q_1 and Q_2. This is a major cause of mergers. For example, we are currently witnessing a consolidation in the food distribution business. Companies like Kraft, Sara Lee, and ConAgra sell a variety of meat products, hot dogs, sausage, and lunchmeats because they can derive economies of scope by distributing these products together. Once you set up a distribution network, you can easily pump more products through the network without incurring additional costs.

Consider the case of a regional breakfast sausage manufacturer in 1997. The firm used 18 trucks and a single distribution center serving retail customers located in 21 southern and midwestern states. Unfortunately, the demand for breakfast sausage is seasonal, with peaks in November and December and troughs in the eight months from March to September. During the heavy winter months, the firm must pay outside carriers a premium to handle excess product, but for the eight trough months, it must idle half of its trucking fleet.

The company finds itself at a competitive disadvantage with respect to Kraft, Sara Lee, and ConAgra, which ship full truckloads of a wide variety of meats, thus smoothing out the seasonal consumption peaks, at significantly lower cost. In addition, overall consumption of breakfast sausage is declining by 2% per year, and the company's strategy of expansion into new geographic areas is costly because of the low volumes associated with new product penetration.

Because the firm sells only a single product—breakfast sausage—it cannot exploit the scope economies associated with distributing a fuller product line. The firm has two choices. It could sell out to one of the larger, full-line companies, like ConAgra. Such a company could exploit the scope economies associated with distribution, thus placing a higher value on the firm. Or it could outsource its distribution function. Several regional and nationwide distribution companies distribute a variety of food products, and these companies could realize scope economies by distributing a full line of meat products.

Our sausage maker eventually decided to outsource its distribution, but after it sold its trucking fleet, it was held up by the distributor. It was a good idea, but poorly executed.

SUMMARY & HOMEWORK PROBLEMS

SUMMARY OF MAIN POINTS

- The **law of diminishing marginal returns** states that as you try to expand output, your marginal productivity (the extra output associated with extra inputs) eventually declines.
- Increasing marginal costs eventually cause increasing average costs and make it difficult to compute break-even prices. When negotiating contracts, it is important to know what your costs curves look like; otherwise, you could sell product at unprofitable prices.
- If average cost falls with output, then you have **increasing returns to scale.** In this case you want to focus strategy on securing sales that enable you to realize lower costs. Alternatively, if you offer suppliers big orders that

allow them to realize **economies of scale**, try to share in their profit by demanding lower prices.

- If your average costs are constant with respect to output, then you have **constant returns to scale.** If average costs rise with output, you have **decreasing returns to scale** or **diseconomies of scale.**
- **Learning curves** mean that current production lowers future costs. It's important to look over the life cycle of a product when working with products characterized by learning curves.
- If the cost of producing two outputs jointly is less than the cost of producing them separately—that is, $\mathrm{Cost}(Q_1,Q_2) < \mathrm{Cost}(Q_1) + \mathrm{Cost}(Q_2)$—then there are economies of scope between the two products. This can be an important source of competitive advantage and can shape acquisition strategy.

MULTIPLE-CHOICE QUESTIONS

1. As a golf club production company produces more clubs, the average total cost of each club produced decreases. This is because
   a. total fixed costs are decreasing as more clubs are produced.
   b. average variable cost is decreasing as more clubs are produced.
   c. there are scale economies.
   d. total variable cost is decreasing as more clubs are produced.

2. What might you reasonably expect of an industry in which firms tend to have economies of scale?
   a. Exceptional competition among firms
   b. A large number of firms
   c. Highly diversified firms
   d. A small number of firms

3. Following are the costs to produce Product A, Product B, and Products A and B together. Which of the following exhibits economies of scope?
   a. 50, 75, 120
   b. 50, 75, 125
   c. 50, 75, 130
   d. All of the above

4. According to the law of diminishing marginal returns, marginal returns
   a. diminish always prior to increasing.
   b. diminish always.
   c. diminish sometimes.
   d. diminish eventually.

5. A company faces the following costs at the respective production level in addition to its fixed costs of $50,000:

Quantity	Marginal Cost	Sale Price	Marginal Return
1	$10,000	$20,000	$10,000
2	$11,000	$20,000	$9,000
3	$12,000	$20,000	$8,000
4	$13,000	$20,000	$7,000
5	$14,000	$20,000	$6,000

How would you describe the returns to scale for this company?
   a. Increasing
   b. Decreasing
   c. Constant
   d. Marginal

INDIVIDUAL PROBLEMS

7-1. Scale and Scope
What is the difference between economies of scale and economies of scope?

7-2. Brand Extensions
Suppose Nike's managers were considering expanding into producing sports beverages. Why might the company decide to do this under the Nike brand name?

7-3. Average and Marginal Costs
Describe the change in average costs and the relationship between marginal and average costs under the following three conditions as quantities produced increase:

	Average Cost	Marginal Cost versus Average Cost
Constant returns to scale	Rising Falling Flat	Higher Lower Equal
Decreasing returns to scale	Rising Falling Flat	Higher Lower Equal
Increasing returns to scale	Rising Falling Flat	Higher Lower Equal

7-4. Learning Curves
Suppose you have a production technology that can be characterized by a learning curve. Every time you increase production by one unit, your costs decrease by $6. The first unit costs you $64 to produce. If you receive a request for proposal (RFP) on a project for four units, what is your break-even price? Suppose that if you get the contract, you estimate that

you can win another project for two more units. Now what is your break-even price for those two units?

7-5. Multiconcept Restaurants Are a Growing Trend

A multiconcept restaurant incorporates two or more restaurants, typically chains, under one roof. Sharing facilities reduces costs of both real estate and labor. The multiconcept restaurants typically offer a limited menu, compared with full-sized, stand-alone restaurants. For example, KMAC operates a combination Kentucky Fried Chicken (KFC)/ Taco Bell restaurant. The food preparation areas are separate, while orders are taken at shared point-of-sale (POS) stations. If Taco Bell and KFC share facilities, they reduce fixed costs by 30%; however, sales in joint facilities are 20% lower than sales in two separate facilities. What do these numbers imply for the decision of when to open a shared facility versus two separate facilities?

GROUP PROBLEMS

G7-1. Economies of Scale

Describe an activity or process or product of your company that exhibits economies or diseconomies of scale. Describe the source of the scale economy. How could your organization exploit the scale economy or diseconomy? Compute the profit consequences of the advice.

G7-2. Learning Curves

Describe an activity or process or product of your company characterized by learning curves. Describe the source of the learning curve. How could your organization exploit the learning curve? Compute the profit consequences of the advice.

G7-3. Economies of Scope

Describe two activities inside your organization, or one inside and one outside your organization, that exhibit economies (or diseconomies) of scope. Describe the source of the scope economies. How could your organization exploit the scope economy or diseconomy? Compute the profit consequences of the advice.

- Microsoft kept the price for its DOS product relatively low. As more consumers purchased DOS computers, more companies made applications that ran on DOS computers, increasing future demand for DOS software.

In contrast to controllable factors are uncontrollable ones.

*An **uncontrollable factor** is something that affects demand that a company cannot control.*

Uncontrollable factors include, among other things, income, weather, interest rates, and prices of substitute and complementary products owned by other companies.

Even though you can't control these variables, you need to understand how they will affect the industry in which you compete because they will affect your own profitability. The risk of a massive power outage following the start of 2000 was an uncontrollable factor that affected demand for portable electric generators. Understanding how both controllable and uncontrollable factors affect your own profit requires that you learn how to manipulate demand and supply curves, a topic to which we now turn.

Because we only have two variables on our demand graph—price and quantity—the only way to represent a change in a third variable is with a ***shift of the demand curve***. For example, if the price of a substitute product increases, then industry demand for a product will increase. We represent this as a rightward shift in the demand curve, as in Figure 8-1.

In this case, at every price, demand shifts rightward, or increases, by four units. In contrast, a decrease in a substitute's price would decrease demand.

SHIFTS IN SUPPLY

***Supply curves** describe the behavior of sellers and tell you how much will be sold at a given price.*

The construction of supply curves is similar to that of demand curves; we arrange sellers by the prices at which they are willing to sell. Every person willing to sell at a price below the given prices "supplies" product to the market. For example, suppose we have nine sellers, with values of {$4, $5, $6, $7, $8, $9, $10, $11, $12}; at a price of $4, one seller would be willing to sell; at a price of $5, two sellers; and so on, until, at a price of $12, all nine sellers would be willing to sell. This supply curve describes these nine sellers' aggregate behavior.

Supply curves differ from demand curves in one very important way.

Supply curves slope upward; that is, the higher the price, the higher the quantity supplied.

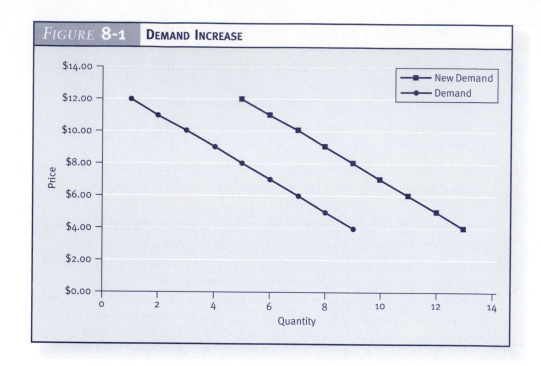

FIGURE 8-1   DEMAND INCREASE

In other words, at higher prices, more suppliers are willing to sell. We plot our aggregate supply curve in Figure 8-2.

As with demand curves, we plot supply curves with price on the vertical axis and quantity on the horizontal axis. In math, we are taught to plot the dependent variable (quantity) on the vertical axis, and the independent variable (price) on the horizontal axis. So the economics convention of plotting quantity on the horizontal axis may confuse those of you who are familiar with graphical analysis. Get used to it.

Also, like demand curves, supply curves shift when a variable other than price changes. Changes in the prices of inputs, changes in exchange rates, technological change, and entry or exit of new capacity or firms will shift supply. Consider the effect of increased input prices. How would that shift the supply curve? Think about an individual seller first—if that producer now has to pay more to produce the same quantity, he or she will require a higher price to cover those increased costs. If other sellers are similarly situated, the aggregate supply curve will shift upward (or to the left)—higher prices are necessary to induce sellers to produce the same quantities. Alternatively, you could say that a smaller quantity will be made available at the previous price.

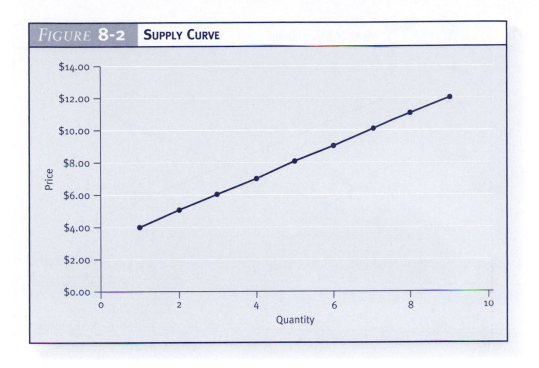

FIGURE **8-2** | **SUPPLY CURVE**

MARKET EQUILIBRIUM

Market equilibrium is the price at which quantity supplied equals quantity demanded.

In other words, at the equilibrium price, the numbers of buyers and sellers are equal, so there's no pressure for prices to change. That's why we call it an "equilibrium." You can see an illustration of market equilibrium in Figure 8-3, where, at a price of $8, five units are demanded and five units supplied.

To understand why this is an equilibrium, see what happens at prices higher or lower than $8. For example, at a price of $11, the quantity demanded (two) is less than the quantity supplied (eight), meaning that eight sellers are chasing only two buyers. Economists call this *excess supply*. Quite naturally, this type of imbalance exerts downward pressure on price.

At a price of $6, the quantity demanded (seven) is greater than the quantity supplied (three)—seven buyers are chasing just three sellers. Economists call this *excess demand*. Quite naturally, this type of imbalance leads to upward pressure on price. Only at $8 are the numbers of buyers and sellers equal, exerting no pressure on price to change. This is why we call $8 an *equilibrium price*.

At the equilibrium price, only buyers with values above $8 buy, and only sellers with values below $8 sell. No one else wants to buy or sell.

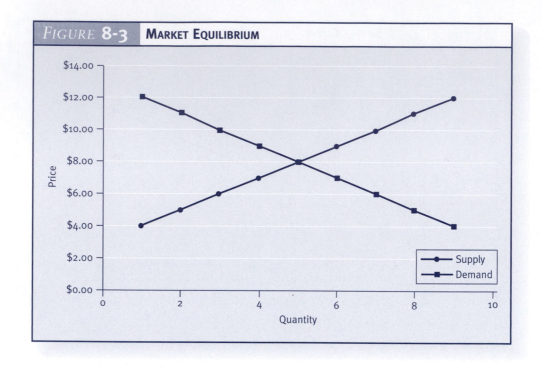

FIGURE 8-3 | **MARKET EQUILIBRIUM**

In market equilibrium, there are no unconsummated wealth-creating transactions.

Another way of thinking about this is that the market has identified the high-value buyers and the low-value sellers, brought them together, and set a price at which they can exchange goods. The market moves goods from lower- to higher-valued uses and thus creates wealth. Economists often characterize market forces as the work of the "invisible hand"[2] of the market.

USING SUPPLY AND DEMAND

We can use supply and demand curves to describe changes that occur at the industry level. In Table 8-1 and Figure 8-4, we begin with a simple example of how an increase in demand changes price and quantity. This increase in demand could arise from an increase in income, a decrease in the price of a complement, or an increase in price of a substitute.

We see the initial equilibrium of $8, where quantity demanded equals quantity supplied (five units) in the first three columns of Table 8-1, as indicated by the shaded numbers in the fifth row. After the demand shift, the new equilibrium is $10, where quantity demanded equals quantity supplied

---

[2] Credit for the invisible hand metaphor goes to Adam Smith and his renowned *The Wealth of Nations*.

TABLE 8-1	MARKET EQUILIBRIUM ANALYSIS			
	Price	**Demand**	**Supply**	**New Demand**
	$12	1	9	5
	$11	2	8	6
Equilibrium 2	$10	3	7	7
	$9	4	6	8
Equilibrium 1	$8	5	5	9
	$7	6	4	10
	$6	7	3	11
	$5	8	2	12
	$4	9	1	13

FIGURE 8-4	MARKET EQUILIBRIUM FOLLOWING DEMAND SHIFT

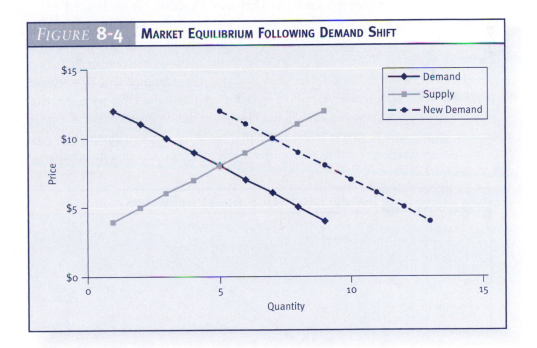

(seven units). The shaded numbers in columns 1, 3, and 4 of the third row show this second equilibrium.

Again, the mechanism driving price to the new equilibrium is competition among buyers to buy and sellers to sell. At the old price of $8, there is excess demand—more buyers than sellers. This imbalance puts upward pressure on price until it settles at the new equilibrium price of $10. Notice that, as the price increased from $8 to $10, quantity also increased from five to seven units.

Again, you'll probably never have the necessary information to plot an entire demand curve or to accurately predict quantitative changes in price and quantity. Nevertheless, the ability of demand and supply analysis to explain and predict qualitative changes in an industry is extremely useful. In addition, demand–supply analysis has become part of the business lexicon. To communicate, you have to learn this analysis.

To illustrate the usefulness of demand and supply, let's return to the changes in the electric generator industry that occurred around 1999. Using demand–supply analysis, we can explain exactly what happened. We can see this analysis in Figure 8-5.

In the graph, we see the change from 1998 to 1999 as the change from A to B (denoted A→B) when both demand and supply increased. Supply shifted outward as firms invested in cost reductions and capacity increases, while demand increased owing to anticipation of power outages in 2000. Because price increased by 21%, we know that the increase in demand must have exceeded the decrease in supply. Both shifts contributed to the quantity increase of 87%.

In 2000, when demand returned to its 1998 level (denoted B→C), it would have been easy to forecast that prices would drop below the 1998 level, but that quantity would stay above the 1998 level owing to the supply increase. Although it is relatively easy to predict these kinds of *qualitative* changes, predicting exact *quantitative* changes is a different matter altogether. For accurate quantitative

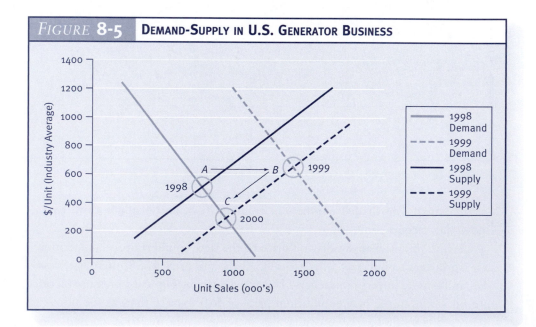

FIGURE 8-5 **DEMAND-SUPPLY IN U.S. GENERATOR BUSINESS**

predictions, you'd need information about the exact magnitudes of the supply and demand shifts, information that is exceedingly difficult to obtain. In fact, you should be very suspicious of consultants who claim they can provide accurate quantitative forecasts.

Nevertheless, we can learn much from simple qualitative analysis. WRM's managers should have been able to predict the movement in price and quantity A→B→C, as shown in Figure 8-5; then they could have taken steps to prepare for the changes. For example, knowing that the demand shift was temporary, they could have hired temporary workers, or even outsourced the extra production, to avoid making investments that would become unprofitable once price fell below its 1998 levels. Like John Deere's managers in Chapter 5, they could have chosen a low-fixed-cost technology, thereby better positioning themselves to adjust to the demand changes.

Let's test our understanding of the analysis thus far. Try to explain the increase in the quantity of personal computers and the decline in price over the past decade using shifts in the demand or supply curves.

To do this, you have to explain two points in time. On a graph, the initial point has a high price and small quantity. The final point has low price and large quantity. You can explain this phenomenon with a simple rightward shift in the supply curve. In Figure 8-6, as supply increases, the equilibrium price falls from P_0 to P_1 and the equilibrium quantity increases from Q_0 to Q_1.[3]

Demand and supply analysis is also useful for explaining changes in international trade. For example, in August 1998, the Mexican peso was devalued from 7.8 to 10.15 pesos per dollar. Try to predict the effect of the peso

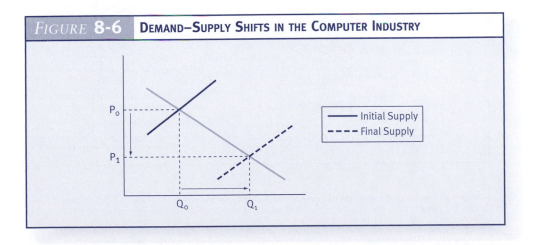

FIGURE 8-6	DEMAND–SUPPLY SHIFTS IN THE COMPUTER INDUSTRY

[3] Note that an increase in demand could explain the increase in quantity but not the decrease in price.

devaluation on the demand and supply of golf in Tijuana and in San Diego, "sister" towns on either side of the Mexico–United States border.[4]

To begin, note that two sets of consumers determine demand for golf in Tijuana: Mexicans who play golf and U.S. citizens who play golf. For both groups, playing golf in the United States is a substitute for playing golf in Mexico. Following the peso devaluation, demand for golf in Mexico increased for two reasons: Mexicans found that they needed more pesos to play golf in the United States, and U.S. citizens found that they needed fewer dollars to play golf in Mexico. Both sets of consumers substitute cheaper Mexican golf for more expensive U.S. golf.

We represent these changes graphically in Figure 8-7. The key to understanding the changes is to look at the change in each area separately, using local currency to denote changes in prices. Since the short-run supply of golf is fixed, the supply curve is relatively inelastic, indicated by a nearly vertical line. Because quantity cannot adjust, we'd expect a relatively large adjustment in price. The price of golf in Tijuana, as measured in pesos, *increases,* and the price of golf in San Diego, as measured in dollars, *decreases.*

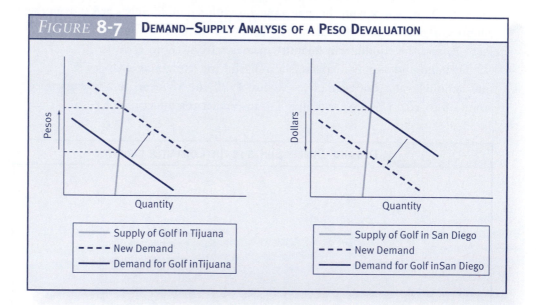

FIGURE 8-7   DEMAND–SUPPLY ANALYSIS OF A PESO DEVALUATION

Supply of Golf in Tijuana
New Demand
Demand for Golf in Tijuana

Supply of Golf in San Diego
New Demand
Demand for Golf in San Diego

[4] To help you understand the effects of currency devaluations, put yourself in the place of different people in the economic system. First, consider a Mexican consumer. This consumer earns pesos through employment and has the option of buying domestic products (in pesos) or imports (in dollars). Prior to the devaluation, a $10 U.S. product would cost 78 pesos; after the devaluation, the same product would cost 101.5 pesos. A devaluation, then, has the effect of making imports relatively more expensive compared with domestic goods. For the U.S. consumer, the effect is the opposite. Mexican goods (imports) become relatively cheaper ($10 in earnings can now buy 101.5 pesos worth of goods).

The devaluation was a benefit to Mexican golf-course owners who "export" a portion of their product to U.S. consumers. In general, devaluations benefit exporters and harm importers.

Currency devaluations help exporters because they make exports less expensive in the foreign currency; they hurt importers because they make imports more expensive in the domestic currency.

PRICES CONVEY VALUABLE INFORMATION

Markets play a significant role in collecting and transmitting information between buyers and sellers. In a sense, prices are the primary mechanism that market participants use to communicate with one another. Buyers signal their willingness to pay, and sellers signal their willingness to sell, with prices.

To illustrate how information is transmitted through prices, let's examine the changes that occurred when a pipeline carrying gasoline to Phoenix broke.[5] The break could have been disastrous because Arizona has no refineries of its own; it obtains gasoline primarily through two pipelines, as shown in Figure 8-8. One pipeline starts in Los Angeles and supplies gasoline from West Coast refineries to the majority of Phoenix's gasoline terminals. The other pipeline starts in El Paso

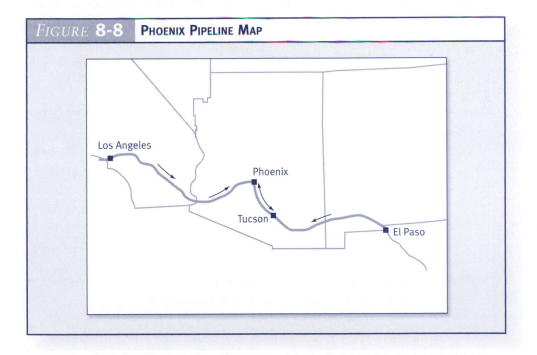

FIGURE 8-8 | **PHOENIX PIPELINE MAP**

[5] Federal Trade Commission, *Gasoline Price Changes: The Dynamics of Industry Supply and Demand* (Washington, D.C.: U.S. Government Printing Office, 2005).

and supplies gasoline from refineries in Texas and New Mexico. Upon entering Arizona, that pipeline travels first to terminals in Tucson and then to terminals in Phoenix.

On July 30, 2003, the Tucson-to-Phoenix section of the pipeline from El Paso ruptured, closing that section of the line from August 8 until August 23, when partial service resumed.

Using supply–demand analysis, you should now be able to analyze what happened in the daily market for gasoline in Phoenix. Following a decrease in supply to Phoenix, the price should go up and quantity should go down. Indeed, the Phoenix price went from less than $1.60 to over $2.10 per gallon. What is less obvious is that the *Tucson* price also increased. Given the location of the pipeline break, it would seem that Tucson should now have an increase in supply, thus reducing Tucson prices. Instead, Tucson prices increased from about $1.60 to $1.80 per gallon.

What happened? The tank wagon owners who normally deliver gas from terminals in Tucson to Tucson gas stations discovered that delivering gas to Phoenix was more profitable than delivering it to Tucson. Tank wagons waited for as much as six hours at the terminal in Tucson to buy gasoline to deliver to Phoenix. The high prices in Phoenix conveyed information to sellers in Tucson that it was more profitable to sell in Phoenix. So supply actually decreased in Tucson—hence the price increase in that city. Likewise, supply decreased in Los Angeles as sellers found it more profitable to divert gasoline to Phoenix, leading to a price increase in that city as well. So next time you hear a politician complaining about the "high price of gas," tell her that she should be celebrating high prices—without those high prices, consumers would consume too much, and suppliers would supply too little. If politicians set prices instead of markets, prices would not convey the valuable information from sellers to buyers and from buyers to sellers that facilitate the movement of gasoline from lower- to higher-valued uses.

The information conveyed by prices is especially important in financial markets, where each market participant possesses a little piece of information about the prospects for a traded security. By trading, they reveal their information to the market. For example, the price of a stock is a good predictor of the discounted flow of profit that will accrue to the stockholder. Likewise, prices of S&P futures are good predictors of the future level of the S&P 500 Stock Market Index, and foreign exchange futures are good predictors of future exchange rates. The information contained in these prices has obvious uses to companies and individuals trying to make decisions based on an uncertain future.

In fact, market prices are so good at forecasting the future that companies like Hewlett Packard, Eli Lilly, and Microsoft are setting up internal markets to help forecast demand for their products.[6] They set up an automated trading platform and let employees buy and sell contracts that pay off according to how much the company will earn or sell in the future. The prices of the contracts tend to be much more accurate than traditional forecasting methods and are being used to plan production. The accuracy of these prices in forecasting future sales can also help firms design compensation schemes for sales people; for example, sales people could be rewarded for increasing sales relative to the forecast quantity.

MARKET MAKING

In the supply–demand analyses in this chapter, we've been ignoring the costs of making a market. Buyers and sellers don't simply appear in a trading pit and begin transacting with one another. Instead, someone has to incur costs to identify buyers and sellers, bring them together, and devise ways of profitably facilitating transactions among them. The economies of Chicago, New York, London, and Tokyo depend largely on the profit earned from making markets. These profits are the "costs" of making a market that, when significant, can prevent prices from moving to equalize demand and supply.

In this section, we show exactly how a "market maker" makes a market—by buying cheap and selling dear. Consider a market maker facing the demand and supply curves in shown in Figure 8-9: nine buyers have values {$12, $11, $10, $9, $8, $7, $6, $5, $4}, and nine sellers are willing to sell at the same prices. If there were but a single (monopoly) market maker, how much would she offer the sellers (the bid), and how much would she charge the buyers (the ask)? How many transactions would occur?

Note that if the market maker bought and sold at the competitive price ($8), she would earn zero profit. To earn profit, the market maker must buy low (at the bid) and sell high (at the ask). The market maker has no desire to *hold inventory,* meaning that the number of buyers equals the number of sellers. For example, if the market maker were going to engage in, say, three transactions, she would offer sellers $6 (from the supply curve, three sellers will sell if the price is at least $6) and charge buyers $10 (from the demand curve, three buyers are willing to pay at least $10). Consequently, there are five obvious bid–ask price combinations:[7]

---

[6] Barbara Kiviat, "The End of Management?" *Time,* July 12, 2004, "Inside Business" section.

[7] Note that it makes sense to make this market only for five transactions or fewer. For quantities greater than this, the demand curve lies below the supply curve. So to complete seven transactions, for example, the market maker would have to offer sellers $10 (see the supply curve) and charge buyers $6 (see the demand curve) for a net loss of $4 per transaction.

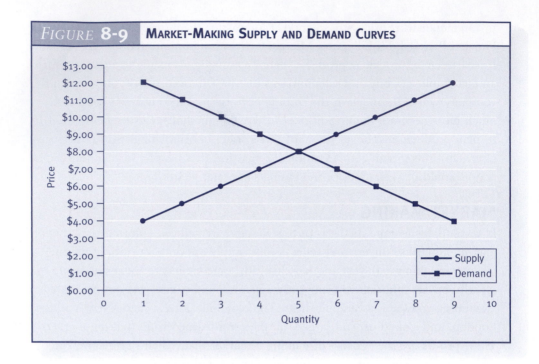

FIGURE 8-9 | **MARKET-MAKING SUPPLY AND DEMAND CURVES**

- Buy at $8 and sell at $8 (five transactions).
- Buy at $7 and sell at $9 (four transactions).
- Buy at $6 and sell at $10 (three transactions).
- Buy at $5 and sell at $11 (two transactions).
- Buy at $4 and sell at $12 (one transaction).

Note that the market maker faces a familiar trade-off. She can consummate fewer transactions but earn more on each transaction; or she can consummate more transactions but earn less on each transaction. In Table 8-2, we calculate the

TABLE 8-2 | **OPTIMAL SPREAD IN MARKET MAKING**

Bid	Ask	Quantity	Profit
$8	$8	5	$0
$7	$9	4	$8
$6	$10	3	$12
$5	$11	2	$12
$4	$12	1	$8

optimal bid–ask spread for the market maker: Either buy at $6 and sell at $10, or buy at $5 and sell at $11. Both earn profit of $12.

Now suppose that competition among several market makers forces the bid–ask spread—the price of a transaction—down to the costs of market making, which we suppose to be $2 per transaction. Now what is the competitive bid and ask?

In this case, each market maker would buy at $7 and sell at $9. Those offering worse prices wouldn't make any sales, and those offering better prices wouldn't cover costs. In this case, competition forces price down to cost, thereby raising the number of transactions from three to four.

Normally, we expect that prices will be forced down to cost in highly competitive markets. But this is not always the case. On May 26, 1994, *The Wall Street Journal* and the *Los Angeles Times* reported on academic research by Bill Christie showing that Amgen, Apple, Microsoft, Cisco, and Intel stocks rarely traded at odd-eighths (fractions ending in 1/8 or $0.125) and thus had bid–ask spreads of at least 1/4 ($0.25). Christie and coauthor Paul Schultz concluded that

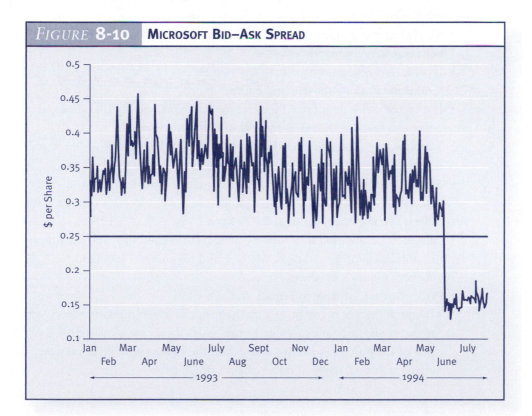

FIGURE 8-10 **MICROSOFT BID–ASK SPREAD**

the behavior was the result of a price-fixing conspiracy by the market makers that kept bid–ask spreads abnormally high.

The following day, market makers in these stocks stopped avoiding odd-eighth quotes. As a consequence, average spreads narrowed dramatically to just over $0.125. We can see this situation illustrated in Figure 8-10—a graph showing the average bid–ask spread of Microsoft stock.

By ruling out cost-based explanations for the collapse, Christie[8] and his coauthors concluded that publicizing the conspiracy led to its collapse. We'll return to this theme later on when we examine the forces of competition and how firms attempt to control them.

SUMMARY & HOMEWORK PROBLEMS

SUMMARY OF MAIN POINTS

- A market has a product, geographic, and time dimension. Define the market before using supply–demand analysis.
- *Market demand* describes buyer behavior; *market supply* describes seller behavior in a competitive market.
- If price changes, *quantity demanded* increases or decreases (represented by a *movement along* the demand curve).
- If a factor other than price (like income) changes, we say that demand curve increases or decreases (a *shift* of demand curve).
- **Supply curves** describe the behavior of sellers and tell you how much will be sold at a given price.
- **Market equilibrium** is the price at which quantity supplied equals quantity demanded. If price is above the equilibrium price, there are too many sellers, forcing price down, and vice versa.
- Currency devaluation in a country increases demand for exports (supply to another country) and decreases demand for imports (demand for another country's products).
- Prices convey valuable information.
- Making a market is costly, and competition between market makers forces the bid–ask spread down to the costs of making a market. If the costs of making a market are large, then the equilibrium price may be better viewed as a spread rather than a single price.

[8] William G. Christie, Jeffrey H. Harris, and Paul H. Schultz, "Why Did NASDAQ Market Makers Stop Avoiding Odd-Eighth Quotes?" *Journal of Finance* 49, no. 5 (December 1994): 1841–1860.

MULTIPLE-CHOICE QUESTIONS

1. If the market for a certain product experiences an increase in supply and a decrease in demand, which of the following results is expected to occur?
  a. Both equilibrium price and the equilibrium quantity could rise or fall.
  b. Equilibrium price would rise, and the equilibrium quantity could rise or fall.
  c. Equilibrium price would fall, and the equilibrium quantity could rise or fall.
  d. Equilibrium price would fall, and the equilibrium quantity would fall.

2. Suppose there are nine sellers and nine buyers, each willing to buy or sell one unit of a good, with values {$10, $9, $8, $7, $6, $5, $4, $3, $2}. Assuming no transactions costs and a competitive market, what is the equilibrium price in this market?
  a. $5
  b. $6
  c. $7
  d. $8

3. If the government imposes a price floor at $9 (i.e., price must be $9 or higher) in the above market, how many goods will be traded?
  a. Five
  b. Four
  c. Three
  d. Two

4. Suppose there is a single market maker in this market. What is the optimal bid–ask spread?
  a. $2 bid; $10 ask
  b. $4 bid; $8 ask
  c. $5 bid; $7 ask
  d. $6 bid; $6 ask

5. Now suppose that competition among several market makers forces the spread down to $2. How many goods are traded?
  a. Five
  b. Four
  c. Three
  d. Two

INDIVIDUAL PROBLEMS

8-1. Widget Market
The widget market is competitive and includes no transaction costs. Five suppliers are willing to sell one widget at the following prices: $30, $29, $20, $16, and $12. Five buyers

are willing to buy one widget at the following prices: $10, $12, $20, $24, and $29. What is the equilibrium price and quantity in this market?

8-2. Demand and Supply of Syndicated Bank Loans

In 1998, the Syndicated Bank Loan market (defined as loans having more than two bank lenders) was a vast and cheap source of debt financing for U.S. corporations. This market was characterized by a large number of financial institutions that aggressively committed capital to debt issuers as a way to build market share and increase earnings.

Over the next three years, however, syndicated loan prices increased dramatically while the quantity of these loans declined. The price increase, measured as a markup over the cost of funds or LIBOR (London Interbank Offered Rate), is illustrated in the figure labeled "All-In Drawn Pricing." For example, the price to BBB-rated companies rose from 37.5 basis points in 1998 to approximately 129 basis points in 2002. This is a 244% increase in the price or spread. Explain these changes using shifts in demand and/or supply.

For Broadly Syndicated Loans Maturing in 2–5 Years Based on S&P Senior Debt Ratings

Over the same time period, in a related lending market, asset-backed commercial paper, we see a huge quantity increase as shown in the "Asset-Backed Commercial Paper" graph. Did prices for these loans increase or decrease? Justify your answer using shifts in supply and demand curves.

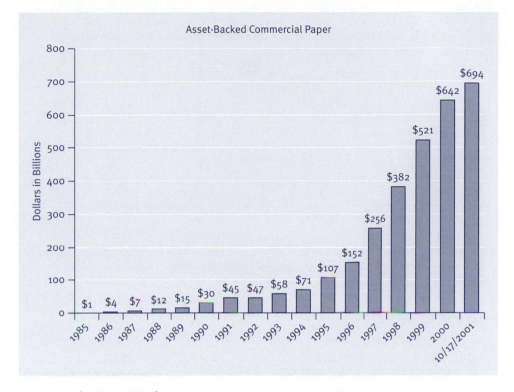

8-3. Candy Bars Market

a. In the accompanying diagram (which represents the market for chocolate candy bars), the initial equilibrium is at the intersection of S1 and D1. Circle the new equilibrium if there is an increase in cocoa prices.

b. In the same diagram, the initial equilibrium is at the intersection of S1 and D1. Circle the new equilibrium if there is rapid economic growth.

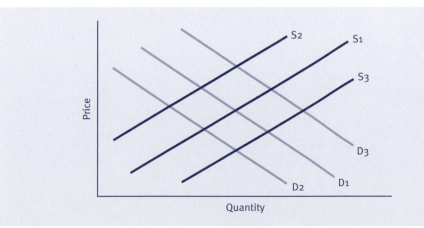

8-4. Demand Shifts

Indicate whether the following changes would cause a shift in the demand curve for Product A and, if so, the direction of the shift.

Change	Demand Curve Shift?	Direction of Shift?
Increase in price of complementary product	Yes No	Increase Decrease N/A
Increase in the price of the Product A	Yes No	Increase Decrease N/A
Launch of effective advertising campaign for Product A	Yes No	Increase Decrease N/A

8-5. Valentine's Day

On Valentine's Day, the price of roses increases by more than the price of greeting cards. Why? (*Hint:* Consider what makes roses and cards different and how that difference might affect supply's responsiveness to price.)

GROUP PROBLEM

G8-1. Supply and Demand

Using shifts in supply and demand curves, describe a change in the industry in which your firm operates. The change may arise from a change in costs, entry/exit of firms, a change in consumer tastes, a change in the macroeconomy, a change in interest rates, or a change in exchange rates. Label the axes, and state the geographic, product, and time dimensions of the demand and supply curves you are drawing. Explain what happened to industry price and quantity by making specific references to the demand and supply curves. If more than one change occurred, then decompose the change into smaller pieces so that your explanation has a step-by-step character to it. (*Hint and warning:* Demand and supply curves are used at the industry level, not at the firm level.)

Chapter 9

How to Keep Profit from Eroding

In 2002, 2003, and 2004, the Oakland A's baseball team won the American League West division with one of the lowest payrolls in baseball. Throughout these seasons, they competed successfully against better-financed teams, like the New York Yankees, which had a $200 million payroll (four times larger than the A's payroll). The team's strategy focused on using statistical methods to better evaluate individual performance.[1] The A's management team found two good measures of individual player productivity, on-base percentage and slugging percentage. More importantly, they found that the first was undervalued by the market. Oakland created a competitive advantage by buying players with high on-base percentages at prices below their value to the team. The advantage didn't last long, however, as other teams soon began copying the strategy, and now, on-base percentage is valued just as highly as slugging percentage. With the erosion of this advantage, the A's failed to win their division in both 2005 and 2006.

Although this example is drawn from the sports world, its lessons are applicable to business competition as well. Succeeding in the face of competition requires that you first find a way to create an advantage and then devise means to protect that advantage. How important is creating and sustaining advantage? Consider this quotation from a recent story on how to identify profitable companies from Motley Fool, an on-line provider of investment advice.

> Warren Buffett was once asked what is the most important thing he looks for when evaluating a company. Without hesitation, he replied, "Sustainable competitive advantage."
>
> I agree. While valuation matters, it is the future growth and prosperity of the company underlying a stock, not its current price that is most important. A company's prosperity, in turn, is driven by how powerful and enduring its competitive advantages are.
>
> Powerful competitive advantages (obvious examples are Coke's brand and Microsoft's control of the personal computer operating system) create a moat around a business such that it can keep competitors at bay and reap

---

[1] This anecdote was adapted from M. Lewis, *Moneyball* (New York: Norton, 2003).

extraordinary growth and profit. Like Buffett, I seek to identify—and then hopefully purchase at an attractive price—the rare companies with wide, deep moats that are getting wider and deeper over time. When a company is able to achieve this, its shareholders can be well rewarded for decades. Take a look at some of the big pharmaceutical companies for great examples of this....

It is extremely difficult for a company to be able to sustain, much less expand, its moat over time. Moats are rarely enduring for many reasons: High profit[s] can lead to complacency and are almost certain to attract competitors, and new technologies, customer preferences, and ways of doing business emerge. Numerous studies confirm that there is a very powerful trend of regression toward the mean for high-return-on-capital companies. In short, the fierce competitiveness of our capitalist system is generally wonderful for consumers and the country as a whole, but bad news for companies that seek to make extraordinary profit over long periods of time.[2]

In this chapter, we show how the forces of competition tend to erode high profit. In the previous chapter, we showed you how to analyze short-run industry-level changes; in this chapter, we show you how to analyze long-run changes. You should learn this material to understand how to formulate long-run strategies to slow down your firm's competitive erosion of profit—in essence how to build a moat around your company so that you can sustain your profitability. We'll also evaluate Buffett's investment strategy.

COMPETITIVE INDUSTRIES

To understand the forces of competition, we first consider the extreme case of a **competitive industry** characterized by these three factors:

- Firms produce a product or service with very close substitutes so they have very elastic demand.
- Firms have many rivals and no cost advantage over those rivals.
- The industry has no barriers to entry or exit.

In short, competitive firms[3] have the worst of all possible worlds. A competitive firm cannot affect price, so its managers choose instead how much to produce. They can sell as much as they want at the competitive price, so the marginal revenue of another unit is equal to the price. If P > MC, they sell more, and if P < MC, less. Fundamentally, industry-level forces determine price and, consequently, firm profitability because individual firms can do nothing but react to price. Thus, a firm's fortunes are closely tied to those of the industry in which it competes.

---

[2] Whitney Tilson (Tilson@Tilsonfunds.com), "Boring Portfolio" column on the Motley Fool site, February 28, 2000, http://www.fool.com/boringport/2000/boringport000228.htm.
[3] These firms are often referred to as "price takers," as they're forced to take whatever price the market is offering. They essentially face a horizontal demand curve. They can sell as much as they like at the market price; however, if they increase price, they will sell nothing. Since price is constant, marginal revenue equals price, and the profit-maximizing condition becomes P = MR = MC.

Several industries come close to being "perfectly" competitive, like commercial printing in the United States, which has nearly 50,000 small commercial printers. But no industry reaches perfect competition because this competition level is a theoretical benchmark. Nevertheless, the benchmark is valuable because it helps us see the forces that move prices and firm profit in the long run.

Suppose industry demand increases for a product in a competitive industry. As a consequence of the demand shift, price goes up and firms in the industry enjoy above-average profit—but only for a while. This "for a while" is the period that economists call the short run. But soon, the above-average profit attracts capital to the industry; existing firms expand capacity or new entrants come into the industry, thereby increasing industry supply. As supply increases, price falls. Entry continues and price keeps falling until firms in the industry are no longer earning above-average profit. At this point, capital flow into the industry stops, and we say that the industry is in **long-run equilibrium.** Since capital can no longer earn a higher rate of return in the industry, it stops moving into the industry.

A storm cloud hovers over any competitive industry: In the long run, no competitive industry can ever earn more than an average rate of return. But this cloud has a silver lining: Neither can a competitive industry ever earn less than an average rate of return. To see this, suppose demand decreases industry-wide for a product in a competitive industry. The demand shift causes prices to go down and firms to suffer below-average profit, but only for a while—the short run. Firms exit the industry, decreasing supply. And as supply decreases, industry price rises. Exit continues, and price continues rising until firms in the industry cease to earn below-average profit. At this point, capital flow out of the industry will stop: The industry is back in long-run equilibrium.

A competitive firm can earn positive or negative profit in the short run but only until entry or exit occurs. In the long run, competitive firms are condemned to earn only an average rate of return.

When firms are in long-run equilibrium, economic profit is zero (including the opportunity cost of capital), firms break even, and price equals average cost. Recall that profit is equal to $(P - AC)Q$; so if Price equals Average Cost, and cost includes a capital charge for the opportunity cost of capital, there's no reason for capital to move because it cannot earn a higher rate of return elsewhere.

In a competitive industry buffeted by demand and supply shocks, prices increase and decrease, but economic profit always reverts to zero. We say that profit exhibits **mean reversion** (what Tilson called "regression toward the mean" in the introduction to this chapter). According to reported estimates, the speed

at which profit moves back toward an average rate of return is 38% per year.[4]
That is, if profit is 20% above the mean one year, it will be only 12.4%
above the mean in the following year.[5] A separate analysis of more than 700
business units found that 90% of both above-average and below-average
profitability differentials disappeared over a 10-year period.[6] Return on
investment, as shown in Figure 9-1, revealed a strong tendency to revert to
the mean level of approximately 20% for both over- and underperformers.

THE INDIFFERENCE PRINCIPLE

We have begun to see the role of entry and exit, or *asset mobility,* as the major
competitive force driving profit to zero. (Remember that economic profit
includes a cost of capital, so economic profit is normally zero.) Positive profit
attracts entry, and negative profit leads to exit. The ability of assets to move
from lower- to higher-valued uses is the force that moves an industry toward

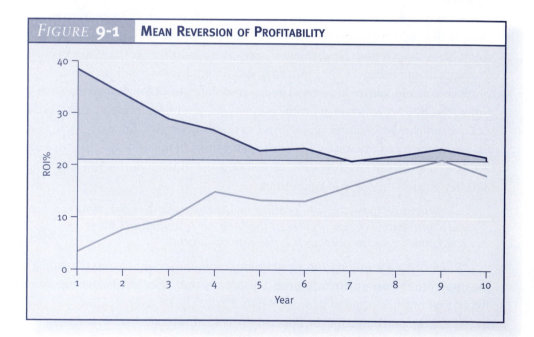

FIGURE **9-1**   **MEAN REVERSION OF PROFITABILITY**

---

[4] Eugene Fama and Kenneth French, "Forecasting Profitability and Earnings," *Journal of Business* (April 2000).
[5] Profitability at time t + 1 = Profitability at time t − (0.38 × Profitability at time t)
     12.4% = 20% − 7.6%.
[6] Source of data and figure: P. Ghemawat, *Commitment* (New York: Free Press, 1991).

long-run equilibrium. Such asset mobility leads to what Steven Landsburg[7] calls the **indifference principle:**

> *If an asset is mobile, then in long-run equilibrium, the asset will be indifferent about where it is used; that is, it will make the same profit no matter where it goes.*

Just to demonstrate the utility of this principle, let's apply it to the problem of choosing a city in which to live. Suppose that San Diego, California, is a much more attractive place to live than Nashville, Tennessee. What do you think will happen?

If labor is mobile, people will move from Nashville to San Diego. This migration will increase the demand for housing in San Diego, driving up those prices while simultaneously reducing housing prices in Nashville. The process will continue until the high price of housing makes San Diego just as unattractive as Nashville. At that point, migration will stop; the two cities are in long-run equilibrium. Both places are now equally attractive, meaning consumers are indifferent about where they live. The lower housing costs in Nashville compensate for enduring Nashville's hot and humid summers.

Similarly, wages adjust to restore equilibrium. The indifference principle tells us that in long-run equilibrium, all professions should be equally attractive, provided labor is mobile. If one profession is more attractive than another, that profession will attract entry—a greater supply of people to that profession. Wages will fall until that profession is just as unattractive as other professions. In equilibrium, differences in wages reflect differences in the *inherent* attractiveness of various professions. We call these wage differences **compensating wage differentials.** Why do embalmers make more than rehabilitation counselors?[8] The higher wages compensate embalmers for working in a relatively unattractive profession. Just as lower-cost housing compensates Nashvillians for living in Nashville, so too do embalmers' higher wages compensate them for spending long hours engaging in the relatively unpleasant task of cleaning and preserving dead bodies.

We can apply the same indifference principle to gain insight into the fundamental principles of finance. We start with the proposition that investors prefer higher returns with lower risk. If one investment earns the same return as another but is less risky, investors will move capital from the more risky investment to the less risky investment and bid up the less risky investment's price. The higher price decreases its expected rate of return[9]—its expected price

---

7 Steven Landsburg, *The Armchair Economist: Economics and Everyday Life* (New York: Free Press, 1993).
8 Median salary of embalmers equals $39,550, and median salary of rehabilitation counselors equals $31,350 according to May 2005 National Occupational Employment and Wage Estimates from the Bureau of Labor Statistics.
9 The percentage return on an investment that is held for one period is equal to $(P_{t+1} - P_t)/P_t$, where P_t is the initial price of the investment. P_{t+1} is the expected price next period, so the difference is the expected return. If the current price increases (i.e., P_t increases), then the expected return decreases.

change—until the lower-risk investment is just as attractive as the more risky investment. In equilibrium, the risky investment will earn a higher rate of return than the less risky investment. The higher return on the risky asset is called a **risk premium** and is analogous to a compensating wage differential. Just as higher wages compensate embalmers for preserving cadavers, so too do higher expected rates of return compensate investors in risky assets.

In equilibrium, differences in the rate of return reflect differences in the riskiness of an investment.

Roger Brinner, managing director and chief economist of the Parthenon Group, uses the indifference principle to derive a predictor of stock prices. The difference between returns on stocks (r_{stocks}) and return on bonds (r_{bonds}) should reflect an equity risk premium (to compensate investors for bearing the higher risk of stocks); that is,

$$r_{stocks} - \text{Equity Risk Premium} = r_{bonds}.$$

If you think of r_{stocks} as Earnings/Price plus growth in earnings and r_{bonds} as bond yield, then

Earnings/Price + Growth − Equity Risk Premium = Bond Yield.

If the (Growth − Risk Premium) component of this equation is relatively stable (over the past two decades it has averaged 1.75%, as shown in Figure 9-2),

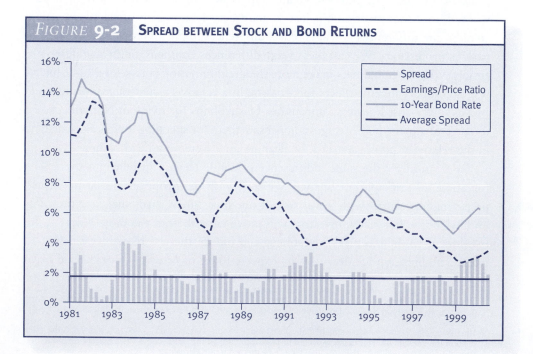

FIGURE 9-2   SPREAD BETWEEN STOCK AND BOND RETURNS

then a relatively stable relationship exists between the inverse of the P/E ratio and the bond yield. This ratio can be used to construct a predictor of stock prices.

Let's take a simple example. Rearranging the equation, we can get

$$\text{Earnings/Price} = \text{Bond Yield} - (\text{Growth} - \text{Equity Risk Premium}).$$

Say the current bond yield is 6%. Using Brinner's data regarding the spread, we would then predict that the Earnings/Price ratio of stocks should be 4.25%.

$$\text{Earnings/Price} = \text{Bond Yield} - \text{Spread}$$
$$\text{Earnings/Price} = 6\% - 1.75\% = 4.25\%$$

As we see in Figure 9-2, the difference between these two series (the "spread" that represents the Growth vs. Equity Risk Premium) exhibits the mean reversion characteristic of competitive equilibrium. When bond yields have exceeded 1.75% above the S&P 500 Earnings/Price ratio, capital has generally moved from stocks to bonds, causing stock prices to fall and bond prices to rise. The fall in stock price increases the Earnings/Price ratio, while the increase in bond prices decreases the yield, driving the spread back toward the average of 1.75%.

We can use this predictor to determine whether the stock market is currently overvalued. Using Brinner's model, we compare the 10-year yield less the 1.75% spread with the S&P 500 Earnings/Price ratio. If the Earnings/Price ratio on stocks is too low, stock prices are too high and are overvalued relative to bonds. In our simple example, say we observed an Earnings/Price ratio of 3.5%. For this ratio to revert to its predicted level of 4.25%, the denominator (price) would have to fall; thus, stocks would be overvalued in this case. The prices of stocks and bonds adjust to reflect buyers' expectations of growth and risk, which generally hover around the equilibrium spread level.

One large caveat is in order here. Brinner's model is a good indicator of whether to buy stocks or bonds *only* as long as the (Growth − Equity Risk Premium) spread stays relatively constant as shown in Figure 9-2. Over a longer time series, however, we see that it has been anything but stable.

In Figure 9-3, we plot the series from 1871 to 2000. There we see much wider variability with a particularly interesting change in 1981, as the Earnings/Price series fell and stayed below the 10-year bond for an extended period. Applying the indifference principle, we know that one or more of the components of the spread must have changed. Stocks became less risky, or bonds became more risky (either of these would decrease the Equity Risk Premium), or expected growth in stock earnings dramatically increased (increasing the growth component of the spread). The change could also have been driven by a combination of any of these three factors. If you had been using Brinner's model, you would have lost money

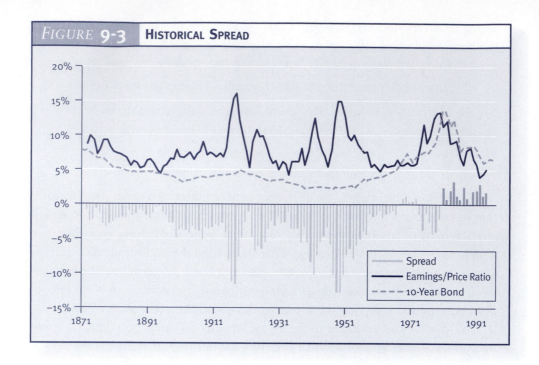

FIGURE **9-3**   HISTORICAL SPREAD

owing to this unpredictable shift in the underlying relationship between the P/E ratio and bond yield. This leads to an obvious maxim:

View all *forecasts with skepticism.*

MONOPOLY

If competitive firms live in the worst of all possible all worlds, **monopoly** firms live in the best. Monopolies have what Tilson called a "moat" around them to protect them from the forces of competition. Monopolies have market power because

- they produce a product or service with no close substitutes,
- they have no rivals, and
- barriers to entry prevent other firms from entering the industry.

Unlike a competitive firm, a monopoly firm[10] can earn positive profit—an above-average rate of return—for a long time. We can interpret this profit as a reward for doing something unique, innovative, or creative—something that gives the firm less elastic demand.

---

[10] In contrast to price takers (competitive firms), monopoly firms are price searchers. These firms face a downward-sloping demand curve; as price increases, quantity sold drops and vice versa. A price searcher "searches" for the optimal price–quantity combination.

However, monopolies are not permanently insulated from the forces of entry and imitation. No barrier to entry lasts forever. Eventually other firms develop substitutes or invent new products that erode monopoly profit. The main difference between a competitive firm and a monopoly is the length of time that a firm can earn above-average profit.

In the long run, even monopoly profit is driven to zero.

To see why this is so, recall from Chapter 6 that a firm will price at the point where $(P - MC)/P = 1/|\text{elasticity}|$. In the very long run, the forces of entry and imitation make the monopolist's demand more elastic. The elastic demand will push price down toward marginal cost and will eventually drive profit to zero.

For example, in 1983, the Macintosh computer's innovative graphical user interface gave Apple Computer a unique, user-friendly product. The elasticity of demand for the Mac was very low and the markups for the product very high. Several years later, Microsoft came up with Windows 3.1, with its own graphical interface. The development of this substitute made demand for Macs more elastic. Later, Windows innovations (95, 98, 2000, and XP) became even better substitutes, making demand for Macs even more elastic. The higher elasticity reduced the Mac's markup over marginal cost, and Apple's profit eroded.

Of course, Apple isn't standing still. Its managers keep improving the product, keeping it innovative and different from substitute products—in a word, unique. The fact that Apple is still making Macs is testament to the company's ability to innovate.

STRATEGY—THE QUEST TO SLOW PROFIT EROSION

Obviously, firms would rather be monopolists than competitors. In fact, if you hire management consultants, they'll advise you to become a monopolist (assuming they're worth their hire). To keep one step ahead of competitors or imitators and keep profit from eroding, firms try to develop strategies to gain *sustainable competitive advantage*. This kind of strategy development is probably the most difficult thing in business to teach, but it's also among the most important to learn.

So what is the key to competitive advantage and generating sustainable economic profit? Two primary schools of thought guide strategic thinking. The first—the industrial organization (IO) economics perspective—locates the source of advantage at the *industry* level. The second—the resource-based view (RBV)—locates it at the *individual firm* level.

In the IO perspective, the industry becomes the fundamental unit to analyze. According to Michael Porter, "The essence of this paradigm is that a firm's performance in the marketplace depends critically on the characteristics of the industry environment in which it competes."[11] Certain industries, owing to their structural characteristics, are inherently more attractive than other industries, and companies within those industries possess market power to generate economic profit. Industry structure determines firm conduct, and that conduct, in turn, determines the firms' performance. Industry structure is defined by the relatively stable dimensions of the industry that provide the context in which competition occurs. Typical structural characteristics of interest to IO researchers include barriers to entry, product differentiation among firms, and the number and size distribution of firms. As an example of the logic of this perspective, IO researchers believe that industries with higher entry barriers are more attractive because competitors find it more difficult to enter the industry and thus force profit down to equilibrium levels.

The IO perspective assumes that the industry structure is the most important determinant of long-run profitability. The key to generating economic profit for a business is its selection of industry. According to Michael Porter's Five Forces Model,[12] the best industries are characterized by

- high barriers to entry,
- low buyer power,
- low supplier power,
- low threat from substitutes, and
- low levels of rivalry between existing firms.

In Figure 9-4, we see support for the IO view because it shows wide differences in profitability across a number of industries.[13] The most profitable industry, pharmaceuticals, exhibits relatively high barriers to entry, arising from significant investments in personnel and technology; moreover, successful products enjoy extended periods of patent protection (legal barriers to entry).

If the IO view told the whole story, we wouldn't expect to find performance differences between firms within particular industries. These differences do exist, however, and the resource-based view (RBV) gained favor in the 1990s as an explanation for these interfirm differences.

The RBV posits that individual firms may exhibit sustained performance advantages owing to their superior resources, where resources are defined[14] as "the tangible and intangible assets firms use to conceive of and implement their

---

[11] M. Porter, "The Contributions of Industrial Organization to Strategic Management," *Academy of Management Review* 6 (1981): 609–620.

[12] M. Porter, *Competitive Strategy* (New York: Free Press, 1980).

[13] Profitability measured by operating income divided by assets over the period 1988–1995. Adapted from P. Ghemawat and J. Rivkin, "Creating Competitive Advantage."

[14] Definition from J. B. Barney and A. M. Arikan, "The Resource-Based View: Origins and Implications," in *The Blackwell Handbook of Strategic Management*, ed. M. E. Hitt, R.E. Freeman, and J. S. Harrison (Oxford: Oxford University Press, 2001), 138.

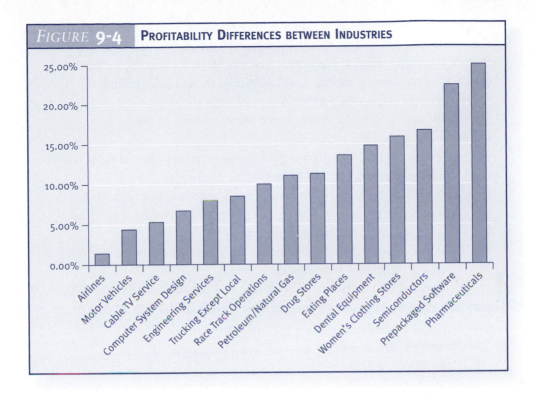

FIGURE 9-4   PROFITABILITY DIFFERENCES BETWEEN INDUSTRIES

strategies." Two primary assumptions underlie the RBV: The first is the assumption of resource heterogeneity (firms possess different bundles of resources); the second is the assumption of resource immobility (since resources can be immobile, these resource differences may persist).

Given the assumption of resource heterogeneity, the RBV[15] provides further guidance on when resources may lead to superior performance, where superior performance is defined as the firm's ability to earn above-average profit. If a resource is both valuable and rare, it can generate at least a temporary competitive advantage over rivals. A valuable resource must allow a business to conceive of and implement strategies that improve its efficiency or effectiveness. Examples include resources that let a firm operate at lower costs than its rivals or charge higher prices to its customers. For a resource to be rare, it must not be simultaneously available to a large number of competitors.

Resources that may generate temporary competitive advantage do not necessarily lead to a sustainable competitive advantage. For such resources to

[15] For an overview of the resource-based view, see J. Barney, "Firm Resources and Sustained Competitive Advantage," *Journal of Management* 17 (1991): 99–120. The explanation contained here draws from that description.

deliver a sustainable advantage, they must be difficult to substitute or imitate. Otherwise, any advantages that those resources deliver will be competed away. Imitation and substitution both erode firm profit. In the first, a competitor matches the resource by exactly duplicating it; in the second, a competitor matches the resources by deploying a different but strategically equivalent resource. We can list several conditions that make resources hard to imitate (*inimitability*):

1. Resources that flow from a firm's unique historical conditions will be difficult for competitors to match.
2. If the link between resources and advantage is ambiguous, then competitors will have a hard time trying to re-create the particular resources that deliver the advantage.
3. If a resource is socially complex (e.g., organizational culture), rivals will find it difficult to duplicate the resource.

So from the RBV perspective, resources and capabilities that are valuable, relatively rare, and difficult to imitate/substitute lie at the core of sustained, excellent firm performance. These resources and capabilities may include

- technology,
- physical capital,
- intellectual assets,
- human capital,
- financial resources, and
- organizational excellence.

THE THREE BASIC STRATEGIES

A firm looking to generate superior economic performance, given its industry and resource base, has three basic strategies it can follow to keep one step ahead of the forces of competition:

- cost reduction,
- product differentiation, or
- reduction in competitive intensity.

Most strategies fall into one of these three categories. The first strategy, cost reduction, is almost self-explanatory. Note, however, that cost reductions generate increases in long-run profitability *only* if the cost reduction is difficult to imitate. If others can easily duplicate your actions, cost reduction will not give you sustainable competitive advantage.

The third strategy, reducing competitive intensity, is also self-evident. If you can reduce the level of competition within an industry and keep new competitors from entering, you may be able to slow the erosion of profitability. (In the chapter on strategic interaction, we'll use game theory to develop strategies that reduce the intensity of competition.)

We can interpret the second strategy, product differentiation, as a reduction in the elasticity of demand for the product. Less elastic demand leads to an increase in price because the optimal markup of price over marginal cost is related to the elasticity of demand; that is, $(P - MC)/P = 1/|e|$. The more unique your product is relative to other market offerings, the less elastic is your product's demand and the higher is the markup of price over marginal cost.

One of the most successful examples of a product differentiation strategy is Perdue Chicken. Frank Perdue took an essentially homogeneous product—chicken—and turned it into a branded product, Perdue Chicken. He did this by exercising quality control over the entire supply chain, from the feed to the final product. Consumers perceive his branded chickens to be of higher quality. Thus, they have less elastic demand, allowing Perdue to charge a higher price. Economies of scale (cost reduction) also have played a part in Perdue's success.

Prelude Lobster's[16] managers tried a product differentiation strategy similar to Perdue's. Although they advertised their superior after-catch handling of the lobsters, customers correctly perceived that, for lobsters, unlike chicken, the supply chain is largely uncontrollable. Prelude was eventually forced out of business by lower-cost competitors who did not advertise.

It's easy to identify successful strategies (and the reasons for their success) or failed strategies (and the reason for their failures) in retrospect. It's much more difficult to identify successful or failed strategies before they succeed or fail.

Before concluding this chapter, let's return to the wisdom of investing in companies with a sustainable competitive advantage. This strategy leads to sustained, above-average profitability for the company, but remember that the stock price also determines the return from investing. If the stock price is high relative to its discounted future earnings, the investment is a bad one, regardless of whether the company has a sustainable competitive advantage. Warren Buffett, for instance, makes money by acquiring companies whose potential future earnings are high relative to their current stock price. He then helps develop strategies to help them realize their high potential earnings by maintaining a sustainable competitive advantage. He doesn't make money simply by investing in companies with a sustainable competitive advantage. The stock price has to be low relative to future earnings.

---

[16] Harvard Business School case number 9-373-052, "Prelude Corp."

SUMMARY & HOMEWORK PROBLEMS

SUMMARY OF MAIN POINTS

- A competitive firm can earn positive or negative profit in the short run until entry or exit occurs. In the long run, competitive firms are condemned to earn only an average rate of return.
- Profit exhibits what is called **mean reversion,** or "regression toward the mean."
- If an asset is mobile, then in equilibrium, the asset will be indifferent about where it is used (i.e., it will make the same profit no matter where it goes). This implies that unattractive jobs will pay compensating wage differentials, and risky investments will pay compensating risk differentials (or a risk premium).
- The difference between stock and bond yields exhibits mean reversion; this difference is a useful indicator of whether the market is overvalued.
- **Monopoly** firms can earn positive profit for a longer period of time than competitive firms, but entry and imitation eventually erode their profit as well.
- The industrial organization economics (IO) perspective assumes that the industry structure is the most important determinant of long-run profitability.
- According to the resource-based view (RBV), individual firms may exhibit sustained performance advantages owing to their superior resources. To be the source of sustainable competitive advantage, those resources should be valuable, rare, and difficult to imitate/substitute.
- Strategy is the art of matching the resources and capabilities of a firm to the opportunities and risks in its external environment for the purpose of developing a sustainable competitive advantage.
- To stay one step ahead of the forces of competition, a firm can adopt one of three strategies: cost reduction, product differentiation, or reduction in the intensity of competition.

MULTIPLE-CHOICE QUESTIONS

1. Which of the following types of firms would face a downward-sloping demand curve?
    a. Both a perfectly competitive firm and a monopoly
    b. Neither a perfectly competitive firm nor a monopoly
    c. A perfectly competitive firm but not a monopoly
    d. A monopoly but not a perfectly competitive firm

2. Which of the following types of firms are guaranteed to make positive economic profit?
   a. Both a perfectly competitive firm and a monopoly
   b. Neither a perfectly competitive firm nor a monopoly
   c. A perfectly competitive firm but not a monopoly
   d. A monopoly but not a perfectly competitive firm

3. If a firm successfully adopts a product differentiation strategy, what should happen to the elasticity of demand for its product?
   a. Increases
   b. Decreases
   c. Becomes unit elastic
   d. Is unaffected

4. A firm in a perfectly competitive market (a price taker) faces what type of demand curve?
   a. Unit elastic
   b. Perfectly inelastic
   c. Perfectly elastic
   d. None of the above

5. Which of the following is critical for a firm adopting a cost reduction strategy?
   a. The firm must be the first to adopt the cost reduction strategy.
   b. The strategy reduces costs by at least 10%.
   c. The strategy is focused on reducing internal production costs.
   d. The methods of achieving cost reductions are difficult to imitate.

INDIVIDUAL PROBLEMS

9-1. Faculty Housing Benefits
At a university faculty meeting in 2000, a proposal was made to increase the housing benefits for new faculty to keep pace with the high cost of housing. What will be the likely effect of this proposal? (*Hint*: Think indifference principle.)

9-2. Entry and Elasticity
Suppose that new entry decreased your demand elasticity from −2 to −3 (made demand more elastic). By how much should you adjust your price of $10?

9-3. MBA Economics Professor
Why do MBA economics professors earn more than regular economics professors?

9-4. Economic Profit
Describe the difference in economic profit between a competitive firm and a monopolist in both the short and long run. Which should take longer to reach the long-run equilibrium?

9-5. Economics versus Business

Describe an important difference in the way an economist and a businessperson might view a monopoly.

GROUP PROBLEMS

G9-1. Compensating Wage Differential

Give an example of a compensating wage differential, a risk premium, or some kind of long-run equilibrium price difference your company faces. How can your company profitably exploit this difference?

G9-2. Strategy

What strategy is your company following (try to classify it into one of the three strategies in the text)? How is your strategy working—how long will it allow you to maintain a competitive advantage?

PRICING FOR GREATER PROFIT

Chapter 10

More Realistic and Complex Pricing

Most Las Vegas casinos offer a variety of gambling ("gaming" in industry parlance) services—slot machines, blackjack tables, sports betting, and so on. They also offer hotel rooms. But when the casino managers set prices for their hotel rooms, they consider how room prices affect demand for their gambling operations. Obviously, if you can attract gamblers to your hotel with low room prices, it seems sensible to forgo some profit on the room, provided you expect to earn that profit back when the room occupants gamble. Such a trade-off is analogous to the loss–leader pricing that grocery stores employ (see Chapter 6: "Simple Pricing"). Just as the grocery stores set low prices for three-liter Coke to attract customers to the grocery store, so too do hotels set low room prices to attract gamblers to the casino.

In both cases (three-liter Coke and hotels), price is set where MR < MC. The grocery store could earn higher profit on soft drinks, and the hotel could earn higher profit on rooms, simply by raising price (and selling fewer units). But the grocery store and the hotel are trying to maximize *total* profit, not profit on their individual product lines. Common ownership of multiple products changes the simple pricing calculus we studied in Chapter 6.

In this chapter, we show you how to extend the simple, single-product analysis of the earlier chapter to more complex and realistic settings, like those involving commonly owned products.

PRICING COMMONLY OWNED PRODUCTS

COMMONLY OWNED SUBSTITUTES

Commonly owned products add a level of complexity to pricing that we can easily understand by once again using marginal analysis. To see this, let's consider how pricing changes after acquisition of a substitute product. Suppose, for example, you purchase a rival video rental store just across the street from your current video store. How does this change the price of video rentals at each store?

With just one store, the pricing calculus is simple. You trade off the benefits of a lower price (more units sold) against the costs of a lower price (less earned on each unit). Marginal analysis balances these two effects and suggests a price where MR = MC to maximize profit.

Common ownership of two substitutes changes this simple pricing calculus. Now, an increase in output at one (through a price reduction) will "steal" some sales from the store across the street. Since you own both stores, you see a reduction in marginal revenue at each store. Recall that MR is the benefit (additional revenue) of increasing output or reducing price. So when MR falls, you should cut back quantity or, equivalently, raise price.

In other words, common ownership of both video stores reduces MR at each because increasing sales of one product (caused by reducing price) decreases demand for the other. And when MR falls below MC, output should be decreased, or, equivalently, optimal price should increase. We summarize this intuition in the following maxim:

> *After acquiring a substitute product, raise price on both products to avoid each product cannibalizing the sales of the other product.*

Put another way: When you price commonly owned products, focus on the change in perspective that joint ownership confers. Your concern changes from earning profit on an individual product to earning profit on both products, which we consider to be a bundle of two goods. Acquiring a substitute makes aggregate demand for the bundle less elastic than the individual demand for either. Remember from Chapter 6 that aggregate demand is less elastic than individual demand as long as the products in the bundle are better substitutes for each other than are products outside the bundle. And with a less elastic aggregate demand, you want to raise price.

So far we haven't said anything about which price to raise more; here, again, marginal analysis can give us some guidance. Recall that the optimal price for a single product is set where the markup of price over cost is proportional to the inverse of the elasticity. Intuitively, the markup is lower on more elastic products because consumers are very sensitive to the price of these products. If you could somehow switch these consumers to the high-margin product, you'd increase profit. You can do this by changing the relative prices of commonly owned products.

> *After acquiring a* substitute product, *raise price on both, but raise price more on the more elastic (low-margin) product.*

As you raise price on the low-margin product, some consumers switch to the higher-margin substitute, thereby increasing your profit.

Recall that marginal analysis tells you which direction to go (raise price on both and raise it more on the low-margin product), but it doesn't tell you by how much. So you get there by taking steps. After raising price, recalculate MR and MC—or simply check to make sure that profit increases—to see if further change is profitable.

After acquiring a substitute product, you can also try to reduce interproduct cannibalization by *repositioning* the products so they don't directly compete with each other—providing that repositioning isn't too expensive. For example, using our video rental retail stores as examples, you might want to stock multiple copies of the most popular videos at one of the stores (add depth) but stock a wider range of titles (add breadth) at the other. Moving the products farther apart can further increase profit derived from acquiring commonly owned substitutes.

COMMONLY OWNED COMPLEMENTS

Common ownership of complementary products leads to the opposite advice. Suppose our video rental store purchases the parking lot next to the store. Before the purchase, both parking lot and video store managers set prices without considering the effect that their actions had on each other's demand.

But after the acquisition, an increase in output at one (through a price reduction) will increase demand at the other. In other words, common ownership of parking lot and video store increases MR at each because increasing sales of one product (by reducing price) increases demand for the other. And when MR rises above MC, output should increase, or, equivalently, optimal price should fall. We summarize this intuition in the following maxim:

> *After acquiring a* complementary product, *reduce price on both products to increase profit.*

Again, we can understand this advice by examining how common ownership changes the aggregate elasticity of demand for the bundle of goods. Acquiring a complement makes aggregate demand more elastic than individual demand. And with a more elastic aggregate demand, you want to reduce price.

The advice on how to change individual prices after acquiring a complementary product is not quite as straightforward as the advice after acquiring a substitute. As with substitute products, the goal is to steer consumers to the high-margin product; however, the analysis is more complicated.

REVENUE OR YIELD MANAGEMENT

Products like cruise ships, parking lots, hotels, and stadiums have several peculiar characteristics that affect their pricing. First, the costs of building capacity are mostly fixed or sunk. Importantly, these costs are very large relative to marginal costs. In addition, firms in the industry typically face capacity constraints; that is, they can increase output only up to capacity, but no further.

To understand how prices are set in these industries, let's begin with the decision of how much capacity to build. This is an extent decision, so we use marginal analysis. The owners have an incentive to keep building capacity (more parking spaces, more hotel or cabin rooms, more seats in a stadium) as long as *long-run* marginal revenue is greater than *long-run* marginal cost, LRMR > LRMC. The owners stop building additional capacity when LRMR = LRMC. Here, the term *long-run marginal revenue* refers to the expected additional revenue that another parking space, hotel or cabin room, or stadium seat would earn over the life of the capacity. Likewise, long-run marginal cost is the expected additional cost of building, maintaining, selling, and using another unit of capacity over the life of the capacity.

Once the hotel, cruise ship, parking lot, or stadium is built and the costs of building capacity have been sunk, the question of how to price arises. As we know from Chapter 3, we should ignore sunk costs when setting price, lest we commit the *sunk-cost fallacy*. In other words, the relevant costs and benefits of setting price are the *short-run* marginal revenue (MR) and *short-run* marginal costs (MC).

In other words, the relevant marginal cost for the pricing decision is much smaller than relevant marginal cost of the capacity decision. If the short-run marginal revenue is close to long-run marginal revenue, then you want to price to fill capacity. This leads to the rather obvious advice:

If MR > MC at capacity, then price to fill available capacity.

Recall that the MR and the MC are the relevant short-run variables that vary with the decision of what price to charge. Because MR > MC, the firm's managers would like to sell more, but cannot because the firm is limited by capacity. So the firm sells as much as it can, or it prices to fill capacity.

To understand this, it helps to use a numerical example. Suppose we are designing a new hotel. We keep adding rooms to the design plan, as long as LRMR > LRMC. We come up with an optimal design of several hundred rooms. At the optimal size, annualized LRMC of building and maintaining the room is about $100,000/year. To annualize fixed costs over the lifetime of a project, we think about how much it would cost to borrow the money from a bank to pay for the construction. Annual interest costs plus the costs of maintaining the room offer a good measure of the annualized long-run marginal costs.

But once the rooms are built—or, more important, from our point of view— once the costs have been sunk, the hotel's owners must decide how much to charge for the rooms. Suppose that 90% of the annualized long-run marginal costs are sunk. This means that the relevant marginal cost is just $10,000 per year. Since the capacity decision is determined by *all* the costs, and the pricing decision *only* by short-run marginal costs, it's likely that MR > MC at the capacity of the hotel. If so, then the hotel's owner should price to sell all available rooms.

To do this, simply choose a price such that demand equals capacity. If demand is known, this is relatively easy to do. For example, it's easy to set price for a parking lot in a downtown business area in which business starts at roughly 9 A.M. Every day, you look to see what time it fills up. If the lot fills up before 9 A.M., then raise price; and if the lot is still empty at 9 A.M., then reduce price. If the lot fills up near 9 A.M., the price is just right. A higher price would leave unused parking spaces, while a lower price would allow you to raise price and still fill available capacity. The relatively constant demand and the daily observation of demand make this easy to do.

Conversely, if demand is difficult to predict, pricing to fill capacity becomes much more difficult. For example, each time a cruise ship sails, no one knows what demand will be. To determine optimal price, the cruise line's managers balance the costs of overpricing (lost profit on unfilled rooms) against the cost of underpricing (lower margins on all the rooms).

In this case, an optimal price would minimize the expected costs of these two mistakes. If the lost profit from these two pricing mistakes is symmetric, then the firm should price so that expected (predicted) demand is just equal to capacity. However, if the lost profit from overpricing is greater than the lost profit from underpricing, then the firm should underprice, and *vice versa*. This will lead, on average, to more underpricing mistakes than overpricing mistakes, simply because the cost of overpricing mistakes is higher.

> *If the lost profit from overpricing (unused capacity) is bigger than the lost profit from underpricing (lower margins), then price lower than would fill capacity, and vice versa.*

The precise degree of over- or underpricing depends not only on the costs of under- and overpricing, but also on the probability of under- and overpricing. In the chapter on uncertainty we will illustrate this difference more clearly.

Obviously, the better forecasts you can make about demand, the fewer errors of either type you'll make. Fewer errors mean more profit because the ship is filled as close to capacity as possible—and at the best possible price. To better match demand to available capacity, cruise ships managers often adjust prices up until the time the ship sails. If it looks like capacity is going unused, they reduce price; and if it looks like capacity will be more than filled, they raise price.

But charging different prices to passengers who purchase at different times is costly for two reasons. First, if consumers realize that they may get a lower price if they wait to purchase, then you create an incentive for them to wait. And this phenomenon makes it more difficult to match demand to capacity—the whole point of adjusting price. To eliminate the late-booking incentive, many cruise line managers reduce price only slightly or reduce price only by offering cabin upgrades, so that consumers don't realize they're paying less. In a related problem, once some passengers realize they paid more than their fellow passengers who booked at different times, they may become angry and demand a refund or disparage the cruise line to future customers. We discuss this phenomenon in a section of the chapter on price discrimination titled "Only Fools Pay Retail." No one wants to be a fool.

ADVERTISING AND PROMOTIONAL PRICING

In your marketing class, you'll learn that there are at least four dimensions to competition, the so-called Four P's of marketing: Price, Product, Placement, and Promotion. *Product* refers to product design; *Placement* refers to the distribution channel (retail stores, catalog sales, discount stores, Internet sales, or distributors); and *Promotion* refers to advertising, discount coupons, end-of-aisle displays, and any other expenditures that increase demand for your product. In this section, we use marginal analysis to show you how to price in conjunction with advertising or promotional expenditures.

The most important thing to realize is that different types of promotional expenditures affect demand in different ways. For pricing, it is most important to know whether promotional expenditures make demand more or less price elastic.

> *If promotional expenditures make demand more (less) price elastic, then you should reduce (increase) price when you promote the product.*

Consider the simplest kind of advertising—information about the price of your product. Typically, this kind of advertising informs some consumers about the price of your product relative to substitute products. Coupons, end-of-aisle displays in grocery stores, and weekly advertising inserts in the newspaper fall into this category. By informing consumers about relative prices, you also make them more sensitive to price differences. Put another way, consumers are more sensitive to price differences when they know about those differences. When you see this kind of promotion, you also typically see a reduction in the price of the promoted good. And this makes sense. If you make demand more elastic, you want to reduce price to attract more customers.

On the other hand, advertising designed to increase the inherent attractiveness of the product makes demand less elastic. Advertising that influences consumer perceptions about the inherent product quality or associates the product with a celebrity or desirable activity falls into this category. When you run this kind of promotional campaign, the seller is trying to reduce the customer's sensitivity to price. In this case, it makes sense to *increase* price.

A final cautionary note about pricing and quality: A higher price may influence consumer perceptions about the quality of the product. If you know nothing else about the product except its price, you may infer that it is of high quality. In other words, a high price may signal high quality. In this case, you'd want to price high to signal quality. Many wines are priced high for this reason.

But low prices can also signal quality. For example, restaurant owners sometimes keep prices too low, thus generating long queues of customers willingly waiting to get in. The long lines signal that the price is low relative to the quality of the meal. Long lines tell customers who don't know anything about the restaurant that quality is high relative to price. We'll discuss signaling further in Chapter 16.

SUMMARY & HOMEWORK PROBLEMS

SUMMARY OF MAIN POINTS

- After acquiring a substitute product, raise price on both products to avoid each product cannibalizing the sales of the other product.
- After acquiring a substitute product, raise price more on the low-margin (more elastic demand) product.
- After acquiring a substitute product, reposition the products so that there is less substitutability between them.
- After acquiring a complementary product, reduce price on both products to increase demand for both products.
- If fixed costs are large relative to marginal costs, and capacity is fixed, price to fill available capacity.
- If the costs of underpricing are smaller than the costs of overpricing, then underprice, on average, and vice versa.
- If promotional expenditures make demand more elastic, then reduce price when you promote the product, and vice versa.

MULTIPLE-CHOICE QUESTIONS

1. You own two products, each of which is a substitute for the other. You raise price on the first product. What happens to marginal revenue?
  a. MR for the first product falls but increases for the second.
  b. MR rises for both products.
  c. MR falls for both products.
  d. MR for the second product falls but increases for the first.

2. Your company produces and sells Product A, which has an associated elasticity of demand of −1.8. You acquire as a substitute product B, which has an associated elasticity of demand of −2.0. How should you handle pricing?
  a. Raise price on both products with a larger increase on Product A.
  b. Raise price on both products with a larger increase on Product B.
  c. Reduce price on both products with a larger decrease on Product A.
  d. Reduce price on both products with a larger decrease on Product B.

3. Your company is in the same position as that in the previous question, but Products A and B are now complements. How should you handle pricing?
  a. Raise price on both products with a larger increase on Product A.
  b. Raise price on both products with a larger increase on Product B.
  c. Reduce price on both products.
  d. Reduce price on one product and raise price on the other.

4. A real estate development company is considering building a new office building in downtown. Above 20,000 square feet, the company's managers believe they can generate approximately $600,000 in additional lease payments for every additional 1,000 square feet built. This $600,000 represents
  a. Long-run economic profit
  b. Long-run marginal revenue
  c. Long-run marginal cost
  d. Long-run average additional revenue

5. Local retailers and producers often use weekly mailed circulars to promote their products to local consumers. The circulars feature a variety of products and make consumers aware of pricing advantages of the products available at local establishments. How would you expect one of the retailers to handle pricing for a product that appears in the circular?
  a. Maintain price and allow the promotion to drive sales.
  b. Raise price to capitalize on the additional potential traffic.
  c. Reduce price to take advantage of the benefits of the promotion.
  d. The advertising and pricing decisions should be unrelated.

INDIVIDUAL PROBLEMS

10-1. Pricing Commonly Owned Substitute Products

Branded drugs face generic entry by rival drugs that typically take 80% of sales away from the branded drug within three years. This loss occurs because generic drugs are much cheaper than branded drugs, and most insurance companies won't pay for a branded drug if a generic is available. But in one instance, the branded-drug maker sued the generic entrant for violating its patent. In the settlement negotiations that ensued, the branded-drug maker offered to pay the generic entrant $10 million to settle the patent dispute by staying out of the industry. Why would the branded drug offer to pay the generic drug to stay out of the industry?

10-2. Pricing Commonly Owned Complementary Products

You are a hospital administrator trying to raise capital to refurbish the hospital. Your local bank is reluctant to lend to you because you already have a large mortgage on the property on which the hospital complex lies. But your bankers tell you that they can lend you more if you reduce your debt by selling your parking lot to some private investors who'll lease it back to you for the next 50 years. And you'll have to renegotiate the price of the lease every five years. What concerns might you have about this sale-and-lease-back contract?

10-3. Yield or Revenue Management 1

Suppose your elasticity of demand for your parking lot spaces is –2, and price is $8/day. If your MC is zero, and your capacity is 80% full at 9 A.M. over the last month, are you optimizing?

10-4. Yield or Revenue Management 2

Suppose your elasticity of demand for your parking lot spaces is –0.5, and price is $20/day. If your MC is zero, and your capacity at 9 A.M. is 96% full over the last month, are you optimizing?

10-5. Yield or Revenue Management 3

Suppose your parking lot has two different consumers who use it at two different times. Daily commuters use it during the daytime, and sports fans use it at different times to park at sporting events. Daily commuter demand is variable, yet stable and known. Demand for sporting events is uncertain, and depends on the quality of the match, as well as on unpredictable events, like the weather. How would you price these two events differently?

GROUP PROBLEMS

G10-1. Pricing Commonly Owned Products

Describe a pricing decision your company made involving commonly owned products. Was it optimal? If not, why not? How would you adjust price? Compute the profit consequences of the change.

G10-2. Yield or Revenue Management

Describe a pricing decision your company made that involved a product or service with fixed capacity. Was price set optimally? If not, why not? How would you adjust price? Compute the profit consequences of the change.

Chapter 11

Direct Price Discrimination

INTRODUCTION

PRICING FOR CLINICAL CONFERENCES

The American Association for Clinical Chemistry (AACC) sponsors numerous three-day conferences in different U.S. cities throughout the year. At these conferences, laboratory professionals get to acquaint themselves with the latest in research and technology, all for a flat rate of $750 per attendee. Attendance figures for these conferences are usually quite high, and the conferences represent a significant source of revenue for the association. But an analysis of demographic data from the AACC's last three conferences revealed that more than 90% of the attendees either lived in the conference city or in the surrounding region—the conferences attracted few participants from distant states or foreign countries. To attend conferences, participants who live far away must incur greater travel costs, longer travel times, and time-consuming hassles, such as applying and interviewing for travel visas. In addition, potential attendees from foreign countries can attend conferences hosted by competing organizations in their own countries.

To increase attendance, the AACC proposed to reduce prices for more distant participants while maintaining prices to local attendees who seem satisfied with the conferences. Offering different prices to different customers would allow the AACC to increase the overall profitability of sponsoring conferences.

PRICING FOR CELL PHONES

In 1997, a global cell phone manufacturer—let's call it Ideal Roaming Kinetics (or IRK)—was losing market share in the Philippines because its competitors were selling phones at significantly lower prices. Since IRK charged a uniform worldwide price of $120 and sold primarily in Western Europe, competitors could undercut it in important, but less lucrative, markets like the Philippines.

In addition, the Philippine market was growing fast, and IRK wanted to position itself for future growth. Experience had shown that a 10% penetration point was critical in terms of future penetration. According to this rule of thumb, the manufacturer with the largest market share at 10% penetration will see market share growth by 40% when the entire market penetration reaches 30%. Why? Because "word-of-mouth" marketing occurs when consumers encounter new products. When consumers choose a particular brand of cell phone, they're largely copying what their colleagues and neighbors have chosen.

In 1997, Philippine market penetration was just 5%, and IRK's market share was below 10% (see Figure 11-1). To raise market share before market penetration reached the critical 10% threshold, IRK's Philippine division wanted to price IRK's cell phones below its worldwide price. However, IRK was worried about the fallout from such discriminatory pricing.

Potentially, both the AACC and IRK could benefit by charging different prices to different consumer groups. In the first case, the AACC could increase profit by offering lower prices to foreign conference participants; in the second, IRK could increase profit by selling cell phones for less in the Philippines.

However, discriminatory pricing carries with it attendant risks. In this chapter, we discuss ways of profitably designing and implementing **price discrimination** schemes, in which sellers charge different prices to different consumers—not on the basis of differences in costs but, rather, on differences in consumer demand.

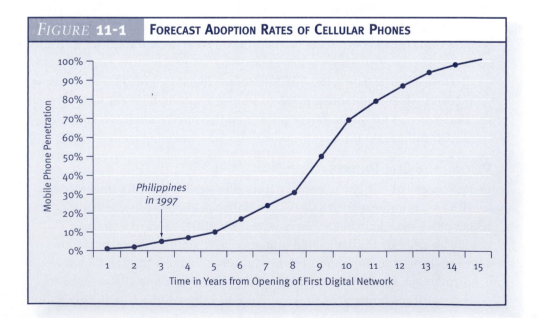

FIGURE **11-1**   **FORECAST ADOPTION RATES OF CELLULAR PHONES**

WHY (PRICE) DISCRIMINATE?

To see how price discrimination increases profit, let's look at the simple aggregate demand curve in Chapter 6 where seven consumers are willing to pay {$7, $6, $5, $4, $3, $2, $1} for a good that costs $1.50 to make. There we saw that the profit-maximizing price is $5. At this price, the company sells three units. We calculate total profit ($10.50) as revenue ($15) minus cost ($4.50).

At the optimal price of $5, low-value consumers—those willing to pay $4, $3, and $2—don't purchase, even though they're willing to pay more than the cost of producing the good. These three consumers represent unconsummated wealth-creating transactions. The one lesson of business tells us to find a way to profitably consummate these transactions.

Suppose you could identify the customers who would buy the product at lower prices; say, they live in a certain part of town, they are older, or they have children. You could offer each a price reduction, respectively, by sending discount coupons to residents in a certain ZIP code, by offering discounts to senior citizens, or by offering discounts for families with children.

To see how this would affect profit, we lump all three customers into one group—those willing to pay $4, $3, or $2. If we can charge a separate price to these low-value consumers, we face a second demand curve, illustrated in Figure 11-2.

As shown in Table 11-1, we could price at $4 and sell one more unit (profit of $2.50), price at $3 and sell two more units (profit of $3), or price at $2 and sell

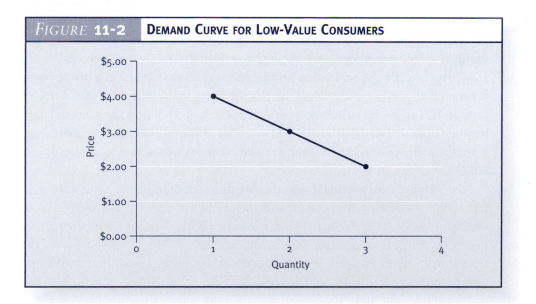

| FIGURE **11-2** | **DEMAND CURVE FOR LOW-VALUE CONSUMERS** |

TABLE 11-1	OPTIMAL PRICE FOR LOW-VALUE CONSUMERS				
Price	Quantity	Revenue	MR	MC	Profit
$4	1	$4	$4	$1.50	$2.50
$3	2	$6	$2	$1.50	$3
$2.00	3	$6	$0	$1.50	$1.50

three more units (profit of $1.50). Obviously, we should sell two more units at a price of $3 and earn an extra $3.

This is the motivation for price discrimination: It allows a firm to sell items to low-value customers who otherwise would not purchase because the price is too high.

Price discrimination is the practice of charging different prices (that are not cost-justified) to different people or groups of people.

Charging lower prices to low-value consumers also means that you charge high-value customers higher prices, making the practice controversial. Often, however, pricing that looks discriminatory (based on demand differences) results instead from the different costs of serving different consumers. Small drugstores, small grocery stores, and small bookstores pay higher prices than do large chains like Wal-Mart because supplying such big stores costs less. Big customers order full truckloads, thus reducing transportation costs; they also invest in information technology that reduces ordering and inventory costs and eases product distribution. If the higher prices arise from the higher costs of serving small mom-and-pop shops, then the higher prices are not discriminatory.

To make price discrimination profitable, you still have to sell at a price above the marginal cost of production. The more unique, innovative, and useful the product is, and the fewer substitutes the product has, the bigger the potential gap between price and marginal cost—and the more profit you can make by designing a price discrimination scheme. Products like software, music, drugs, and books all fall into this category.

To discriminate, you must also identify different customer groups with different price elasticities of demand for the product or service. Obviously, you'd target for discounts the group(s) with the more elastic demand and charge a higher price to the group with the less elastic demand. This creates an incentive for the high-priced group to try to purchase at the lower prices offered to the group with more elastic demand. If too many high-value customers are able to do this, then they can make the price discrimination scheme unprofitable.

DIRECT PRICE DISCRIMINATION

We can draw a distinction between *direct* and *indirect* discrimination schemes. In a **direct price discrimination scheme,** we can identify members of the low-value group, charge them a lower price, and prevent them from reselling their lower-priced goods to the higher-value group. In an indirect discrimination scheme, we can neither perfectly identify the two groups nor prevent arbitrage, so we must find indirect methods of setting different prices to the two different groups. This distinction will become clearer in the next chapter when we describe various indirect discrimination schemes.

As we've learned in previous chapters, we should price high to consumers with less price-elastic demands and price low to those with more price-elastic demands. In particular, we want a direct price discrimination scheme charging different prices to two groups of consumers that sets prices as follows:

$$(P_1 - MC_1)/P_1 = 1/|elasticity_1| \quad and$$
$$(P_2 - MC_2)/P_2 = 1/|elasticity_2|$$

Note that the marginal cost of selling to the two different groups can be different—that is, $MC_1 \neq MC_2$. But as long as the price elasticities differ, we can't explain the price difference by costs alone. In other words, the markup of price over marginal cost is higher to the low elasticity group.

For example, senior citizens have more price-elastic demand for a variety of reasons (lower incomes, lower opportunity cost of time, etc.). Consequently, older people often pay lower prices in movie theaters than do younger people. The theater managers are able to recognize low-value customers by the age indicated on an ID card. Theater managers prevent arbitrage by making sure that those admitted on a senior citizen's ticket do not resell their tickets to younger customers.

Likewise, airlines discriminate between business and leisure travelers. Business travelers have less elastic demands than do leisure travelers for several reasons. Business travelers don't pay for their own tickets; they have very specific time and geographic demands for a flight ("I have to be in Dallas, Texas, at 8:00 A.M. on Tuesday"); and they have schedules that can change at the last minute, so they need the flexibility of changing their tickets up until flight time. Airlines exploit the differences between the two consumer groups to design price discrimination schemes. The airline is able to identify the leisure travelers because they're willing to buy tickets in advance, and they're willing to stay over a Saturday night.

While the airline can't prevent some business customers from buying tickets with these characteristics (which makes this more like an indirect discrimination scheme), most want the flexibility of a fully refundable ticket with no restrictions on it. If enough business travelers take advantage of discounts for an advance purchase and a Saturday night stay, they can render the price discrimination scheme unprofitable, analogous to arbitrage between the two groups. In this case, the inability to identify the two groups can make the discrimination unprofitable.

It's also possible that the opportunity cost of holding a seat open for a business traveler with an uncertain demand (the probability that the seat will go unused is higher) can justify the higher price paid for a refundable, or business class, ticket. If so, the price difference arises from differences in costs and therefore is not discrimination.

ROBINSON–PATMAN ACT

There is a tension in the law about the effects of price discrimination. On the one hand, if a firm offers an array of different prices to consumers, it consummates more transactions and thus creates more wealth. On the other, if you charge prices closer to what consumers are willing to pay for a good, you also reduce consumer surplus.

The **Robinson–Patman Act** is part of a group of laws collectively called the *antitrust laws* governing competition in the United States. Under the Robinson–Patman Act, it's illegal to give or receive a price discount on a good sold to another business. This law does not cover services and sales to final consumers. The U.S. Congress passed the Robinson–Patman Act in 1936 in response to complaints from small grocery stores facing competition from lower-cost competitors, like A&P, the first grocery store chain. Sometimes called the Anti-Chain-Store Act, Robinson–Patman tries to protect independent retailers from chain-store competition by preventing the chains from receiving supplier discounts. Small retailers have sued book publishers, large book retailers, large drugstore chains, Wal-Mart, and similar large retailers (together with their suppliers) for giving and receiving price discounts.[1] Economists have criticized the act throughout its history because it protects *competitors* rather than the process of *competition*. By penalizing those who give or receive price discounts, the act often has the perverse effect of reducing competition and raising prices, thus hurting consumers.

Suppose someone sues you for giving or receiving a price discount. In this case, you have two defense alternatives: You can claim that the price discount was cost-justified or that the price discount was given to meet the competition. In sum:

---

[1] European countries have laws with similar prohibitions to Robinson–Patman.

Charge all customers the same price, unless the cost of serving them varies. But feel free to cut price to any customer to meet the lower price of a competitor.[2]

Antitrust economists have long recognized that the Robinson–Patman Act discourages discounting. If companies have to offer the same price to every customer, they are less likely to reduce price to their most valuable customers. Fortunately, many practices, such as offering promotional allowances to large retailers, may shield companies from this kind of antitrust liability, making them more willing to compete by offering discounts.

IMPLEMENTING PRICE DISCRIMINATION SCHEMES

Now that we know how price discrimination works and what legal constraints limit the actual practice, we can discuss how to do it. We focus on the two price discrimination opportunities described in the introduction.

PRICING FOR CLINICAL CONFERENCES

In the AACC case, it's obvious that more distant potential attendees exhibit more highly elastic demand for the conferences than do those living nearby. This difference in elasticity suggests a policy of abandoning the uniform price of $750 in favor of a multitiered price structure based on distance from the conference, like that shown in Table 11-2.

With these prices, the AACC can attract professionals who would otherwise attend a competing organization's conference closer to home. To implement this pricing scheme, AACC could mail regional editions of conference brochures containing different prices to different customers. To prevent regional and domestic conference attendees from taking advantage of the lower international rate, the AACC could require a foreign mailing address to qualify for the international rate. Also, AACC should mail all conference materials to registrants

TABLE 11-2	AACC CONFERENCE PRICING BY LOCATION	
	Region	**Price**
	Local	$800
	National	$600
	International	$400

---

[2] John H. Shenefield and Irwin M. Stelzer, "Common Sense Guidelines," *The Antitrust Laws: A Primer*, 3rd ed. (Washington, D.C.: AEI Press, 1998), 123–126.

prior to the conference date so that any U.S. resident who registers using a false international address would receive no conference packet.

PRICING FOR CELL PHONES

In early 1998, IRK, our cell phone manufacturer, abandoned its global uniform pricing and reduced the price of low-end models sold in the Philippines from $120 to $90. Since the Philippines uses the same communication standard as most of the world (GSM), the pricing decision created an arbitrage opportunity that threatened sales in higher-priced countries (15 million units annually). To prevent arbitrage, the firm sold the $90 phones with incorporated SIM-locks—encrypted mathematical algorithms that allow the phones to operate only in local networks—which made those cell phones useless outside the Philippines.

In the past, Turkish hackers had managed to break some SIM-lock algorithms and reprogram small numbers of the phones to work in other networks. To defeat the hackers, the firm developed new, more complex algorithms for the SIM locks. The hackers managed to break the algorithm codes twice during 1998, but they were able to ship just 15,000 phones to Western European markets before IRK changed the algorithms.

During 1998, IRK sold 200,000 phones to the Philippines. Without the price discrimination scheme, sales would have been only 50,000 units. Its market share went from below 10% to over 25% in one year. The competitors didn't respond because they were already selling their phones at a significant loss. Then, in early 1999, IRK returned to the global uniform pricing policy, raising the cell phone prices in the Philippines back to $120. Competitors followed by raising their prices to the same level. In 2000, cell phone penetration in the Philippines surpassed 12%, and IRK's market share rose to 34%.

ONLY FOOLS PAY RETAIL

Research[3] has shown that consumers don't like knowing that they're paying a higher price than other consumers. This is summed up in popular sayings like "Only fools pay retail [prices]." If low-elasticity consumers know they're being discriminated against, they may even refuse to purchase. A study of on-line pricing showed that when shoppers are asked whether they have any discount coupons (thus revealing the existence of a price discrimination scheme), the click-through rate to completion[4] of the sale dropped enough to make the price discrimination scheme unprofitable.

---

[3] Richard L. Oliver and Mikhael Shor, "Digital Redemption of Coupons: Satisfying and Dissatisfying Effects of Promotion Codes," *Journal of Product and Brand Management* 12, no. 2 (2003): 121–134.

[4] *Click-through rate to completion* refers to "clicking through" all of the checkout screens to complete an order.

So, if you're price discriminating, it's important to keep the scheme secret if you can. Otherwise, you may lose your high-value customers to rivals who don't price discriminate.

SUMMARY & HOMEWORK PROBLEMS

SUMMARY OF MAIN POINTS

- If a seller can identify two groups of consumers with different demand elasticities, and it can prevent arbitrage between two groups, it can increase profit by charging a higher price to the low-elasticity group.
- **Price discrimination** is the practice of charging different people or groups of people different prices that are not cost-justified.
- A **direct price discrimination scheme** is one in which we can identify members of the low-value group, charge them a lower price, and prevent them from reselling their lower-priced goods to the higher-value group.
- It can be illegal for business to price discriminate when selling goods (not services) to other businesses unless
  - price discounts are cost-justified, or
  - discounts are offered to meet competitors' prices.
- Price discrimination schemes may annoy customers who know they're paying more than others and can make them less willing to buy because they know someone else is getting a better price.

MULTIPLE-CHOICE QUESTIONS

See the end of the next chapter for multiple-choice questions.

INDIVIDUAL PROBLEMS

See the end of the next chapter for individual homework problems.

GROUP PROBLEMS

See the end of the next chapter for group homework problems.

Chapter 12

Indirect Price Discrimination

In 2000, Hewlett-Packard (HP) sold about $9 billion worth of printers; it also sold $9 billion worth of ink and supplies. Despite the revenue similarities, HP earned about three times as much profit from sales of ink cartridges (sold at a 50% markup over marginal cost) than it did from sales of printers (sold at a 15% markup). The relatively low margin on printers and the high margin on cartridges are similar to the margins on razor blades and razors, on movies and popcorn, and other similar complementary item pairs. Perhaps the most famous example of this kind of pricing involves Barbie dolls and dresses, inspiring the name of the general practice: *Barbie Doll marketing*—you give away the dolls and sell the dresses at very high markups.

We can best understand this kind of pricing, the topic of this chapter, as a type of *indirect* price discrimination. Recall from Chapter 11 that price discrimination is the seller's effort to set different prices for different groups of customers with different price elasticities of demand. But how can you set prices for different groups if you can't tell who belongs in which group? The trick is setting prices that induce the consumers to identify themselves by their behavior.

Suppose that HP's low-value customers consume one cartridge each year and are willing to pay $100 for printing capability (printer plus one cartridge). High-value customers consume two cartridges each year and are willing to pay $200. What price should HP charge?

If HP priced printers at $50 and cartridges at $50, then low-value users would pay $100, but high-value consumers would pay just $150. The firm could do much better by giving away the printer and charging $100 for each cartridge. In this case, the low-value customers pay $100 and the high-value customers, $200. The manufacturer ends up making more money through this scheme than in one based on equal markups for printers and cartridges.

This pricing strategy works because the high-value consumers identify themselves by the number of cartridges they consume. Since HP charges a relatively high price for the cartridges, high-value customers end up paying a higher margin on printing services (printer + cartridges) than do low-value consumers, who consume fewer cartridges.

Likewise, high-value consumers buy more razor blades (replacing them more frequently as they become dull), more popcorn, and more Barbie outfits. Lower-value consumers buy fewer razors, forgo popcorn at the movies, and buy fewer doll accessories.

This kind of indirect price discrimination is more difficult to design and implement than the direct price discrimination strategies we discussed in Chapter 11 because it's more difficult to sort consumers into separate groups. Consequently, you can easily misclassify consumers. You might end up charging a high-value customer too low a price or a low-value customer too high price. In the former case, you're leaving money on the table; in the latter, the customer may decide not to purchase.

INDIRECT PRICE DISCRIMINATION

When a seller cannot directly identify low- and high-value consumers or cannot prevent arbitrage between two groups, the seller can still discriminate by designing products or services that appeal to different consumer groups. To see how this works, let's look at a series of examples.

Take grocery stores. High-income shoppers are typically less price-sensitive than are low-income consumers, at least for low-priced items. To discriminate between low- and high-price elasticity shoppers, grocery stores offer weekly coupon promotions, usually in newspapers. Low-value customers (those with a higher price elasticity of demand) identify themselves by clipping coupons out of the newspapers. The grocery store effectively reduces prices to the low-value consumers because high-value customers don't clip coupons—they consider their time too valuable.

This **indirect price discrimination scheme** differs from the direct method because high-value customers *could* clip coupons if they wanted to. If this scheme is to be profitable, the store must prevent high-value consumers from regarding coupon clipping as worthwhile. Fear of cannibalizing high-priced sales by offering low-priced items is characteristic of many indirect price discrimination schemes.

Another problem that plagues both direct and indirect discrimination schemes is the risk of creating profitable entry opportunities for rival firms. Take printer manufacturers, for example. Rivals may try to enter the toner cartridge business or provide toner refill kits. Unless the firm can find a way to prevent competitors from selling lower-priced cartridges, say, by "tying" the sales of new cartridges to sales of printers, this kind of competition can render the firm's price discrimination scheme unprofitable. But such ties can run afoul of the antitrust laws.[1]

Like grocery stores and printer manufacturers, software manufacturers discriminate indirectly. They distinguish between commercial and home users, and then they design versions of software that appeal to each group. To charge the more highly price-elastic home consumers a lower price, software manufacturers design a low-priced disabled version lacking the features a business user desires. Here, the cannibalization threat is apparent—the manufacturer must price the full-featured version low enough so high-value business consumers prefer it to the disabled version.

Suppose your marketing department does a survey of potential users. The results, shown in Table 12-1, indicate the values that home and commercial users place on the two versions of the software.

Now suppose that the numbers of home and commercial users are equal; say, you have one of each type. You can see three obvious pricing strategies, as illustrated in the Table 12-2. (Assume that the MC of production is zero, as the cost of producing one more unit, copying the software, is negligible).

The first two strategies are obvious and reflect the usual trade-off. You can price high but sell fewer units or price low and sell more. And the third strategy is, by now, an obvious alternative as well. The much less obvious part of Table 12-2 is why, in the implementation of Strategy 3, you charge just $450 for the full-featured version. First, recall that buyers will choose a product that offers them the most consumer surplus. Commercial users have two purchase options, either the full-featured or the disabled version. Buying the disabled version gives commercial users $50 worth of surplus ($200[value] − $150[price]). What happens if you price the full-featured version at $500? Buying the full-featured version at $500 gives commercial users $0 surplus ($500[value] − $500[price]).

TABLE 12-1	DEMAND FOR SOFTWARE	
Software Version	**Home Users**	**Commercial Users**
Disabled version	$150	$200
Full-featured version	$175	$500

---

[1] *Do not tie the sale of one product to another.* Such arrangements are only legal in a few rare instances—to ensure effective functioning of complicated equipment, to name one. But they are generally against the law. See John H. Shenefield and Irwin M. Stelzer, "Common Sense Guidelines," *The Antitrust Laws: A Primer*, 3rd ed. (Washington, D.C.: AEI Press, 1998), 123–126.

T_{ABLE} **12-2**	**P**OTENTIAL **S**OFTWARE **P**RICING **S**CHEMES	
Strategy	**Implementation**	**Total Profit**
1. Sell only to commercial users at a single high price.	Price full-featured version at $500; do not sell home version.	$500
2. Sell to all users at a single low price.	Price full-featured version at $175.	$175 + $175 = $350
3. Price discriminate: Price high to the commercial users; price low to the home users.	Price disabled version at $150; price full-featured version at $450.	$150 + $450 = $600

Comparing the amount of surplus available under each option, commercial users will buy the disabled version because it offers $50 more surplus than the full-featured version. With the disabled version priced at $150, you have to offer the high-value commercial users at least $50 worth of surplus to get them to purchase the commercial version. This limits the price you can charge for the commercial version to $450 ($500[value] − $450[price] = $50 surplus). Put another way, you have to price the full-featured version low enough so commercial users get at least as much consumer surplus (value minus price) as they do from the disabled version. In contrast, if you don't offer the disabled version at all (Strategy 1), you can charge commercial users exactly what they're willing to pay ($500) so they earn zero surplus (they don't have another option that offers more surplus).

This price discrimination scheme works because the software manufacturer uses two tactics to encourage businesses to buy the commercial version: (1) It makes the home version unattractive by disabling some of its business applications features; (2) it prices the commercial version such that business users receive at least as much buyer surplus as they could get from purchasing the disabled version.

This example illustrates the potential for what marketers call *cannibalization*.

When you offer a low-priced version of a good, you have to be careful that you do not cannibalize *sales of the high-priced good.*

If you offered both the disabled and full-featured versions at a price both commercial and home users were willing to pay ($500 and $150, respectively), sales of the disabled version would cannibalize sales of the full-featured version. That is, those inclined to purchase the full-featured version would now purchase the disabled version. Some cannibalization is inevitable. But if too much cannibalization occurs, setting a single price (either price high and sell to high-value consumers only, or price low and sell to everyone) may be more profitable than price discrimination.

VOLUME DISCOUNTS AS DISCRIMINATION

So far, we've been discussing ways of price discriminating among different *customers*—that is, setting different prices to different people or groups of people. Here, we consider the case of a single customer who demands more than one unit of a good. To price discriminate toward this customer, we have to find a way to set different prices for each unit consumed.

Consider a single customer who's willing to pay $7 for the first unit, $6 for the second, $5 for the third, and so on, as in our earlier demand curve example. If the price is set at $7, this consumer will purchase one unit; if the price is set at $6, two units; $5, three units; and so on. Each price represents the value that the consumer places on each unit consumed; that is, the consumer values the first item at $7, the second at $6, and so on. Notice the difference from the aggregate demand curve. There, each point represented a different consumer with a different value for a single unit of the good. Here, we are speaking of the marginal value of each additional unit to a single customer.

Individual demand curves slope downward because the marginal value, the value placed on an extra unit of the good—and therefore the amount a consumer is willing to pay for it—declines with each purchase. For example, a retailer who purchases from a manufacturer may find that the first few items are relatively easy to sell, but to sell more, she may have to lower the price, "hold" the item in inventory for a longer period of time, or spend money promoting the item. All of these activities reduce the amount that the retailer is willing to pay for additional items.

If a seller is setting a single price, it doesn't matter whether she faces an aggregate or an individual demand—the profit calculus is the same. She'll sell all items where MR > MC—in this case, three units at a price of $5. And, just as in the aggregate demand curve, we see unconsummated wealth-creating transactions at the optimal price. At the profit-maximizing price of $5, our representative consumer purchases only three items. The low-value extra goods— those worth $4, $3, and $2—are not purchased even though the consumer would pay more for these extra goods than the marginal cost ($1.50) of producing them. These three extra units represent unconsummated wealth-creating transactions. Remember, the one lesson of business is to figure out how to profitably consummate these transactions.

The trick to profitably selling more units is to find a way to sell these additional units without dropping the prices of the earlier units. We can identify several ways to do this.

- Offer volume discounts; for example, price the first good at $7, the second at $6, the third at $5, and so on.
- Use two-part pricing. Charge a unit price low enough to consummate all wealth-creating transactions (in this example, $1.50); then bargain over how to split the resulting consumer surplus. The consumer's total value for six units is $27 (= $7 + $6 + $5 + $4 + $3 + $2), and six units cost just $9 to produce. Bargain over how to split the $18 worth of surplus between buyer and seller.
- Bundle the goods—offer six units at a bundled price of $27. The consumer values the first unit at $7, the first two units at $13, the first three at $18, the first four at $22, and the first five at $25, and the first six at $27.

Notice that this bundled pricing resembles that of the timber tract pricing discussed in Chapter 4 on extent decisions. If you set a bundled price of $27, the consumer purchases the whole bundle. This is analogous to the logger who harvests all the trees under a fixed payment of $15,000. Instead of charging by the tree—and letting the logger choose how many trees to consume—the tract owner makes more money by bundling all the trees together and selling them for a lump sum.

This example illustrates a very important lesson for pricing:

When bargaining with a customer, do not bargain over unit price; instead, bargain over the bundle price.

First figure out how much the consumer would demand if price were set at marginal cost; then bargain over the bundled price for this amount. This strategy ensures that you're bargaining over how to split the largest possible pie.

BUNDLED PRICING

We can also use bundling in a slightly different context—when consumers have different demands for different items. Consider a movie theater with two groups of customers whose preferences for two films—a horror film and an adventure film—are different.[2] The theater owners cannot engage in direct price discrimination because they cannot identify the movie preferences of particular consumers ahead of time. But they can bundle the films together in a double feature, thereby accomplishing the same thing.

---

[2] See http://www.nytimes.com/2001/07/26/business/26SCEN.html?pagewanted=print.

Suppose the theater has 100 potential customers: One half would be willing to pay $3 to see the horror film and $2 to see the adventure film; the other half would pay $2 to see the horror film and $3 to see the adventure film.

If the theater sets a single price for both films, it faces the usual trade-off. It can sell to all the consumers at a price of $2 (revenue = $200), or it can sell to half of the moviegoers at a price of $3 (revenue = $150). Since both films have the same aggregate demand, the movie theater could set the price at $2 and earn $200 for each film or $400 in total.

But look what happens when the theater bundles both films together in a double feature. Each customer values the bundle at $5, so the theater can sell to all customers at the bundled price of $5 (revenue = $500).

In this case, bundling makes customers more homogeneous (they're willing to pay the same amount for the bundle), so the seller doesn't have to make significant cuts in the price of the bundle to attract additional customers. Intuitively, bundling makes it easier for the theater to extract consumer surplus with a single price for the bundle.

Bundled pricing[3] can allow a seller to extract more consumer surplus if willingness to pay for the bundle is more homogeneous than willingness to pay for the separate items in the bundle.

SUMMARY & HOMEWORK PROBLEMS

SUMMARY OF MAIN POINTS

- When a seller cannot identify low- and high-value consumers or cannot prevent arbitrage between two groups, it can still discriminate, but only indirectly, by designing products or services that appeal to groups with different price elasticities of demand, who identify themselves based on their purchase patterns.
- If you offer a low-value product that is attractive to high-value consumers, you may cannibalize sales of your high-price product.
- When bargaining with a customer, do not bargain over unit price; instead, bargain over the price of a bundle.
- Bundled pricing can allow a seller to extract more consumer surplus if willingness to pay for the bundle is more homogeneous than willingness to pay for the separate items in the bundle.

[3] Bundling can be accomplished in different ways. *Pure* bundling describes a situation where the commodities in a bundle are not offered for sale separately, whereas *mixed* bundling refers to a pricing strategy where the bundled goods can also be purchased separately.

MULTIPLE-CHOICE QUESTIONS

1. The individual demand curve slopes downward because
  a. the value an individual places on an extra unit of the good decreases.
  b. the amount an individual is willing to pay for the additional unit increases.
  c. the total value consumers derive from consuming a product increases when they consume more units.
  d. All of the above.

2. The strategy underlying price discrimination is
  a. to charge higher prices to customers who have good substitutes available to them.
  b. to charge everyone the same price, but limit the quantity they are allowed to buy.
  c. to increase total revenue by charging higher prices to those with the most inelastic demand for the product and lower prices to those with the most elastic demand.
  d. to reduce per-unit cost by charging higher prices to those with the most inelastic demand and lower prices to those with the most elastic demand.

3. Direct price discrimination may be based on
  a. the age groups of buyers.
  b. the location of buyers.
  c. a buyer's membership in certain clubs or associations.
  d. All of the above.

4. Which of the following statements is consistent with an *indirect* price discrimination scheme?
  a. The seller doesn't have market power.
  b. The seller has no means to identify different customer groups with different demand elasticities.
  c. The seller cannot prevent arbitrage between the two groups.
  d. None of the above.

5. Bundling helps sellers extract more consumer surplus by
  a. smoothing out different preferences in different buyer groups.
  b. grouping buyers into more heterogeneous segments.
  c. implementing an direct price discrimination scheme.
  d. None of the above.

INDIVIDUAL PROBLEMS

12-1. Newspaper versus Soft Drink Vending Machines
Why do newspaper vending machines allow buyers to take more than one paper while soft drink vending machines dispense just one can of soda at a time?

12-2. Movie Theater Price Discrimination

You run a chain of movie theaters, so you commission a marketing study that categorizes your potential customers into 10 equal-sized groups according to what they're willing to pay for a movie, {$10, $9, $8, $7, $6, $5, $4, $3, $2, $1}. It turns out that the low-value customer groups, those with values {$5, $4, $3, $2, $1}, are all over 65 years old. All the costs of exhibiting movies are fixed except for the $3.50 royalty payment you must make to the film distributor for each ticket sold. What price should you charge for movie tickets? Should you offer senior citizen discounts? If so, how much?

12-3. Amazon Discrimination

In September 2000, Amazon offered a *Planet of the Apes* DVD to customers using a Netscape Web browser for $64.99. Several seconds later, however, a similar search performed with Microsoft's Internet Explorer browser resulted in a price of $74.99 for the same product. Why?

12-4. Amazon Discrimination II

Planet of the Apes isn't the only DVD that has different prices at different times. Recently, on-line shoppers logged onto the DVD Talk Forum, a chat room dedicated to discussions about DVDs. These shoppers noted that Amazon's price for a limited-edition copy of the *Men in Black* DVD could differ, depending on a number of factors. Among the determining factors, they said, were the following: which browser was being used, whether a consumer was a repeat or first-time customer, and which Internet service provider address a customer was using. Were prices higher or lower for repeat buyers? Explain your answer.

12-5. Software Discrimination

Suppose your marketing department does a survey of potential users and finds that these users place the following values on the two versions of your software:

Software Version	Home Users	Commercial Users
Disabled version	$150	$200
Full-featured version	$175	$225

If the numbers of home and commercial users are equal, and you cannot distinguish between commercial and home users, what is the most profitable pricing strategy? Assume the MC of production is zero. Explain your answer.

    a. Sell only to commercial users.
    b. Sell only to home users.
    c. Sell to both groups using a single price.
    d. Sell to both groups at two different prices.

GROUP PROBLEMS

G12-1. Price Discrimination

Describe a price discrimination opportunity your company faces—direct, indirect, or bundling. Tell your company how best to implement the scheme, and compute the profit consequences of implementing the scheme.

G12-2. Price Discrimination Data[4]

Collect a set of price quotes for no fewer than 30 airplane tickets. Examine how these price quotes change as you vary the tickets—one characteristic at time.

For instance, suppose you get a price quote for a ticket on United Airlines from Raleigh-Durham to Chicago, departing on May 17 and returning on May 19. Change the following characteristics, one at time, and get a new price quote:

- Change the time of departure within the same day.
- Change the source of your quote (e.g., from Travelocity to the airline's Web site).
- Change the predeparture interval date (e.g., compare flights bought a couple of days in advance to months in advance).
- Change the class of the ticket and travel restrictions.
- Change the return date to include a Saturday stay-over.
- Change anything else you can think of.

Make sure you get price quotes from airports where one airline has a dominant presence (e.g., Northwest in Minneapolis) and a route presenting stiff competition from a "no-frills" carrier such as Southwest or JetBlue.

In your paper, describe some of the important differences in pricing you observe. Are the pricing differences consistent with the patterns of indirect or direct price discrimination, or are there other explanations? Original, novel, and thoughtful interpretations of the patterns you see in the data are particularly welcome.

---

[4] Taken from Pat Bajari's economics class.

STRATEGIC DECISION MAKING

Chapter 13

Strategic Games

In 1995, in Sanya City, China, the Rural Credit Union, hoping to attract new deposits to the bank, raised interest rates from 9.2% to 10.8% on one-year savings accounts. Instead of attracting deposits, however, the change provoked its closest competitor, the Hainan Development Bank, to increase deposit rates as well. As a result, capital costs increased at both banks, with no corresponding increase in deposits, and profit declined at both banks. In 1996, the Central Bank of China ended this "excessive competition" for deposits by mandating a uniform (and low) interest rate throughout the country. Although we don't know what motivated the Central Bank to act, it's likely that the competing banks asked it to end the interest rate "bidding war" between them.

We now have a glimpse of what can happen when the profit of one firm depends on the actions of another. To analyze this interdependence, we use what is known as *game theory*. In a game, we identify the players, the options or moves available to them, and the payoffs associated with combinations of moves. If each player acts optimally, rationally, and selfishly, we can calculate the likely outcome—or equilibrium—of the game.

Studying game theory doesn't just help you figure out what's likely to happen; it also gives you guidance on how you might be able to change the game to your advantage. For example, it's likely that the Chinese banks realized that neither of them could stop competition for depositors by itself, so the banks asked the government to stop it for them.[1]

Remember the three strategies mentioned in Chapter 9 for slowing profit erosion: reducing costs, differentiating your product, and reducing competitive intensity. Game theory helps you understand the third option. In this chapter, we separate our study of games into three areas: sequential-move games, simultaneous-move games, and repeated games.

---

[1] This is very similar to what the Federal Reserve did in the 1970s with its Regulation Q, fixing deposit rates at 5¼%. As happened in the United States, we would expect nonprice competition for deposits, and competition from foreign banks not subject to the domestic regulations.

SEQUENTIAL-MOVE GAMES

In **sequential-move games,** players take turns, and each player observes what his or her rival did before having to move. To compute the equilibrium of a sequential game, it's important to *look ahead and reason back*. Consider a simple two-move game: By anticipating how the second player will react, the first player can accurately forecast the consequences of her own moves. Each player chooses her best move, knowing how the other will react.

The likely outcome of the game is called the **Nash equilibrium,** named for John Nash, the mathematician (and Nobel laureate in economics) who is the subject of Sylvia Nasar's 1998 book and the Academy Award–winning 2001 movie, *A Beautiful Mind*.

> *A Nash equilibrium is a pair of strategies, one for each player, in which each strategy is a best response against the other.*

In equilibrium, neither player wants to change his or her strategy because each player is doing the best that he or she can given what the other player is doing.

In the games that follow, we represent sequential games using the *extensive* or *tree form* of a game, familiar to anyone who's ever used a decision tree.

ENTRY DETERRENCE

In the game illustrated in Figure 13-1, an entrant is trying to decide whether to enter an industry in competition with an incumbent firm. Beginning on the bottom of the left branch of the tree, we see that if the entrant enters, and the

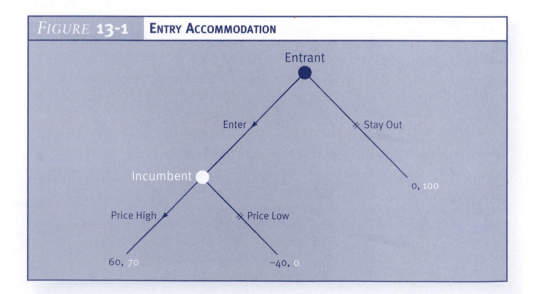

| FIGURE **13-1** | **ENTRY ACCOMMODATION** |

incumbent prices high, the incumbent earns $70. If the incumbent prices low following entry, the incumbent earns nothing. So the incumbent does better by pricing high if the entrant decides to enter.

Once the entrant knows how the incumbent will react, she can compute the profit for both options: If she enters and the incumbent prices high, the entrant earns $60. If the entrant stays out, it doesn't matter what the incumbent does—the entrant earns nothing. So the entrant does better by entering, and the incumbent does better by pricing high. These results form the *equilibrium path* of the game, shown by the arrows leading from the top of the tree to an outcome at the bottom. We compute it by looking ahead to figure out how the incumbent will react and then reasoning back to the entrant's decision.

The analysis doesn't stop here, however. We don't just want to figure out what's likely to happen; we also want some guidance about how to change the game to our advantage. For example, in this game, if the incumbent could figure out how to deter entry, he could end up on the right branch of the tree and earn $100 instead of $70.

One way of deterring entry is to threaten the entrant with a low price following entry. If the entrant believes the threat, she'll stay out because entry, combined with an incumbent's low price, would yield a loss of $40 for the entrant. We diagram the threat by eliminating one of the branches of tree. Suppose the entrant believes the option of the incumbent pricing high has been eliminated; then, if the entrant enters, she'll end up on the branch where the incumbent prices low. On the other hand, if she stays out, she'll earn nothing. By eliminating one of his own options, the incumbent has changed the entrant's behavior. The new equilibrium path is highlighted in the Figure 13-2.

The difficult part if you are the incumbent is figuring out how to convince the entrant you'll price low following entry because pricing low is less profitable than pricing high if entry does occur. So how can you make such a threat credible?

This is very difficult to do. If, for example, the incumbent is able to choose between two technologies—one with a high fixed cost but a low marginal cost, the other with a high marginal cost but a low fixed cost—the incumbent could commit to pricing low by choosing the technology with the low marginal cost. (Recall that in the short run, fixed costs are irrelevant to the pricing decision.) With the low-marginal-cost technology, the incumbent may find it profitable to price low in the event of entry. This choice would change the payoffs, permitting the incumbent to price low in the event of entry.

Remember that this is the whole point of studying game theory. Being able to compute the Nash equilibrium tells you where you are likely to end up, but this

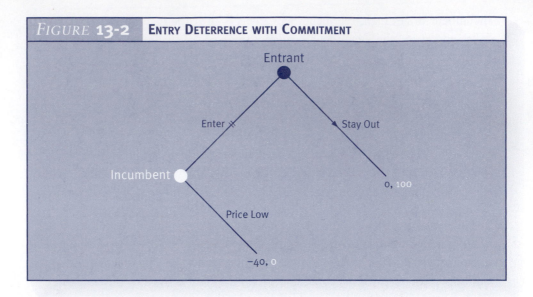

FIGURE **13-2**   **ENTRY DETERRENCE WITH COMMITMENT**

Entrant

Enter ✗   ▲ Stay Out

Incumbent ●   0, 100

Price Low

−40, 0

depends on the payoffs and rules of the game, neither of which is fixed. Analyzing the game helps you figure out how you can restructure the game to your advantage.

SIMULTANEOUS-MOVE GAMES

In **simultaneous-move games,** players move at the same time.[2] To analyze these games, we use the *matrix* or reduced form of a game. As in sequential-move games, likely outcomes are Nash equilibria, a set of strategies such that no player has an incentive to change because all players are doing the best that they can.

HOW TO COMPUTE NASH EQUILIBRIA[3]

In a two-player game, we can represent the payoff as a matrix in which one player (Row) chooses among the row strategies, while the other (Column) chooses among the column strategies, as in Table 13-1. Player Column chooses among the five strategies represented by columns labeled V, W, X, Y, and Z; Player Row chooses among the five strategies represented by rows labeled A, B, C, D, and E. The payoff to each is the two-element entry (row, column) in the corresponding cell. For example, if Player Column chooses V and Player Row chooses B, then Column's payoff is 8 and Row's payoff is 7.

---

[2] For a simultaneous-move game, it is not strictly necessary for the players to move at the same time. It is only necessary that each player not know the other's action before moving.
[3] Adapted from notes by Mikhael Shor, http://mba.vanderbilt.edu/Mike.Shor/courses/game-theory/docs/ lectures0123/Equilibria.html.

TABLE 13-1	SAMPLE PAYOFF MATRIX				
			Player Column		
		V	W	X	Y	Z
	A	9, 9	7, 1	5, 6	3, 4	1, 1
	B	7, 8	5, 2	3, 6	1, 4	3, 3
Player Row	C	5, 6	3, 3	1, 8	9, 7	1, 5
	D	3, 9	1, 9	9, 4	7, 9	5, 9
	E	1, 2	9, 8	7, 7	5, 6	3, 7

To compute equilibrium, we have to ask, "Does either player have an incentive to change his or her strategy unilaterally?" or, equivalently, "Are both players playing a best response to what their rivals are playing?" If not, no equilibrium exists, because at least one player could do better.

Let's start from the perspective of Player Row. For each of Player Column's strategies, select the strategy or strategies that would maximize Player Row's payoff. For example, if Player Column plays V, Player Row's best response is to play A, earning a payoff of 9. Underline this payoff in the game box. Then proceed with Player Column's other strategies. In each column, underline Player Row's best response to each of Player Column's strategies, as shown in Table 13-2.

Now, we can do the same thing for Player Column's best response to Player Row. If Player Row plays D, Player Column is indifferent among V, W, Y, and Z. Note that a best response is not necessarily unique. A player can have a number

TABLE 13-2	IDENTIFYING PLAYER ROW'S BEST STRATEGIES				
			Player Column		
		V	W	X	Y	Z
	A	9, 9	7, 1	5, 6	3, 4	1, 1
	B	7, 8	5, 2	3, 6	1, 4	3, 3
Player Row	C	5, 6	3, 3	1, 8	9, 7	1, 5
	D	3, 9	1, 9	9, 4	7, 9	5, 9
	E	1, 2	9, 8	7, 7	5, 6	3, 7

of strategies, all of which are best responses if each earns the same payoff and earns a bigger payoff than other strategies. In cases such as these, underline all of the best responses. Continue for the rest of Player Row's strategies, as in Table 13-3.

Recall that equilibrium means both players are simultaneously playing their best responses so that neither player has any incentive to change. This is equivalent to saying that a pair of strategies is in equilibrium if both payoffs are underlined.

In the preceding example, we find three equilibria: {A, V}, {E, W}, and {D, Z}. You should convince yourself that, in all three cases, neither player has an incentive to change strategy unilaterally.

Now that you know how to find equilibria, let's consider several different games and their application to common business problems.

PRISONERS' DILEMMA

The **prisoners' dilemma** is perhaps the oldest and most studied game in the history of game theory. It is the story of two parolees, Frank and Jesse, who are caught riding in a car together shortly after someone robbed a nearby bank. The police suspect that Frank and Jesse—known felons—robbed the bank, but they have no direct evidence tying them to the crime. However, association with other felons is a violation of parole, so the district attorney can send them both back to jail to serve out their remaining sentences on their previous crimes. The DA puts Frank and Jesse in separate cells—and creates a nasty dilemma. He offers each prisoner immunity from prosecution in exchange for testimony or evidence to convict the other.

TABLE **13-3**	**ADDING PLAYER COLUMN'S BEST STRATEGIES**				
			Player Column		
		V	W	X	Y	Z
	A	<u>9</u>, <u>9</u>	7, 1	5, 6	3, 4	1, 1
	B	7, <u>8</u>	5, 2	3, 6	1, 4	3, 3
Player Row	C	5, 6	3, 3	1, <u>8</u>	<u>9</u>, 7	1, 5
	D	3, <u>9</u>	1, <u>9</u>	<u>9</u>, 4	7, <u>9</u>	<u>5</u>, <u>9</u>
	E	1, 2	<u>9</u>, <u>8</u>	7, 7	5, 6	3, 7

If only one confesses, that confessor goes free, while the other gets 10 years in jail. If both confess, each receives five years. If neither confesses, each serves two years. We present these payoffs in the matrix shown in Table 13-4.

The only Nash equilibrium is in the upper left corner, {Confess, Confess}. We can verify that this is an equilibrium by making sure that each player's strategy is a best reply to what the other is doing. If Jesse changes his move from "confess" to "say nothing," his payoff goes down, from −5 to −10. And because the game is symmetric, the same thing happens to Frank.

Note the tension between conflict (self-interest) and cooperation (group interest) inherent in the game. If Frank and Jesse could cooperate (both "say nothing"), they could make the group better off by moving to the bottom right corner. However, the cooperative outcome in the bottom right corner {Say Nothing, Say Nothing} is not an equilibrium: If your rival is saying nothing, you can reduce your own sentence by confessing. Cooperation is not an equilibrium. By following their self-interest (by trying to make themselves better off), the players make the group worse off.

Now we can see an opportunity for the group to improve its position. Our subsequent study of the prisoners' dilemma will focus on how to move Frank and Jesse out of the low-payoff equilibrium (upper left) to the high-payoff cooperative square (lower right).

HORIZONTAL PRICING DILEMMA

The pricing dilemma illustrated in Table 13-5 has the same logical structure as the prisoners' dilemma. Both Coke and Pepsi could make more money by pricing high, but {Price High, Price High} is not a Nash equilibrium. Pepsi does better by pricing low, regardless of what Coke does; and Coke does better by pricing low, regardless of what Pepsi does. The only Nash equilibrium is for both to price low, in the upper left corner.

If Coke and Pepsi can find a way to coordinate their pricing, they can get out of this dilemma. However, explicit price coordination is a violation of the

TABLE **13-4**	**PRISONERS' DILEMMA**		
		Frank	
		Confess	Say Nothing
Jesse Confess		−5, −5	0, −10
Say Nothing		−10, 0	−2, −2

TABLE **13-5**	**HORIZONTAL PRICING DILEMMA**	
	Coke	
	Price Low	Price High
Pepsi Price Low	**0**, **0**	**4**, −2
Price High	−2, **4**	2, 2

antitrust laws, as summed up in the following advice from a former antitrust prosecutor.[4]

> *Do not discuss prices with your competitors. That is one of those black-and-white areas. The enforcement authorities can be counted on to bring a criminal prosecution if they learn that you have met with your competitors to fix prices or any other terms of sale. Jail time is increasingly common.*

Another way out of this dilemma is to allocate customers, divide up territories, and agree not to compete in each other's areas. However, these agreements are also illegal.[5]

> *Do not agree with your competitor to stay out of each other's markets. It may be tempting to seek freedom of action in one part of the country by agreeing with a competitor not to go west if he will not come east. Avoid that temptation. The consequences of the discovery of such behavior by the enforcement authorities are likely to be the same as the unearthing of a price-fixing conspiracy.*

Another way out of this dilemma is to buy or merge with your competitor. Again, if the only reason for doing so is to stop competition, the merger may violate the antitrust laws. The Clayton Act outlaws mergers that substantially lessen competition.

Note the similarity of this advice to that given in Chapter 10 on pricing commonly owned substitute products. If you own both substitutes (Coke and Pepsi), your aggregate demand becomes less elastic, so you want to raise price. This is just another way of analyzing the same problem.

PRICE DISCRIMINATION DILEMMA

As you learned in Chapters 11 and 12 on price discrimination, you can always raise profit by charging different prices to different consumers based on their price elasticity of demand—also known as price discriminating. But when you're

---

[4] John H. Shenefield and Irwin M. Stelzer, "Common Sense Guidelines," *The Antitrust Laws: A Primer*, 3rd ed. (Washington, D.C.: AEI Press, 1998), 123–126.
[5] Ibid.

competing against other firms, you may provoke your competitor to retaliate in a way that could make you both worse off. If your competitors begin discriminating in reaction to your decision to discriminate, then everyone's profit can fall below what they would've been had no one price discriminated. You're likely to see this situation when firms can offer price discounts to consumers who prefer a rival brand or location. For example, firms often discriminate through coupon targeting. Supermarkets may circulate coupons in geographic areas closer to that of their rivals, or they may issue coupons at the checkout counter to customers known to live closer to rivals.[6] Some companies offer coupons at supermarket checkouts to customers who have purchased competing brands.[7] Domino's Pizza reportedly targets promotions to customers who live closer to its rivals' stores, a strategy consistent with discrimination based on consumer location.[8] Similarly, long-distance phone service providers offer lower prices to their competitors' customers.[9] In all such cases, we would expect rivals to react by offering lower prices to these targeted customers as well, with the result that equilibrium prices creep closer to costs than they would be without targeted price reductions.

In Table 13-6, we see an illustrative game involving two grocery stores. These stores (Kroger and Safeway) are considering whether to offer targeted discount coupons offering a percentage reduction on their customers' next grocery bills. Customers living close to the store have less price-elastic demand than do customers located farther away. Thus, either grocery store can raise profit by offering bigger discounts to customers who live farther away—and nearer to a competitor's store.

If just one grocery store offers such coupons, then its profit increases. However, if its competitor retaliates and does the same thing, then all the stores wind up with about the same overall sale volume, but at lower prices. In the equilibrium (upper left in Table 13-6), all players are worse off. Intuitively, with the uniform-price strategy, the stores compete vigorously for customers only on

---

[6] Retail scanner data and company loyalty programs sometimes make such discrimination possible. For a detailed analysis of these strategies, see Greg Shaffer and Z. John Zhang, "Competitive Coupon Targeting," *Marketing Science* 14 (1995): 395.

[7] Examples of these so-called pay-to-switch strategies include Coca-Cola's giving a discount on Diet Coke to purchasers of Diet Pepsi and Chesebrough-Pond's giving a discount on Mentadent Toothpaste to purchasers of PeroxiCare. See Greg Shaffer and Z. John Zhang, "Pay to Switch or Pay to Stay: Preference-Based Price Discrimination in Markets with Switching Costs," *Journal of Economics and Management Strategy* 9 (2000): 397, 400.

[8] Ibid.

[9] See ibid. at 399 (noting how AT&T and MCI will offer cash payments to induce customers to switch services). See also Yongmin Chen, "Paying Customers to Switch," *Journal of Economics and Management Strategy* 6 (1997): 877. Drew Fudenberg and Jean Tirole, "Customer Poaching and Brand Switching," *Rand Journal of Economics* 31 (2000): 634. Discrimination based on consumers' spatial positioning also may take place in vertically differentiated settings. For example, private-label or generic firms may offer "choosy" customers a discount on their product, and at the same time branded firms may offer discounts on their products to consumers with lower valuations of quality. See Kenneth S. Corts, "Third-Degree Price Discrimination in Oligopoly: All-Out Competition and Strategic Commitment," *Rand Journal of Economics* 29 (1998): 306.

TABLE 13-6	OLIGOPOLY PRICE DISCRIMINATION DILEMMA	
		Kroger	
		Price Discriminate	Set Uniform Price
Safeway	Price Discriminate	**0**, **0**	**4**, −2
	Set Uniform Price	−2, **4**	2, 2

the boundaries of their market areas. When they discriminate, they compete vigorously over the entire area.

ADVERTISING DILEMMA

Table 13-7 exhibits an advertising dilemma that has the same logical structure as the prisoners' dilemma.

Both RJR and Phillip Morris could make more money by not advertising. Cigarette advertising is predatory; that is, it serves mainly to steal market share from rivals without increasing market size. But the lower right corner in Table 13-7 is not an equilibrium. Each firm could do better by advertising to steal the other's customers. The only Nash equilibrium is for both to advertise and earn lower profits.

When the government banned over-the-air cigarette advertising in the early 1970s, the profitability of the cigarette industry increased because the ban moved the industry from the upper left corner to the lower right corner of the payoff matrix. Ordinarily, however, you can't count on the government to help you out of a prisoners' dilemma, despite the story of the Chinese banks in the introduction.

FREE-RIDING DILEMMA

The game in Table 13-8 illustrates the strategic interdependence typical of an MBA study group. It's also typical of the kinds of payoffs you'd expect in any

TABLE 13-7	ADVERTISING DILEMMA	
		RJR	
		Advertise	Don't Advertise
Phillip Morris	Advertise	**0**, **0**	**4**, −2
	Don't Advertise	−2, **4**	2, 2

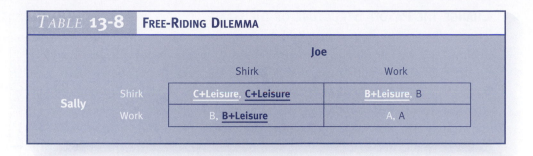

		Joe	
		Shirk	Work
Sally	Shirk	C+Leisure, **C+Leisure**	**B+Leisure**, B
	Work	B, **B+Leisure**	A, A

TABLE 13-8 FREE-RIDING DILEMMA

group or team-based activity. Each player has the option of working hard or shirking. The benefit of working hard is that you raise your grade, but the downside is that you sacrifice leisure time.

To determine the Nash equilibrium of the game, you need to know how study group members rank various outcomes. Assume that both students rank the outcomes as follows:

- A grade of B, with leisure time is better than
- a grade of A and no leisure time, which is better than
- a grade of C plus leisure, which is better than
- a grade of B and no leisure.

With this set of preferences, the Nash equilibrium occurs when each player shirks and receives a C plus leisure time. This outcome is inefficient because students in the group would jointly prefer the A that comes from hard work. However, this outcome is not an equilibrium because once the other group members are working hard, the best response is to shirk. As in the other prisoners' dilemma games, the fundamental conflict lies between competition and cooperation. Successful study groups figure out how to solve the dilemma and reach the preferred cooperative outcome.

WHAT CAN I LEARN FROM STUDYING GAMES LIKE THE PRISONERS' DILEMMA?

The Nash equilibrium of a prisoners' dilemma represents an unconsummated wealth-creating transaction between players. In the pricing dilemma, both players would like to price high. In the advertising dilemma, both would like to advertise less. In the free-riding game, both would like to work harder. However, none of these outcomes is a Nash equilibrium.

The point of studying the prisoners' dilemma is to learn to avoid these bad outcomes or, alternatively, to learn how to consummate these unconsummated wealth-creating transactions between or among the players.

CHANGE THE PAYOFF STRUCTURE OF THE GAME

The implication of the prisoners' dilemma for long-run strategy is clear: Try to *avoid* games with the logical structure of a prisoners' dilemma. Instead, work on developing long-run strategies that change the structure of the game to make your own payoffs less dependent on your rivals' actions. Try one of the strategies mentioned in the text: Differentiate your product by providing something novel that your competitors can't easily imitate, or figure out a way to lower your costs.

If you have no other option, try to reduce the intensity of competition without running afoul of the antitrust laws. We also discuss next how you can escape the dilemma when the game is repeated.

HOW BEST TO GET OUT OF A REPEATED PRISONERS' DILEMMA

If the game with the logical structure of a prisoners' dilemma is played only once, it is difficult to find your way out of it. But if the game is repeated, only a fool (or someone who hasn't read this book) would stay stuck in a bad equilibrium.

To determine the best way to play a repeated prisoners' dilemma, economist Robert Axelrod[10] had a novel idea—he ran a tournament with a cash prize. Asking professors of political science, mathematics, psychology, computer science, and economics to submit strategies as programmable functions, Axelrod was able to run simulated tournaments among the strategies. Consider one strategy as an example: You price high unless your opponent prices low, and if your rival prices low, punish him by pricing low for the next 10 periods. Axelrod was able to characterize the features of the strategies that earned the highest profit:

- *Be nice*: No first strikes.
- *Be easily provoked*: Respond immediately to rivals.
- *Be forgiving*: Don't try to punish competitors too much if they defect from a good outcome.
- *Don't be envious*: Focus on your own slice of the profit pie, not on your competitor's.
- *Be clear*: Make sure your competitors can easily interpret your actions.

The tit-for-tat strategy—doing what your opponent did last period—was the winning strategy. It exhibits all of the characteristics of a successful strategy just listed. Tit-for-tat never strikes first, and it responds immediately to defection, but punishment is limited to times when a rival is not cooperating. It is focused on

---

[10] Robert Axelrod, *The Complexity of Cooperation: Agent-Based Models of Collaboration and Competition* (Princeton, N.J.: Princeton University Press, 1997), http://pup.princeton.edu/titles/6144.html.

maximizing the player's profit, not on limiting competitor's profits, and it is easily understood by rivals.

Consider another similar situation. Company B and Company C produce automobile carburetors. The demand for carburetors is declining, largely because fuel injection technology has superseded carburetor technology. However, people with older automobiles still demand carburetors. Direct competition between the two companies is minimal because Company B produces a bronze-finish carburetor, whereas Company C specializes in a chrome finish. Consumers wouldn't dream of considering the products to be close substitutes. "Muscle" car owners desire the more expensive chrome carburetors almost exclusively because chrome enhances the appearance of the car. Other owners are content with bronze carburetors, which are functional but have no cosmetic appeal.

Company B hired a recent MBA who decided to go after C's customers by producing a new chrome-finish carburetor. Company C then retaliated by offering a bronze-finish carburetor. Both companies' profits suffered. What should the companies do?

When you analyze this game in Table 13-9, you can easily see what happened. The parties started off in the lower right corner, the cooperative outcome, each earning high profit. Then, Company B became envious, coveting the high profit it could earn from entering the chrome-finish carburetor market. Company B's entry into C's business essentially moved the game from the lower right to the lower left. Company C, thus provoked, immediately retaliated by entering B's core business. They ended up in the Nash equilibrium outcome, upper left, each competing in the other's market and earning low profit. Both companies' managers could have foreseen, without much sophisticated thought, the undesirable consequences of this outcome—which is about as self-destructive as starting a price war. In general, it's a bad idea to compete using easily copied strategies like lowering price.

To get out of this dilemma, Company B should announce its withdrawal from the chrome market and hope that C follows suit. If C doesn't follow suit, B should consider further actions against C—actions that would allow C's managers to see

TABLE 13-9   CARBURETOR PRODUCER DILEMMA

		Company B	
		Offer both types	Offer only bronze
Company C	Offer both types	0, 0	4, −2
	Offer only chrome	−2, 4	2, 2

clearly that they must leave the bronze-finish market to make high profit. Whatever actions B takes should be in compliance with antitrust laws. As we noted earlier in this chapter, explicit agreements to allocate customers, divide up territories, and agree not to compete in each other's areas are illegal.

OTHER GAMES

GAME OF CHICKEN

In the classic game of chicken, two teenage boys—say, James and Dean—drive their cars straight toward each other. If both go straight, they crash and die. If both swerve, they're better off because they live, albeit with the shame of chickening out. The best outcome for a boy is to go straight, while his opponent swerves. And, of course, the boy who swerves has to suffer humiliation, losing credibility and respect among his peers. In Table 13-10, you can verify for yourself that the game of chicken has two equilibria in the off-diagonal entries of the matrix—in one, James goes straight while Dean swerves; in the other, Dean goes straight while James swerves.

Of the two equilibria in the game, game theory is silent on which is more likely. Note that each party prefers one of the equilibria. This implies an obvious strategy: Commit to a position, and make sure your rival understands your commitment to your position. Coordination here is important so that the players don't end up killing each other.

The game of chicken has business applications as well (see Table 13-11). In 2000, a biotechnology company (A) had a choice of developing hybrid grapes to grow in either South Africa or Italy. The company could afford to develop only one grape variety. The Italian market is much bigger than the South African market, so A's managers would prefer to serve the Italian market. However, A's only rival (B) is also developing hybrid grapes and faces the same choices. Both would prefer to be the sole entrant in a market, and both prefer Italy to South

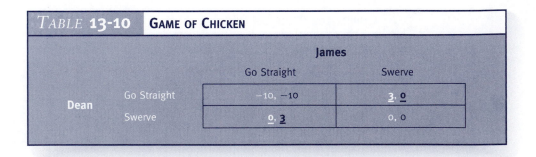

TABLE **13-10**	**GAME OF CHICKEN**		
		James	
		Go Straight	Swerve
Dean	Go Straight	−10, −10	**3**, **0**
	Swerve	**0**, **3**	0, 0

TABLE **13-11**	**MARKET ENTRY GAME OF CHICKEN**	
	A	
	Italy	South Africa
B — Italy	0, 0	**100, 50**
B — South Africa	**50, 100**	−50, −50

Africa. This game has the same logical structure as the game of chicken, with two equilibria, where one company invests in each country.

As in any chicken-game situation, coordination is very important. Moreover, this kind of game lends itself to first-mover advantages. If A can move first or commit to going into Italy, it will force B into South Africa. By moving first, A turns the simultaneous-move game into a sequential-move game with a "first-mover advantage" in which it gets to "choose" the favorable equilibrium. We graph this outcome in Figure 13-3.

DATING GAME

The dating game shares the tension between group interest (cooperation) and self-interest (conflict) inherent in a prisoners' dilemma. The game is about a couple with different interests—Sally likes ballet, and Joe likes wrestling. But each likes

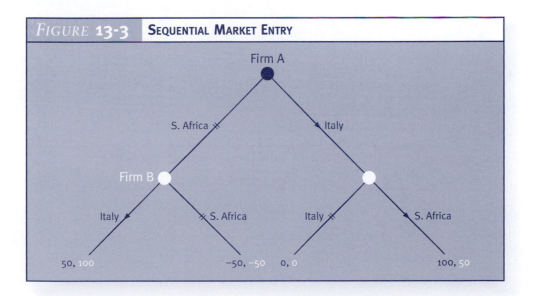

FIGURE **13-3**	**SEQUENTIAL MARKET ENTRY**

Firm A

S. Africa ✗   ↑ Italy

Firm B ○   ○

Italy ↑   ✗ S. Africa   Italy ✗   ↑ S. Africa

50, 100   −50, −50   0, 0   100, 50

the other's company and would prefer attending events together, regardless of what the event is. The group (Sally and Joe) would be best served if Sally and Joe could agree to attend an event together (group payoff of 5), but neither coordination possibility—both attend the ballet or both attend wrestling match— is a Nash equilibrium. The only Nash equilibrium is the lower left in Table 13-12, where Joe goes to the wrestling match and Sally goes to the ballet. As in the prisoners' dilemma, the idea is to find a way to change the rules of the game so both players can earn higher payoffs.

One easy way to increase the joint payoffs is to take turns by attending a different event together each week. This solution gives a higher group payoff (5) than the Nash equilibrium (4). Note the similarity of this solution to the repeated prisoner's dilemma—if you repeat the game, you'll find it relatively easy to figure a way out of the dilemma.

The dating game also gives you a way to analyze the tension between divisions within a corporation. Suppose Saturn and Cadillac—two separate divisions under the same parent company, General Motors (GM)—receive a volume discount if they purchase common tires from a single supplier. However, Saturn and Cadillac cannot agree on a common supplier because each has its own preference: Saturn wants Goodyear Tires, while Cadillac wants Michelin. This interdivision conflict negatively affects company-wide profit (see Table 13-13).

TABLE **13-12**	**DATING GAME**		
		Joe	
		Wrestling Match	Ballet
Sally	Wrestling Match	1, **4**	0, 0
	Ballet	**2, 2**	**4**, 1

TABLE **13-13**	**CORPORATE DIVISION DATING GAME (EXTERNALITY)**		
		Saturn	
		Goodyear Tires	Michelin Tires
Cadillac	Goodyear Tires	1, **4**	0, 0
	Michelin Tires	**2, 2**	**4**, 1

Interdivision conflict is more likely to arise when the parent company runs each division as a separate profit center. Finding a way to cooperate, for the good of the parent company, is management's problem. In this case, GM might offer some kind of profit sharing or payoff from one division to another (e.g., Cadillac could pay Saturn to use Michelin tires).

SHIRKING/MONITORING GAME

We can consider the problem of how to efficiently manage workers as a game between an employer and an employee. Using game theory helps us understand how to manage self-interested employees.

Consider the most basic situation: A self-interested employee would prefer to work less (shirk), but he can only shirk if his manager is not monitoring what he does. His employer wants him to work hard, but she must incur costs to monitor the employee's behavior. To make this concrete, think of the employee as a bank teller and the employer as the bank manager. The employee has some incentive to embezzle (steal) funds from the bank, and the manager can conduct costly audits of employee behavior (monitor) to detect embezzlement. More generally, you can think of this as any game between an employee who prefers working less (shirking) to working hard and his manager who has to incur costs to monitor the employee's behavior.

Table 13-14 is a diagram of the shirking/monitoring game. Try to find an equilibrium. If the manager monitors, then the employee does better by working hard. If the employee works, the manager does better by not spending resources to monitor employee behavior. But if the manager doesn't monitor, then the employee does better by shirking. And so on. This game has no pure strategy equilibrium.

In these kinds of games, the players play mixed strategies; that is, they choose which strategy to play randomly. The idea is to use the element of surprise to keep your opponent from taking advantage of your strategy. By choosing actions

TABLE 13-14	SHIRKING/MONITORING GAME		
		Employee	
		Shirk	Work Hard
Manager	Monitors	−**1**, 0	5, **5**
	No Monitoring	−10, **10**	**10**, 5

randomly, neither player can take advantage of the other. The employer randomly monitors the employee's behavior, and the employee randomly shirks. It turns out that the probability of monitoring depends on how much the employee gains by shirking, and the probability of shirking depends on how much it costs the employer to monitor the employee's behavior. If the employee's shirking gains are large, or if the employer's monitoring expenses are great, the probability of shirking will be higher.

Now that we understand behavior in this game, let's try to figure out how to change the outcome to our advantage. The employer can reduce shirking by combining monitoring with an incentive compensation scheme. When the employer monitors and finds the employee is working hard, the employer can reward the employee with a bonus; or, equivalently, when the employer monitors and finds the employee is shirking, the employer can punish him with a fine, like demotion or dismissal. This combination of monitoring and incentive compensation can reduce the costs of controlling self-interested employees. We'll return to this problem in a future chapter when we discuss aligning employee incentives with the goals of the firm.

SUMMARY & HOMEWORK PROBLEMS

SUMMARY OF MAIN POINTS

- In **sequential-move games,** players take turns, and each player observes what his or her rival did before having to move.
- A **Nash equilibrium** is a pair of strategies, one for each player, in which each strategy is a best response against the other.
- When players act rationally, optimally, and in their own self-interest, it's possible to compute the likely outcomes of games. By studying games, we learn where the pitfalls are and how to avoid them.
- Sequential games include a potential first-mover advantage, or disadvantage, and players can change the outcome by committing to a future course of action. Credible commitments are difficult to make because they require that players threaten to act in an unprofitable way—against their self-interest.
- In **simultaneous-move games,** players move at the same time.
- In the **prisoners' dilemma,** conflict and cooperation are in tension—self-interest leads the players to outcomes that no one likes. Studying the games can help you figure a way to avoid these bad outcomes.

- In repeated games, it is much easier to get out of bad situations. Here are some general rules of thumb:
  - Be nice: No first strikes.
  - Be easily provoked: Respond immediately to rivals.
  - Be forgiving: Don't try to punish competitors too much.
  - Don't be envious: Focus on your own slice of the profit pie, not on your competitor's.
  - Be clear: Make sure your competitors can easily interpret your actions.

MULTIPLE-CHOICE QUESTIONS

1. What is the equilibrium of the following game?

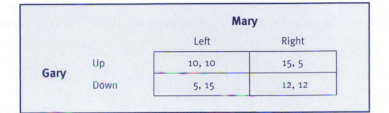

  a. Up, Left
  b. Down, Left
  c. Up, Right
  d. Down, Right

2. In a strategic game, if the other player has adopted a Nash equilibrium strategy, you should
  a. also adopt a Nash equilibrium strategy.
  b. use a strategy that delivers you a higher payoff than the Nash equilibrium strategy.
  c. use either a or b, depending on the specifics of the game.
  d. None of the above.

3. If you find yourself in a repeated prisoner's dilemma, which of the following would be appropriate actions?
  a. Launch a first strike.
  b. Punish your competitor severely.
  c. Respond immediately to your competitor's actions.
  d. Make sure your actions confuse your competitor.

4. The following matrix representation identifies a Nash equilibrium (Black, Even) for a simultaneous-move game between Joe and Sally. If this were a sequential-move game, and Joe had the opportunity to move first, what would the outcome be?

Sally		**Joe**	
		Odd	Even
	Black	Joe makes $40 Sally makes $20	Joe makes $80 Sally makes $60
	White	Joe makes $90 Sally makes $30	Joe makes $100 Sally makes $40

a. Black, Odd

b. Black, Even

c. White, Odd

d. White, Even

5. In the previous game, up to how much, if anything, would Joe be willing to pay to move first?

   a. $0

   b. $10

   c. $80

   d. $90

INDIVIDUAL PROBLEMS

13-1. Study Group Free Riding

1. In the game shown below, change the ranking of values that Sally and Joe place on leisure and grades to change the game from a prisoners' dilemma into a game of chicken with two equilibria.

2. Give advice to Joe about how to change the game to his advantage.

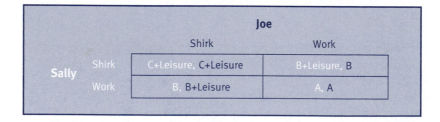

Sally		**Joe**	
		Shirk	Work
	Shirk	C+Leisure, C+Leisure	B+Leisure, B
	Work	B, B+Leisure	A, A

Upper left is an equilibrium if both students rank the outcomes as follows:

   a. A grade of B and leisure is better than

   b. a grade of A and no leisure, which is better than

   c. a grade of C and leisure, which is better than

   d. a grade of B and hard work.

13-2. Coke versus Pepsi

In 1931, Pepsi was almost broke. The Great Depression hit it hard, and Coke had most of the duopoly market for soft drinks in the United States. Pepsi tried many things: marketing campaigns, label changes, and more. Then it came up with the idea of selling 12-ounce bottles for 5¢, which had been the 6-ounce price. Coke could have followed the price per unit down, but it didn't. Total soft drink demand increased, and Pepsi took a larger share of the demand. Why is the equilibrium of this game different from that of a prisoners' dilemma? (*Hint*: Change the payoffs of the prisoners' dilemma to reflect the implied equilibrium.)

13-3. Cell Phone Standards Game

Nokia and Ericsson plan to introduce new handheld communications devices. However, they must decide whether to use their own software standard or a common third-party-developed standard. The respective payoffs are diagrammed here. What is the likely outcome?

		Nokia	
		Own Standard	Common Standard
Ericsson	Own Standard	$15M, $18M	$25M, $10M
	Common Standard	$8M, $29M	$20M, $23M

13-4. Airline Hub Game

Two airlines, A and B, are deciding to choose whether Atlanta or Chicago should be their major hub. Given the diagram here, find all equilibria of this game.

		Airline A	
		Atlanta	Chicago
Airline B	Atlanta	$40M, $40M	$85M, $60M
	Chicago	$60M, $85M	$35M, $35M

13-5. Auditing Game

The manager of a corporate division faces the possibility of an audit every year. She prefers to spend time preparing if she will be audited; otherwise, she would prefer to invest her time elsewhere. The auditor, who gets recognized for uncovering problems, prefers to audit unprepared clients. If the players match their actions (i.e., the manager prepares and the auditor audits, or the manager doesn't prepare and the auditor doesn't audit), the manager wins with a payoff of 20, and the auditor loses with a payoff of −20. If the actions don't match, the auditor wins with a payoff of 20, and the manager loses with a payoff of −20. Diagram this game, and comment on the equilibrium.

GROUP PROBLEMS

G13-1. Simultaneous Game

Describe a simultaneous game within your firm, or between your firm and a competitor, or between your firm and a customer or supplier. Draw a formal 2×2 payoff matrix with the strategy choices clearly labeled, and the payoffs to each of the parties. (Use numbers if you can estimate them; otherwise, describe qualitative rankings among outcomes.). Clearly identify the equilibrium by shading the cell of the table. What advice can you derive from your analysis? Compute the profit consequences of the advice.

G13-2. Sequential Game

Describe a sequential game facing your firm, and represent it in extensive or tree form. Compute and analyze the equilibrium of the game. What advice can you derive from your analysis? Compute the profit consequences of the advice.

G13-3. Repeated Game

Describe a repeated game facing your firm. Compute and analyze the equilibrium of the game, and explicitly show how it differs from the one-shot (nonrepeated) equilibrium. What advice can you derive from your analysis? Compute the profit consequences of the advice.

Chapter 14

Bargaining

In 2003, Blue Cross Blue Shield (a health insurance company covering Rhode Island's state employees) hired PharmaCare to provide pharmaceutical services to 20,000 employees. PharmaCare assembled a limited network of retail pharmacies willing to sell drugs to state employees at a significant discount. The old (expiring) contract had been more liberal, allowing employees to go to any pharmacy in the state, but the new contract saved the state $820,000.

After Blue Cross signed the contract, four pharmacies that were not part of the new PharmaCare network lobbied Rhode Island legislators to allow them to join. Stop & Shop, Target, Walgreen's, and Shaw's Supermarkets said they'd be willing to sell drugs to state employees at the same prices specified in the contract negotiated with PharmaCare. These four pharmacies argued that opening the network would benefit the state employees, as they would have a wider array of stores from which to purchase their medications.

Blue Cross declined the offer to open the network. Scott Frasier, spokesman for Blue Cross said, "Adding all the other stores eliminates the savings you can generate from having a [restricted] network."

The ensuing controversy reignited debate in the state's legislature over the merit of "freedom-of-choice" bills. Such bills would open networks to any pharmacy willing to meet the prices and terms of the negotiated contracts. The governor supported this legislation. He favored expanding the network to include more pharmacies[1] to increase convenience for state workers, who could then go to any pharmacy they wanted.

But the governor failed to understand the way Blue Cross achieved its price reduction. Blue Cross was able to improve its bargaining position (and negotiate a reduced price) only by threatening to exclude some pharmacies from the network. If you take that capability away—which the freedom-of-choice laws do—then Blue Cross loses its ability to negotiate lower prices. Why would a pharmacy owner offer lower prices if she knows that her firm is going to be included in the

---

[1] Liz Anderson, "Blue Cross Rejects a Carcieri Administration Request to Add Pharmacies to the Recently Limited Options for State Workers," *Journal State House Bureau*, January 13, 2004.

network, no matter what price it offers? If the governor had read this chapter, perhaps he would have recognized that the freedom-of-choice laws he supported would lead to higher prices in future negotiations.

In this chapter, we formally study bargaining, using game theory tools discussed in Chapter 13. We present bargaining both as a simultaneous game with two outcomes and as a sequential game, in which the ability to commit can affect the game's outcome. As in Chapter 13, we use game theory not merely to predict what's likely to occur but also to help you position yourself in ways that increase your bargaining payoff.

We also introduce an alternative way of looking at bargaining in which the alternatives to agreement determine the terms of agreement. Under this view of bargaining, changing the outcome to your advantage depends on being able to change the alternatives to agreement.

BARGAINING AS A GAME OF CHICKEN

Here we show how to model bargaining as either a *simultaneous game* with two equilibria or as a *sequential game*, where being able to commit to a position gives one player bargaining power over a rival player.

BARGAINING AS A SIMULTANEOUS GAME

Suppose a company's managers are bargaining with a labor union over the wages the firm will pay its workers. To simplify matters, assume that management and labor are bargaining over a fixed sum of $200 million and that each player has just two possible strategies: *bargain hard* or *accommodate*. If both bargain hard, they'll reach no deal; if both accommodate, they split the gains from trade. If one player bargains hard and the other accommodates, the player who bargains hard takes 75% of the proverbial pie (i.e., the gains from trade).

We see in Table 14-1 that this game has two equilibria: upper right and lower left, each with very different implications for the two parties. Management prefers the lower-left equilibrium, while labor prefers the upper right. If both

TABLE **14-1**	**LABOR NEGOTIATION GAME**		
		Management	
		Bargain Hard	Accommodate
Labor	Bargain Hard	0, 0	__150__, __50__
	Accommodate	__50__, __150__	100, 100

bargain hard, then each earns nothing (upper left), but upper left is not an equilibrium—either party could do better by changing its strategy unilaterally.

Clearly, we have a game of chicken here. Recall that the point of formally modeling a game like this is not necessarily to predict where you're likely to end up; it's to show you how you can manipulate the rules of the game to your advantage. Both parties want to steer the game to their preferred equilibrium, so they'll try to do this by committing to a position. If you convince your rival that you're going to bargain hard, regardless of what your rival does, he will do better by accommodating. Thus, you've successfully steered the game to your preferred equilibrium.

BARGAINING AS A SEQUENTIAL GAME

Committing to a position isn't as easy as it sounds. For your stance to be credible, the other party has to believe you. To see the value of commitment, let's study the same game, but employ sequential moves. Management makes either a generous offer or a low offer; then the union can either strike or accept the offer. If the union accepts the offer, the game ends peaceably; but if the union strikes, each party earns nothing.

We diagram the offers and payoffs in Figure 14-1. To analyze the game, begin at the second stage, and notice that the union does better by accepting whatever is offered in the first stage. Whether the union receives a generous offer or a low offer, accepting the offer gives the union a higher payout than

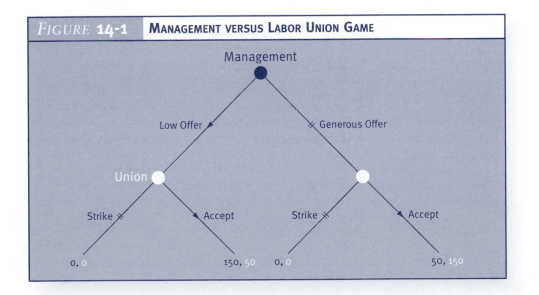

FIGURE **14-1**   **MANAGEMENT VERSUS LABOR UNION GAME**

Management

Low Offer   Generous Offer

Union

Strike   Accept   Strike   Accept

0, 0   150, 50   0, 0   50, 150

striking. Management, looking ahead and reasoning back, realizes that making a low offer is better. You'll find this equilibrium path identified by the arrows in Figure 14-1.

This game illustrates a *first-mover advantage*—by moving first, management has an advantage because it can decide which branch of the tree to go down. The union has the power only to accept or reject management's offer.

Now that the union knows what's likely to happen, can it figure out how to change the game to its advantage? It can change the outcome of the game if it can find a way to credibly threaten a strike if it receives a low offer from management. If management believes the union's threat, it will make a generous offer. As in the entry deterrence game in Chapter 13, by committing to a position, the union eliminates an option, thereby changing the equilibrium of the game. We illustrate the new equilibrium in Figure 14-2.

Although committing to strike sounds simple, it's difficult for the union to persuade management that it will pursue an otherwise unprofitable strategy, like striking. If the threat is not credible, the union might actually have to strike, leading to the following maxim:

The best threat is one you never have to use.

Strikes often occur because management doesn't believe the union's threat. In these cases, the only way for the union to convince management that it's committed to striking is to go on strike.

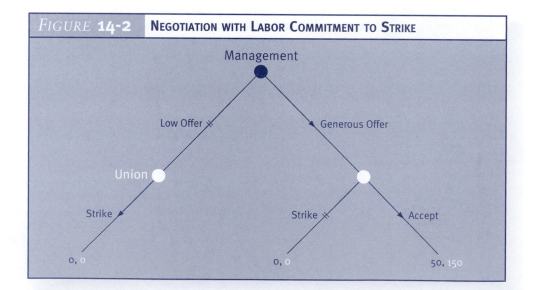

FIGURE 14-2   NEGOTIATION WITH LABOR COMMITMENT TO STRIKE

Management

Low Offer ✗   ▲ Generous Offer

Union

Strike ▲   Strike ✗   ▲ Accept

0, 0   0, 0   50, 150

HOW TO IMPROVE YOUR BARGAINING POSITION

The games just described present a **strategic view of bargaining,** in which the outcome of bargaining games depends on who moves first and who can commit to a bargaining position, as well as whether the other player can make a counteroffer. The dependence of the bargaining outcome on the precise rules of the bargaining game is a little disturbing because real-world bargaining rarely has such well-defined rules. To address this uncertainty, John Nash, the mathematician whose work was popularized by the book[2] and subsequent movie *A Beautiful Mind,* characterized what he thought should be "reasonable" outcomes to any bargaining game. He then proved that any reasonable outcome, z, would maximize the product of the bargainer's surpluses:

$$[S_1(z) - D_1] \times [S_2(z) - D_2],$$

where $S_i(z)$ is the value of reaching agreement z, and D_i is the "disagreement value," or payoff if no agreement is reached. Each bracketed term is the player's increased gain from reaching agreement relative to the payoff he receives from having no agreement.

Nash's characterization of the bargaining game leads immediately to a split-the-difference outcome, in which two parties end up dividing the total surplus in half. For example, imagine two players bargaining over how to split a dollar, both receiving nothing if they don't reach agreement. If they reach an agreement, then Player 1's surplus is z, and Player 2's surplus is $1 - z$. Here z is the agreed-on split of the dollar. Nash's bargaining outcome is for the parties to agree to a 50:50 split of $1.[3]

The Nash outcome is useful because it tells us how the bargaining outcome is likely to change as circumstances change. Suppose, for example, that Player 1 receives a $0.50 bonus for reaching agreement. As before, Player 1 is bargaining against Player 2 over how to split a dollar. The total gain to reaching agreement has now risen to $1.50 from $1.00. The Nash bargaining outcome is for the two players to split the total gains from agreement between them. In this case, Nash's outcome predicts that both players receive $0.75. In essence, Player 1 "gives" away half of his $0.50 bonus to Player 2. When you increase the first player's gains to reaching an agreement, you make him more eager to reach agreement, and his eagerness results in his agreeing to a smaller share of the original dollar ($0.25 instead of $0.50).

Bonuses like this $0.50 are a type of incentive compensation—similar to the kind a company adopts to induce its salespeople to increase sales. Offering

---

[2] S. Nasar, *A Beautiful Mind* (New York: Simon and Schuster, 1998).
[3] In this case, the disagreement values are 0, and the problem is to maximize $z(1 - z)$, where z is the amount that Player 1 receives, and $(1 - z)$ is the amount that Player 2 receives.

salespeople bonuses for making sales increases their eagerness to reach agreement, and this inducement makes them weaker bargainers. If you give your salespeople an incentive bonus like this, you can expect lower prices when they negotiate with customers.

The other interesting feature of the Nash bargaining solution is that it highlights the role that outside alternatives to agreement (D_1 and D_2) play in determining the terms of agreement. This leads immediately to the following advice:

> To improve your own bargaining position, increase your opponent's gain from reaching agreement, $S_2(z) - D_2$, or reduce your own gain from reaching agreement, $S_1(z) - D_1$.

By increasing your opponent's gain from reaching agreement, you make him more willing to compromise to reach an agreement, weakening his bargaining position. Likewise, reducing your own gain from reaching agreement makes you less willing to compromise, improving your bargaining position.

Analyzing games using the Nash bargaining solution suggests changing the alternatives to agreement to improve your bargaining position. We call this a **nonstrategic view of bargaining** because you don't have to analyze the explicit rules of the game to understand the likely outcome of the bargaining between the players.

To understand how advice gleaned from Nash's bargaining outcome differs from advice gleaned from analyzing bargaining as a strategic game of chicken, let's return to the union/management game we just considered. The strategic view of bargaining emphasized the role of commitment and timing in affecting the outcome of a game. For example, a union's commitment to strike in the event of a low offer, or the ability to move first, changes the equilibrium of the strategic game. But these two strategies don't affect the gains from reaching agreement, so neither would affect the Nash bargaining outcome. Only a strike that hurts management more than it hurts the union can improve the bargaining position of labor. This is why strikes threats are more common during seasonal peaks in demand, when it would hurt the firm more than it would hurt the union. By changing the alternatives to agreement for management (bigger loss during a strike), the union can increase management's willingness to reach agreement.

The Nash bargaining outcome also tells you that if you can *decrease* your own gains to reaching agreement, you become a tougher bargainer—you have less to gain by reaching agreement. For example, the best time to ask for a raise is when you already have an attractive offer from another company. Because you have a good alternative [(D_1 is big or $S_1(z) - D_1$ is small], your gain to reaching agreement is relatively small, thus improving your bargaining position. Note the similarity of this idea to *opportunity cost*. The opportunity cost of staying in your current job is the offer you give up if you stay. If you have a good alternative offer, your opportunity cost of staying is high, putting you in a stronger bargaining position.

The next time you shop for a car, keep in mind that salespeople typically get their commissions at the end of the month. So shopping for a car near the end of the month means that the salesperson can earn an immediate commission for any sale. This immediacy raises the gain to reaching agreement (remember that current dollars are worth more than future dollars due to the time value of money), increasing the likelihood that you'll receive a better offer. You can also shop for cars at unpopular times, like Christmas Eve, when few other customers are around. Because selling to you is the forgone opportunity to sell to someone else, the salesperson's gains from reaching agreement with you are higher if no one else is around.

Mergers or acquisitions can also weaken your opponent's bargaining position. Suppose a managed care organization (MCO) or insurance company puts together a network of hospitals to serve its client base. The MCO bargains with individual hospitals over whether to include them in the network and what price they'll charge if included in the network. To get better prices, the MCO threatens to exclude one hospital in favor of a nearby substitute hospital. But if the two hospitals merge and bargain together, the MCO's bargaining alternatives are much worse. If the MCO fails to reach agreement with the merged hospitals, then its managers must go to the next best alternative, which might create a big hole in its network. Such a hole could reduce the attractiveness—and profitability—of the network.

Let's use a numerical example. Suppose an MCO can market its network to an employer for $100 if the network contains one of two merging hospitals and for $120 if it contains both, but the MCO cannot market the plan at all without at least one of the hospitals. The gain to the MCO from adding either of the hospitals to its network when it already has the other is $20. By threatening each of the merging hospitals with being dropped from the network, the gain from striking a bargain with a second hospital is just $20, which the Nash bargaining solution predicts is evenly split. Thus, before the merger, each hospital gets $10 for joining the MCO network. Now suppose the hospitals merge and bargain together. The MCO can no longer drop one of the hospitals, so the gain from striking a bargain with the merged hospital is the full $120, which is also evenly split in the Nash bargaining solution. The merged hospitals thus receive $60, while the separate merging hospitals would have only received $20.[4]

4 Gregory Werden and Luke Froeb, "Unilateral Competitive Effects of Horizontal Mergers II: Auctions and Bargaining," in *Issues in Competition Law and Policy*, ed. W. Dale Collins (forthcoming).

Mergers can similarly increase the bargaining power of pharmaceutical manufacturers petitioning to get on a list of approved drugs (formularies) for use by an HMO or hospital. Just as a merger can improve the bargaining position of the merged hospitals, so too can a merger improve the bargaining position of two substitute drugs. If failure to reach agreement with the merged drugs generates a product gap in the drug formulary (because the next best alternative medication is significantly less effective), then the merged company can improve its bargaining position. Note, however, that both the Department of Justice (DOJ) and Federal Trade Commission (FTC) have challenged mergers as anticompetitive if the mergers are predicted to raise prices significantly.

Let's close this chapter by analyzing the strategy that the excluded pharmacies employed in the Rhode Island case mentioned in the introduction. To improve their bargaining position in negotiations with the state, the excluded pharmacies tried to change the law to force the state to accept either all pharmacies or none. By taking away the state's ability to form limited networks, the law would have increased the state's gain from reaching agreement, which would have made the state a weaker bargainer. The FTC has found that states that restrict the ability of firms to form limited networks have higher medical expenditures,[5] and it has warned the Rhode Island legislature against passing the law.[6] Apparently, they listened.

SUMMARY & HOMEWORK PROBLEMS

SUMMARY OF MAIN POINTS

- Bargaining can be modeled as either a simultaneous or sequential game.
- A player can gain an advantage by shifting a simultaneous-move game to a sequential-move game.
- Credible commitments are difficult to make because they require players to commit to a course of action against their self-interest. Thus, the best threat is one you never have to use.
- The **strategic view of bargaining** focuses on how the outcome of bargaining games depends on who moves first and who can commit to a bargaining position, as well as whether the other player can make a counteroffer.

---

[5] Michael Vita, "Regulatory Restrictions on Selective Contracting: An Empirical Analysis of 'Any Willing Provider' Regulations," *Journal of Health Economics* 20 (2001): 955–966.
[6] See http://www.ftc.gov/os/2004/04/ribills.pdf.

- The **nonstrategic view of bargaining** does not focus on the explicit rules of the game to understand the likely outcome of the bargaining. This view focuses on the gains from bargaining relative to alternatives.
- The gains from bargaining relative to the alternatives to bargaining determine the terms of any bargain.
- Anything you can do to increase your opponent's gains from reaching agreement or to decrease your own will improve your bargaining position.

MULTIPLE-CHOICE QUESTIONS

1. For threats or commitments to be effective, they must be
  a. irrational.
  b. rational.
  c. credible.
  d. None of the above.

2. How many pure strategy equilibria does the following game have?

		Labor	
		Bargain Hard	Be Nice
Mgmt.	Bargain Hard	0, 0	20, 10
	Be Nice	10, 20	15, 15

  a. 0
  b. 1
  c. 2
  d. 3

3. Consider a vendor–buyer relationship. Which of the following conditions would lead to the buyer having more bargaining power?
  a. Lots of substitutes for the vendor's product are available.
  b. There are relatively few buyers and many vendors.
  c. It costs little for buyers to switch vendors.
  d. All of the above.

4. Pete and Lisa are entering into a bargaining situation in which Pete stands to gain up to $5,000 and Lisa stands to gain up to $1,000. Who is likely to be the better bargainer?
  a. Pete
  b. Lisa
  c. They will be equally effective
  d. The potential gains will have no impact on bargaining

5. The game of chicken has
   a. a second-mover advantage.
   b. a first-mover advantage.
   c. no sequential-move advantage.
   d. potential sequential-move advantages, depending on the players.

INDIVIDUAL PROBLEMS

14-1. Ultimatum Game

You are given an offer to split a $20 bill. The other player offers you $1. If you accept the offer, you keep the $1, and the other player keeps $19. If you reject the offer, neither of you will get anything. Do you take the offer?

14-2. Ultimatum Game Continued

How could you take the advantage away from the other player in the ultimatum game?

14-3. Newspaper Bargaining

Two equal-sized newspapers have overlap circulation of 10% (10% of the subscribers subscribe to both newspapers). Advertisers are willing to pay $10 to advertise in one newspaper but only $19 to advertise in both, because they're unwilling to pay twice to reach the same subscriber. What's the likely bargaining negotiation outcome if the advertisers bargain by telling each newspaper that they're going to reach agreement with the other newspaper, so the gains to reaching agreement are only $9? Suppose the two newspapers merge. What is the likely postmerger bargaining outcome?

14-4. Price Matching

ElectroWorld and Galaxy Appliance are competing retail stores that tacitly bargain with each other in deciding pricing policies. Each can either price high or price low. If both price high, payoffs to each are $50 million; if one prices high and the other low, the low-pricer gains $70 million and the high-pricer gains $30 million. If both price low, each gains $40 million. Model this situation as a 2 × 2 game, and identify the equilibrium. How would this change if each of the retailers, as part of the bargaining, committed to a price-matching guarantee, where one would match any low price from the other?

14-5. House Closing

You've entered into a contract to purchase a new house, and the closing is scheduled for next week. It's typical for some last-minute bargaining to occur at the closing table, where sellers often try to sweeten their deal. You have three options for the closing: (1) attend yourself, (2) send an attorney authorized to close only per the previously negotiated terms, or (3) presign all the closing documents per the current terms and do not attend the closing. Which of these would be most advantageous from a bargaining position?

GROUP PROBLEMS

G14-1. Sequential Bargaining

Describe a bargaining game within your firm, or between your firm and a competitor, or between your firm and a customer or supplier. Draw a formal game tree with the choices and payoffs to each of the parties. (Use numbers if you can estimate them; otherwise, describe qualitative rankings among outcomes.) Clearly identify the equilibrium path of the game. What advice can you derive from your analysis? Compute the profit consequences of the advice.

G14-2. Repeated Bargaining

Describe a repeated bargaining game your firm faces. Compute and analyze the equilibrium of the game, and explicitly show how it differs from the one-shot (nonrepeated) equilibrium. What advice can you derive from your analysis? Compute the profit consequences of the advice.

G14-3. Test Your Bargaining Skill[7]

How do different bargaining strategies influence the final purchase price of a new car? In particular, determine whether having better information, being willing to walk away from a deal, or being male affects the price that you receive.

Each group will be assigned one make of car (e.g., Toyota); then the group should pick a particular model (e.g., a Toyota Corolla), with a fixed set of options that is identical for each member of the group. Each person should go into a dealership alone and bargain over the price of the car. Assign the following four types of bargainers:

1. Someone who's researched the dealer cost on the Internet
2. A patient bargainer who tells the salesperson he "needs time to think about it" and returns to negotiate at a later date
3. A man who doesn't follow strategies 1 or 2
4. A woman who doesn't follow strategies 1 or 2
5. Another strategy?

When bargaining, please make sure to follow these rules:

1. The group should send no more than two people to a single dealership.
2. Do not disclose that you're doing this for a homework assignment.
3. Make sure to bargain for an identical car within the group, but each group should choose a different manufacturer (e.g., one group will buy a Toyota, one a Ford, one a Chevrolet, etc.).

After you're finished, the group should write an assignment together. Compare and contrast the prices you were able to get. What were the differences in the final prices you paid versus the predictions of bargaining theory? How did your experience of bargaining differ across group members?

---

[7] From Pat Bajari's economics class.

UNCERTAINTY

Chapter 15

Making Decisions with Uncertainty

Historically, TeleSwitch, a large telecommunications manufacturer, sold switching equipment to its customers (phone companies) only through distributors. But in 2000, the distributors' largest customers began pressuring TeleSwitch to deal directly with them. Dissatisfied with the level of distributor support, the large customers thought they'd get quicker access to the latest technology if they dealt directly with the manufacturer. The large customers threatened to switch to a competing supplier if the manufacturer would not sell direct.

Meanwhile, the distributors, alarmed by the potential loss of their most lucrative clients to direct sales from TeleSwitch, threatened to change to a competing supplier as well. The distributors would find such a switch costly because they'd have to invest significantly in additional technical training to gain expertise with the new supplier's equipment.

The large customers' request put the telecommunications manufacturer in a dilemma: If TeleSwitch dealt directly with its large customers, it might lose its distributors (together with many small customers). If it didn't go direct, it might lose its large customers. Although the probability of losing distributors was lower (because they would have to incur costs to change suppliers), losing them would be catastrophic because the distributors represented a large share of TeleSwitch's profit.

This quandary illustrates the uncertainty inherent in most significant business decisions. In this section, we look at how to quantify uncertainty, thereby helping you better weigh the benefits of a decision against its costs. In particular, we model missing pieces of information as *random variables*; that way, we can compute the *expected costs* and *expected benefits* of various decisions.

In addition to leading to better decisions, this kind of analysis identifies the sources of risk, and it may even suggest ways to mitigate those risks. The analysis also tells us what kind of information we most need to gather to make better decisions.

RANDOM VARIABLES

You'll never have as much information as you want—especially when you're faced with a significant decision. This means that you cannot simply compute the costs and benefits of a decision (as we did in Chapter 3) because both costs *and* benefits will be uncertain. Instead, we use random variables to explicitly take account of the uncertainty. A **random variable** is simply a way of representing numerical outcomes that occur with different probabilities. In this chapter, we will work with discrete random variables, which can assume only a limited (countable) number of values.[1] This approach allows us to use the information we know or can estimate: the potential outcomes and the likelihood of each of those outcomes occurring. When we're uncertain about what value a variable will take, we list all possible outcomes, assign a probability to each outcome, and compute expected values, or *average outcomes,* using a weighted average, where the weights are the probabilities. Random variables that can take only two or three values are special cases that we will use extensively in this chapter.

> *A binomial random variable, X, is one that can take two values, {x1, x2} with probabilities {p, 1 − p}. The mean or expected value of a binomial random variable is E[X] = p × x1 + (1 − p)x2.*

> *A trinomial random variable, X, is one that can take three values, {x1, x2, x3} with probabilities {p1, p2, 1 − p1 − p2}; the mean is E[X] = p1 × x1 + p2 × x2 + (1 − p1 − p2)x3.*

As a simple example of how to use random variables to calculate likely outcomes, suppose, while at a carnival, you're offered the opportunity to bet on the outcome of spinning the Wheel of Cash. The wheel works like a simple roulette wheel, which has three pielike wedges, or thirds. On each wedge one of three values appears: $100, $75, or $5. If the cost to play is $50, should you take a chance on the game?

First note that you have three possible outcomes: $100, $75, and $5. If the wheel is fair—that is, if each outcome has an equal probability of occurring—then the *expected value* of playing the game is (1/3)($100) + (1/3)($75) + (1/3)($5) = $60. So it looks like a really good deal. On average, you'll earn $10 every time you play. But before playing, you should remember this maxim:

> *If a deal seems too good to be true, it probably is.*

If players could really earn, on average, $10 per spin by playing the game, we'd expect to see a very long line of players eager to take their chances. Likewise, we'd expect to see the carnival losing money on the game. What's more likely

---

[1] A continuous random variable assumes an uncountably infinite number of values corresponding to the points on an interval (or more than one interval).

is that the wheel is *not* fair and that it lands on the $5 slice more frequently than on the other two slices. For example, if the wheel is twice as likely to land on the $5 slice than on the other two, then the expected value of playing is only $(1/6)(\$100) + (1/6)(\$75) + (2/3)(\$5) = \$32.50$.

Now, let's return to the quandary facing our telecommunications manufacturer, TeleSwitch. Total company profit is currently $130 million, split between large customers ($30 million) and small customers ($100 million). If the firm sells directly to large customers, TeleSwitch managers estimate that they have a 20% probability of losing distributors (as well as their capacity to serve small customers), but they keep their large customers. If they don't sell directly, they estimate a 60% probability of losing large customers, but they keep their distributors. What should the TeleSwitch do? We diagram the consequences of the decision in Figure 15-1.

Look first at the left branch of the decision tree in Figure 15-1. If TeleSwitch decides to sell directly to large customers, it doesn't know whether its distributors will leave. The firm quantifies its uncertainty by estimating a 20% probability that its distributors will leave if it does sell direct, in which case firm profit drops to $30 million. If distributors stay, profit remains the same at $130 million. Thus, the sell-direct option has an expected value of $110 million in profit.

Now check out the right branch of the tree. If TeleSwitch elects to sell only through dealers, its managers estimate a 60% probability that its large customers will leave, in which case firm profit drops to $100 million. If the large customers

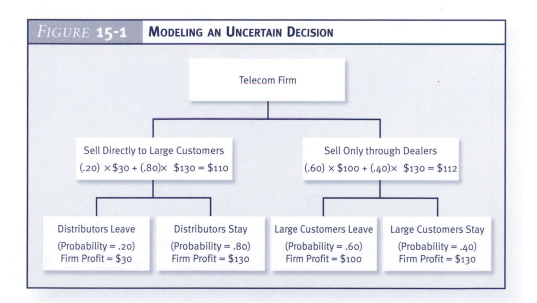

FIGURE 15-1   MODELING AN UNCERTAIN DECISION

Telecom Firm

Sell Directly to Large Customers
$(.20) \times \$30 + (.80) \times \$130 = \$110$

Sell Only through Dealers
$(.60) \times \$100 + (.40) \times \$130 = \$112$

Distributors Leave
(Probability = .20)
Firm Profit = $30

Distributors Stay
(Probability = .80)
Firm Profit = $130

Large Customers Leave
(Probability = .60)
Firm Profit = $100

Large Customers Stay
(Probability = .40)
Firm Profit = $130

stay (40% probability), profit remains unchanged at $130 million. The option of selling only through dealers has an expected value of $112 million in profit.

This is a close call. Just $2 million in expected profit separates the alternatives—less than 2% of total expected profit. It's unlikely that the firm has measured probabilities precisely enough to distinguish between the two alternatives. Thus, TeleSwitch may want to gather better information—perhaps by surveying large end users and distributors in hopes of estimating outcome probabilities more precisely.

This kind of analysis clearly identifies two separate risks that TeleSwitch should try to avoid. First, the firm should try to find a way to retain its dealers, even if it does deal directly with large customers—perhaps by giving them a cut of the profit from large customer accounts. Or TeleSwitch should try figure out how to prevent large customers from leaving if it sells only through dealers—perhaps by providing large customers with in-house company-trained technicians.

Now let's return to the entry-deterrence example in Chapter 14. Suppose that the potential entrant is uncertain about whether the incumbent will price low if it enters, and it quantifies this uncertainty by placing a 50% chance on a low price following entry. So the entrant faces a 50% chance of earning $60, but also a 50% chance of losing $40. The expected value of entering is $(0.5)\$60 + (0.5)(-\$40) = \$10$. The expected value of staying out of the industry is $0. So the expected benefits are $10 larger than the expected costs. We illustrate this decision with a tree in Figure 15-2.

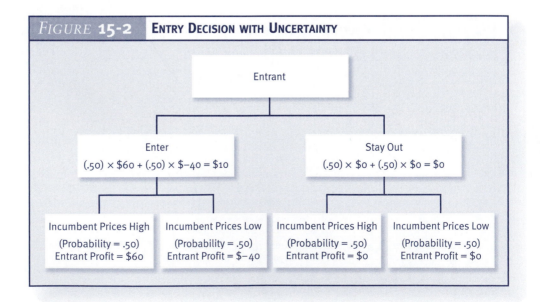

FIGURE **15-2**   **ENTRY DECISION WITH UNCERTAINTY**

Entrant

Enter
$(.50) \times \$60 + (.50) \times \$-40 = \$10$

Stay Out
$(.50) \times \$0 + (.50) \times \$0 = \$0$

Incumbent Prices High
(Probability = .50)
Entrant Profit = $60

Incumbent Prices Low
(Probability = .50)
Entrant Profit = $-40

Incumbent Prices High
(Probability = .50)
Entrant Profit = $0

Incumbent Prices Low
(Probability = .50)
Entrant Profit = $0

We've seen that using probability distributions rather than point estimates to do benefit–cost analysis identifies sources of risk as well as pointing out ways to mitigate them. But we have another very good reason for doing this kind of analysis: If things don't turn out well, we have a good excuse for making the wrong decision. When you use a distribution that includes a worst-case scenario, you can always say that you correctly foresaw the possibility and that things went wrong because the firm was unlucky. Also, by presenting decision makers with analyses that account for uncertainty, you alert them to the riskiness of the decisions they face.

Finally, suppose your Uncle Joe invites you to invest in a real estate venture. He gives you a prospectus that shows how much money you'll make if you invest. The prospectus is based on estimates of future interest rates and future housing demand in the area. How should you analyze the prospectus?

If you're uncertain about the future, you need to rework the analysis using best- and worst-case scenarios. You have two sources of risk here—both future demand and future interest rates—so you should rework the analysis on a spreadsheet, allowing you to vary the assumptions about the future.

Uncle Joe has most likely given you a best-case scenario (low interest rates/ high demand). Add other scenarios (low interest rates/low demand, high interest rates/high demand, high interest rates/low demand), and assign probabilities to each scenario. Compute profit under each possible outcome, and calculate expected profit as the weighted sum of the possible outcomes. Almost certainly, Uncle Joe will do well under all four scenarios; you, however, will do well under only one (low interest rates/high demand). Don't invest. Or, alternatively, suggest that Uncle Joe accept a payoff that rewards him only if the venture does well. If Joe declines, then most likely he doesn't believe his own forecasts.

UNCERTAINTY IN PRICING

If you don't know your demand, you face uncertainty in pricing. One of the easiest ways to model uncertainty is to classify the number and type of customers who come to your retail store. Suppose you run a marketing survey and find you have two types of customers: high-value customers willing to pay $8 and low-value consumers willing to pay just $5. Your survey tells you that there are equal numbers of high- and low-value customers.

Obviously, you have two possible price options: Price high ($8) and sell only to the high-value group, or price low ($5) and sell to everyone. Which price should you choose? The answer is "It depends." In this case, it depends on your costs, which we'll set at $3 per unit for illustrative purposes.

Plot the decision tree as in Figure 15-3. If you price high, you earn $8 − $3 = $5, provided you get a high-value customer. And such sales happen only 50% of the time, so expected profit is $2.50. If you price low, you sell all the time, and you earn $5 − $3 = $2. So price high and sell half as many goods, but earn an *expected* $0.50 more on each unit you sell.

Note that with this high-price strategy, you're left with unconsummated wealth-creating transactions—the low-value customer is willing to pay $5 for a good that costs you $3 to produce. To consummate these transactions, we turn again to a strategy of price discrimination (see Chapters 11 and 12).

PRICE DISCRIMINATION

If you can identify the two types of customers, set different prices for each group, and prevent arbitrage between the two types, then you can price discriminate. Sell at a price of $8 to the high-value customers and a price of $5 to the low-value customers. However, once your customers learn you're discriminating, high-value customers will try to defeat your price discrimination scheme by mimicking the behavior or appearance of low-value customers. Figuring out how to correctly identify low- and high-value customers is critical for any price discrimination scheme.

To see how identification matters, consider car salespeople. By making customers wait at the dealership before offering them a price discount, salespeople can identify low-value customers. The longer you're willing to wait,

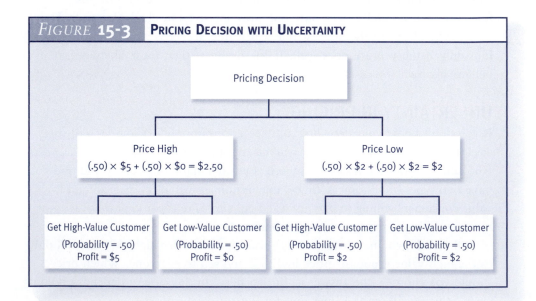

FIGURE 15-3   PRICING DECISION WITH UNCERTAINTY

Pricing Decision

Price High
$(.50) \times \$5 + (.50) \times \$0 = \$2.50$

Price Low
$(.50) \times \$2 + (.50) \times \$2 = \$2$

Get High-Value Customer
(Probability = .50)
Profit = $5

Get Low-Value Customer
(Probability = .50)
Profit = $0

Get High-Value Customer
(Probability = .50)
Profit = $2

Get Low-Value Customer
(Probability = .50)
Profit = $2

the bigger your price discount. This discrimination scheme works because the opportunity cost of time is high for high-value customers. Only low-value customers are willing to wait for better offers.

To defeat this kind of discrimination, try to mimic the behavior of low-value customers. If it's too difficult for you, or if you're too impatient, hire a negotiating agent who can bargain for you.

According to a 1995 article[2] in the *American Economic Review,* new-car salespeople tend to give worse offers (higher prices) to women and minority buyers. The article described a study employing "testers" who were given identical credit histories and bargaining scripts. The study found that women and minority testers received worse offers than their nonminority male counterparts.

Surprisingly, these offers did not vary with the race or gender of the salesperson—minority and female salespeople discriminated against minority and female car buyers, just as their male and nonminority counterparts did. The article concluded that the discrimination did not arise from racial or gender bias but, rather, that it was a profit-increasing price discrimination scheme.

Why, then, do salespeople think women and minority buyers are willing to pay more? It could be that nonminority men are better bargainers because they have better access to information about the costs of the car or perhaps that they simply have a "taste" for bargaining.

ORAL AUCTIONS

Let's continue with the problem of setting prices when you don't know what buyers are willing to pay. But instead of computing the best price, or trying to design a discriminatory pricing scheme, we consider how to sell using an auction.

*In an **oral** or **English auction,** bidders submit increasing bids until only one bidder remains. The item is awarded to this last remaining bidder.*

Every bidder is willing to bid up to his value, but no higher. Bidding proceeds until only two bidders remain. The low-value bidder stops bidding at a price equal to his value. Thus, the high-value bidder wins the item at a price at, or slightly above, the value of the second-highest bidder.

Suppose there are five bidders with different values: $5, $4, $3, $2, and $1. In this case, the high-value bidder will win and pay a price close to $4. Note that the winning bidder earns one dollar's worth of surplus—he's willing to pay $5, but he has to pay only $4 to outbid the losing bidders.

---

[2] Ian Ayres and Peter Siegelman, "Race and Gender Discrimination in Negotiation for the Purchase of a New Car," *American Economic Review,* 84 (1995): 304. For a further discussion of the results, see http://islandia.law. yale.edu/ayers/carint.htm.

Economists love auctions. Not only do auctions identify the high-value bidder (efficiency), but they also set a price for the item, thereby avoiding costly negotiation. Auctions are especially valuable for selling unique or customized items, like art or antiques. For such items, it's difficult to identify the high-value buyer and to set appropriate prices. An auction will move these unique items to their highest-valued use without wasting bargaining time.

Contrast the use of auctions to the pricing scheme we used earlier for your retail store. Suppose that two bidders show up at an auction. They could be either high-value ($8) or low-value ($5) bidders. The probability of seeing a high-value bidder is .50. What is the expected revenue from the auction?

You can see the possible outcomes of the auction listed in Table 15-1. The last column shows the winning bid, which represents the value of the second-highest bidder. If the auctioneer is lucky, she'll get two high-value bidders, and the winning bid will be $8 because the winning bidder has to outbid the losing bidder whose value is $8. However, this outcome occurs only 25% of the time. The other 75% of the time, the auctioneer can expect one high-value bidder at most, so the winning bidder can win the auction by bidding just $5. The expected revenue of the auction is the weighted average of these outcomes, where the weights are the probabilities of each outcome: .75($5) + .25($8) = $5.75.

Now suppose that three bidders show up at an auction. As before, they could be either high-value ($8) or low-value ($5) bidders. What is the expected revenue from the auction?

The possible outcomes of the auction are listed in Table 15-2. Again, if the auctioneer is lucky, two or more high-value bidders will show up, so the winner has to bid $8 to win, but this outcome occurs only 50% of the time. The other 50% of the time, we expect at most one high-value bidder, so the winning bidder has to bid just $5 in order to win. So expected revenue is (.5)($8) + (.5)($5) = $6.50.

Comparing Table 15-1 and Table 15-2, we see that more bidders raise the expected price.

Bidder 1	Bidder 2	Probability	Winning Bid
$5	$5	.25	$5
$5	$8	.25	$5
$8	$5	.25	$5
$8	$8	.25	$8

TABLE 15-1 ORAL AUCTION WITH TWO BIDDERS

TABLE 15-2	ORAL AUCTION WITH THREE BIDDERS			
Bidder 1	**Bidder 2**	**Bidder 2**	**Probability**	**Winning Bid**
$5	$5	$5	.125	$5
$5	$5	$8	.125	$5
$5	$8	$5	.125	$5
$8	$5	$5	.125	$5
$5	$8	$8	.125	$8
$8	$5	$8	.125	$8
$8	$8	$5	.125	$8
$8	$8	$8	.125	$8

The stronger the losing bidders are, the higher the winning bid is.

For example, on eBay, auctions that are open for 10 days return 42% higher prices than do auctions that are open for just 3 days because the longer auctions attract a larger number of bidders.[3]

Note that if two bidders who have the same value show up at an auction, neither can expect any surplus because each has to bid up to his or her values to win.

SECOND-PRICE AUCTIONS

*A **Vickrey** or **second-price auction** is a sealed-bid auction in which the item is awarded to the highest bidder, but the winner pays only the second-highest bid.*

Why would an auctioneer use an auction that seems to leave money on the table? Why not force the highest bidder to pay his or her bid amount? The answer is that a second-price auction induces bidders to bid more aggressively than they would in a first-price auction. Why are bidders willing to bid more aggressively in a second-price auction? Bidders are willing to bid up to their values because they know their bid only determines whether they win, not the price they pay. The price paid is determined by the bid of the second-highest bidder. Under these conditions, it is an optimal[4] strategy for bidders to bid their true values.

If all bidders bid their values, the high-value bidder gets the item at a price equal to the second-highest value. This outcome is identical to the outcome from an oral auction, so auctioneers end up making just as much money as they would in an oral auction,[5] with the advantage that second-price auctions are easier to run.

---

[3] See www.u.arizona.edu/~dreiley/papers/PenniesFromEBay.pdf.
[4] This strategy weakly dominates all other strategies.
[5] The so-called revenue equivalence theorem requires risk neutrality.

William Vickrey shared (together with James A. Mirrlees) the 1996 Nobel Prize in Economics for his work in inventing the Vickrey auction and establishing its equivalence to oral auctions. Recently, however, economists have discovered that second-price auctions were common methods for selling rare stamps as early as 1893.[6] To accommodate bidders who didn't want to pay to travel to an auction, stamp dealers held second-price auctions. Vickrey auctions predated Vickrey by nearly a century!

Internet auction sites eBay, Yahoo!, and Amazon.com use formats[7] that resemble second-price auctions because they employ "bidding agents" that automatically raise bids for you. Bidders need not log on frequently to change their bid. They simply tell the computer, which acts as a bidding agent, how much they are willing to pay; then the bidders can just forget about the auction. The bidding agents automatically raise bids to just above what rivals are willing to pay. This feature allows these auctions to be run remotely and asynchronously over the Internet. More than one million auctions close each day on eBay and Amazon.[8]

Second-price auctions are also useful for auctioning off multiple units of the same item—say, 10 laptop computers. As in a single-unit second-price auction, the highest losing bid determines the price. In this case, however, the highest losing bid is the 11th-highest[9] bid. As in the second-price auction, you'll find it optimal to bid your value and wait for the outcome because the bid you make has no link to the price you pay.[10]

SEALED-BID AUCTIONS

*In a **sealed-bid first-price auction**, the highest bidder gets the item at a price equal to the highest bid.*

In a sealed-bid first-price auction, your bid determines what you have to pay, in contrast to a second-price auction. Consequently, each bidder faces a trade-off. She can bid higher and raise the probability of winning, but doing so lowers her surplus if she does win. In equilibrium, each bidder *shades* her bid; that is, she balances these two effects by bidding below her value. In these auctions, experience is the best teacher.[11] In general, you should bid more aggressively— shade your value less—if the competition is stronger.

---

[6] See http://www.u.arizona.edu/~dreiley/papers/VickreyHistory.pdf.

[7] See http://www.u.arizona.edu/~dreiley/papers/InternetAuctions.pdf for more on Internet auctions.

[8] In 2001, Amazon began a withdrawal from its auction business.

[9] If bidders can bid for multiple items, then the price is the highest rejected bid, not made by one of the winning bidders.

[10] See http://www.u.arizona.edu/~dreiley/papers/DemandReduction.pdf for experimental evidence on how to design multiunit second-price auctions.

[11] For practice in sealed bidding, try http://www.antitrust.org/simulation/simulation.html.

BID RIGGING

Assume an oral auction in which bidders have values of $5, $4, $3, $2, and $1; but in this case, the two high-value bidders form a bidding ring or *cartel*—that is, they decide not to bid against each other. What is the winning bid?

A cartel earns money by eliminating competition among the cartel members. Here, the two high-value bidders, those willing to pay $5 and $4, decide not to bid against each other. To win the auction, they have to outbid the highest noncartel member, whose value is just above $3.

Had the bidding been competitive, the winning price would have been $4. So the cartel "earns" $1. This dollar is the difference between $4 (what the price would have been without the cartel) and $3 (the price with the cartel). The cartel members split the $1 between them.

This kind of agreement between bidders in an auction, called *bid rigging* or *collusion,* is a criminal act in the United States and most other developed countries. In a typical bid-rigging scheme, antique dealers, for example, will refrain from bidding against one another at an estate sale. Then they retire to the back of the auction hall or to a hotel room to "re-auction" the goods they won among themselves. The difference between what the good sold for in the general auction and what it sold for in the second or "knockout auction" is profit that the cartel members split among themselves.

The informal *quid pro quo* bidding behavior associated with a bid-rotation scheme is probably more common than the kind of explicit collusion just described. In a bid rotation scheme, bidders refrain from bidding against one another, or submit very weak bids, in return for similar consideration when it's their "turn" to win an item.

> *Collusion is more likely in oral and second-price auctions than in sealed-bid auctions.*

In a sealed-bid auction, collusion requires the cooperation of *all* the cartel members; that is, the cartel members must figure a way out of a prisoners' dilemma. If any of the cartel members raises his bid above the agreed-on price, he could win the item for himself at a very low price. This temptation often leads cartel members to cheat on the cartel.

In an oral auction, however, no dilemma presents itself because cheating on the cartel offers no benefit. All cartel members can immediately see when one of their own tries to bid higher than the agreed-on price. In retaliation, the other cartel members will begin bidding competitively. The cheater cannot expect to win the item at a low price because the other cartel members will bid up the price to the competitive price, thereby eliminating any extra profit for the cheater.

In a bid rotation scheme, each cartel member must wait for her turn to win. Lumping all the contracts together into a single big auction raises the gains derived from cheating on the cartel by bidding slightly above the agreed-on bid. This provides our second observation about bid rigging:

Collusion is more likely in small, frequent auctions than in big, infrequent ones.

The graph in Figure 15-4 plots the average winning price of a conspiracy that collapsed when a grand jury began investigating auctions to supply the navy with frozen fish. The price dropped 23% after the conspiracy collapsed. The investigators computed the effect of the conspiracy by *backcasting* (the opposite of forecasting) from the competitive period to the collusive period (the darker line in Figure 15-4), allowing them to determine what prices would have been during the collusive period had bidders behaved competitively.

Among the reasons for the conspiracy was a set of "domestic content" rules, which prevented foreign suppliers from bidding on new contracts. Without foreign competition, it was quite easy for the few domestic suppliers of frozen seafood to form a cartel. Another reason was the frequent (up to 10 each week) auctions, which made the bid rotation scheme fairly easy to organize.[12]

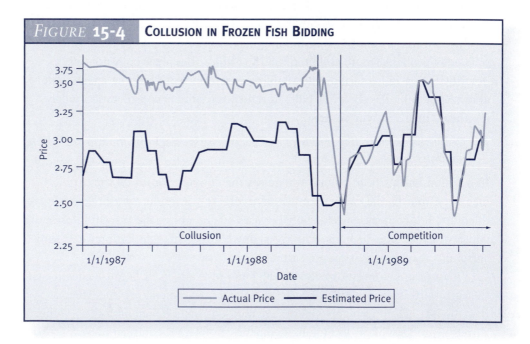

FIGURE 15-4   COLLUSION IN FROZEN FISH BIDDING

[12] The cartel and its collapse are described in L. Froeb, R. Koyak, and G. Werden, "What Is the Effect of Bid-Rigging on Prices?" *Economics Letters* 42 (1993): 419–423.

The government is a frequent victim of bid rigging, and this government experience allows us to draw several lessons:

- Do not rely on purchasing agents who have little interest in buying at a low price. Reward agents only for making good (high-quality and low-price) purchases.
- Do not entangle purchasing agents with masses of red tape. Instead, permit them to negotiate—to bargain with the bidders if they suspect bid rigging.
- Do not use the procurement process to further a social agenda (small business set-asides, public lands, national defense, etc.) that is irrelevant to purchasing goods at low prices.
- Keep information away from any potential cartel.
- If you suspect collusion,
  - do not hold open auctions;
  - do not hold small and frequent auctions;
  - do not disclose information to bidders—do not announce who the other bidders are, who the winners are, or what the winning bids are.

COMMON-VALUE AUCTIONS

*In a **common-value auction**, the value is the same for each bidder, but no one knows what it is. Each bidder has only an estimate of the unknown value, and the value is the same for everyone.*

Offshore oil tracts, for instance, have a common value to each bidder. The amount of oil on the tract determines the value of the tract—which is the same for all bidders. However, no one knows how much oil is in the tract; each bidder has only an estimate of the amount of oil contained in the tract.

Winning in a common-value auction can be bad news: It means that yours was the highest and most optimistic estimate of the unknown value of the item. Such a win is an affliction known as the **winner's curse**. To avoid the curse (losing money), you must bid as if your information is too optimistic and shade your estimated value by an amount that increases with the number of bidders against whom you're bidding.

The winner's curse problem worsens as the number of bidders increases.

Why should this be? Because when you outbid a large number of bidders, you learn that your information was more optimistic than everyone else's. The more bidders there are, the more optimistic your information must have been if you won.

The winner's curse is especially bad when rival bidders have better information about the unknown common value than you do. For example, some bidders for offshore oil tracts own neighboring tracts and have better estimates of the amount of oil—and therefore the value—than those without neighboring tracts.

When others have better information than you do, you'll win only when others think the item isn't worth much, or when you overbid. This is an extreme form of the winner's curse. It's seldom a good idea to bid in auctions when others have better information than you do.

If you're the auctioneer, you want to encourage everyone to bid aggressively. To diminish the bid-dampening effects of the winner's curse, release as much information as you can about the value of the item. By reducing uncertainty about the value of the item, you mitigate the winner's curse and encourage bidders to bid closer to their estimated values. Even if you have adverse information about an item, you should still release it; if you don't, bidders will correctly infer that the information is bad.

Oral auctions return higher prices in a common-value setting.

One way to release information in a common-value auction is to hold an oral auction. In an oral auction, each bidder reveals her information by how aggressively she bids. Reducing uncertainty about the item's value reduces the magnitude of the winner's curse and results in higher bids and higher prices.

If releasing information is good for the auctioneer, it must be bad for the bidders. We see this conclusion in some eBay auctions, for example. There, bidders *snipe*; that is, they wait until the last minute of the auction to submit bids.[13] If the auction has a common-value component, rivals learn something about the item's value by observing your bid, thereby creating an incentive for you to hide your bid. By submitting bids at the last minute, bidders can effectively hide their bids and turn what resembles an oral auction into a sealed-bid auction.

---

[13] See http://slate.msn.com/id/22998/.

SUMMARY & HOMEWORK PROBLEMS

SUMMARY OF MAIN POINTS

- When you're uncertain about the costs or benefits of a decision, assign a simple probability distribution to the variable and compute expected costs and benefits.
- When customers have unknown values, you face a familiar trade-off: Price high and sell only to high-value customers, or price low and sell to all customers.
- If you can identify high-value and low-value customers, you can price discriminate and avoid the trade-off. To avoid being discriminated against, high-value customers will try to mimic the behavior and appearance of low-value customers.
- In **oral** or **English auctions,** the highest bidder wins but only has to outbid the second-highest bidder. Losing bidders determine the price.
- A **Vickrey** or **second-price auction** is a sealed-bid auction in which the high bidder wins but pays only the second-highest bid. These auctions are well suited for use on the Internet.
- In a **sealed-bid first-price auction,** the high bidder wins and pays her value. Bidders must balance the probability of winning against the profit they will make if they do win. Optimal bids are less than bidders' private values.
- Bidders can raise profit by agreeing not to bid against one another. Such collusion or bid rigging is more likely to occur in open auctions and in small, frequent auctions. If collusion is suspected,
  - do not hold open auctions;
  - do not hold small and frequent auctions;
  - do not disclose information to bidders—do not announce who the winners are, who else may be bidding, or what the winning bids were.
- In a **common-value auction,** bidders bid below their estimates to avoid the winner's curse. Oral auctions return higher prices in common-value auctions because they release more information.

MULTIPLE-CHOICE QUESTIONS

1. You've just decided to add a new line to your manufacturing plant. Compute the expected loss/profit from the line addition if you estimate the following:
- There's a 70% chance that profit will increase by $100,000.

- There's a 20% chance that profit will remain the same.
- There's a 10% chance that profit will decrease by $15,000.

a. Gain of $100,000

b. Gain of $71,500

c. Loss of $15,000

d. Gain of $68,500

2. You have two types of buyers for your product. The first type values your product at $10; the second values it at $6. Forty percent of buyers are of the first type ($10 value); 60% are of the second type ($6 value). What price maximizes your expected profit contribution?

a. $10

b. $6

c. $7.60

d. $8

3. Six bidders in an oral auction place the following values on a good: {$6, $5, $4, $3, $2, $1}. In an oral competitive auction, what is the winning price?

a. $3

b. $4

c. $5

d. $6

4. Suppose that the second, third, and fourth bidders from the preceding oral auction form a cartel. What is the new winning price?

a. $3

b. $4

c. $5

d. $6

5. You're considering holding a closed-bid auction for a new technology your company has developed. One of your assistants raises a concern that the potential for a winner's curse may encourage bidders to shade their bid values. How might you address this concern?

a. Release more information about the technology.

b. Switch to an oral auction.

c. Use a second-price auction.

d. All of the above.

INDIVIDUAL PROBLEMS

15-1. Global Expansion

You're the manager of global opportunities for a U.S. manufacturer, who is considering expanding sales into Europe. Your market research has identified three potential market opportunities: England, France, and Germany. If you enter the English market, you have a .5 chance of big success (selling 100,000 units at a per-unit profit of $8), a .3 chance of moderate success (selling 60,000 units at a per-unit profit of $6), and a .2 chance of failure (selling nothing). If you enter the French market, you have a .4 chance of big success (selling 120,000 units at a per-unit profit of $9), a .4 chance of moderate success (selling 50,000 units at a per-unit profit of $6), and a .2 chance of failure (selling nothing). If you enter the German market, you have a .2 chance of huge success (selling 150,000 units at a per-unit profit of $10), a .5 chance of moderate success (selling 70,000 units at a per-unit profit of $6), and a .3 chance of failure (selling nothing). If you can enter only one market, and the cost of entering the market (regardless of which market you select) is $250,000, should you enter one of the European markets? If so, which one? If you enter, what is your expected profit?

15-2. Two Bidder Auction
You hold an auction on eBay and expect two bidders to show up. You estimate that each bidder has a value of either $5 or $8 for the item, and you attach probabilities to each value of 50%. Your own value for the item is zero. You can set a reserve price, a price below which you will not accept bids for the item. What reserve price should you set, and what are your expected profit (surplus) from auctioning the item with a reserve price?

15-3. Vickrey Auction
Suppose after submitting your sealed bid in a Vickrey auction, you find out that you have lost the auction (you were not the highest bidder); however, you have the opportunity to revise your bid. Would you go ahead and change your bid? Why or why not?

15-4. Hot Dog Uncertainty
You want to invest in a hot dog stand near the ballpark. You have a .35 probability that you can turn your current $15,000 into $50,000 and a .65 probability that fierce competition will drive you to ruin, losing all your money. If you decide not to enter, you keep your $15,000. Would you enter the market?

15-5. Lottery Expected Value
Tennessee just instituted a state lottery. The initial jackpot is $100,000. If the first week yields no winners, the next week's jackpot goes up, depending on the number of previous players who placed the $1 lottery bets. The probability of winning is one in a million (1×10^{-6}). What must the jackpot be before the expected payoff is worth your $1 bet? Assume that the state takes 60% of the jackpot in taxes, that no one else is a winner, and that you are risk-neutral (i.e., you value the lottery at its expected value).

GROUP PROBLEM

G15-1. Uncertainty
Describe a decision your company has made when facing uncertainty. Compute the expected costs and benefits of the decision. Offer advice on how to proceed. Compute the profit consequences of the advice.

Chapter 16

The Problem of Adverse Selection

When a manufacturing firm in South Carolina, Rivets & Bolts, Inc. (R&B), hires assembly workers, it wants employees whose work ethic is strong. Because work ethic is an intangible quality that is difficult to measure, firms like R&B often mistakenly hire workers who can best be described as "shirkers." Shirkers are difficult to manage and have high absentee rates. Shirkers also reduce worker morale and ultimately raise production costs.

To improve the quality of its workforce, R&B devised a clever plan. R&B's Human Resources managers asked candidates to go through a pre-hire process (24 hours of classes over eight days during a four-week period). The HR managers told potential employees that this process would be the final step before full-time employment and that candidates would receive no pay for attending these classes. The candidates thought the pre-hire classes served as an orientation to the company; however, the firm used the classes to weed out less-motivated candidates. Candidates who missed a class—or showed up late—were sent home and not allowed to return. On average, R&B's managers dismissed two in each class of thirty people for not coming in on time. This pre-hire screening has been very successful; just 10 of the 1,300 workers hired under the program have exhibited significant attendance problems. The program reduced the rate of bad hires from about 8% to less than 1%.[1]

This story illustrates the problem known as **adverse selection.** Adverse selection arises when one party to a transaction is better informed than another—in this case, workers know more about their work habits than does their employer. Unless employers can distinguish good from bad workers, they end up hiring both.

In general, adverse selection arises in any transaction in which one party to a transaction has better information than the other.[2] In this chapter we show you how to anticipate the adverse selection problem, protect yourself from its consequences, and, in some cases, how to solve it.

---

[1] R&B's screening process may also be illegal if, for example, it has a discriminatory impact. Before trying something like it, you may want to consult an attorney to ensure that you are in full compliance with all labor laws.

[2] Adverse selection problems are often characterized as being problems of "hidden information."

INSURANCE AND RISK

We can illustrate the adverse selection problem most clearly by looking at the insurance industry. To understand the demand for insurance, we have to return to our discussion of random variables. A lottery is a random variable with a payment attached to each outcome. Say I agree to pay you $100 if a fair coin lands heads-up and $0 otherwise; in this instance, you face a random payoff with an expected value of $50. Your attitude toward risk determines how you value this risky payoff.

> A *risk-neutral* consumer values a lottery at *its expected value*. A *risk-averse* consumer values a lottery at less *than its expected value*.

Consider the possibility of trade between a risk-averse seller and a risk-neutral buyer. For instance, a risk-averse consumer would be willing to sell the ($0, $100) lottery at $40, while a risk-neutral consumer would be willing to pay $50 for the same lottery. If the two of them transact at a price of, say $45, they have created wealth by moving an asset—the lottery—to a higher-value use. After the transaction, the risk-averse seller has $45, a sure payout that he values more than the lottery, while the risk-neutral buyer has a lottery that she values at $50, five dollars more than she paid for it.

Similarly, insurance is a wealth-creating transaction that transfers risk from someone who doesn't want it (the risk-averse consumer) to someone who doesn't mind it (the risk-neutral insurance company). The only difference from our lottery example is that the risk-averse sellers face a lottery over *bad* outcomes instead of *good* ones.

Suppose, for example, a student, Andee, owns a $100 bicycle that might be stolen. The possibility of theft means that the payoff from owning the bicycle is like that of a lottery: Lose $100 if the bike is stolen and lose nothing if it isn't. If the probability of theft is 20%, the *expected* cost of the lottery is $(0.2) \times (\$100) = (\$20)$.

If Andee purchases insurance, say for $25, that reimburses her for the value of her stolen bicycle, she eliminates the risk. By voluntarily transacting, both Andee and her insurance company are better off. After the transaction, Andee pays $25 to the insurance company, which now "owns" a lottery with an expected cost of just $20. The insurance company earns $5 on the transaction, on average.

Insurance is not the only way of moving risk from those who don't want it to those who don't mind it. One of the financial industry's main functions is to move risk from lower- to higher-valued uses. For example, farmers face uncertain future prices for their crops. To get rid of the risk, they sell forward contracts to grain companies. The buyer of the contract takes possession of the crop on a specified delivery date and accepts the possibility that the crop may be worth less than the company paid for it. Selling crops before they are planted moves risk from the farmer to the grain company.

ANTICIPATING ADVERSE SELECTION

Let's extend our bicycle insurance example. Suppose that we now have two different types of consumers, each facing different risks. One type of consumer lives in a secure area, where the probability of theft is 20%. The other type lives in a less secure area, where the probability of theft is higher—say 40%. As above, each consumer is risk-averse and would be willing to buy insurance for $5 more than its expected cost; that is, the low-risk consumer would be willing to pay $25 for insurance, and the high-risk consumer would be willing to pay $45.

Let's see what happens when an insurance company tries to sell policies to consumers who know more about their own risks than the company does. If the company offers to sell insurance at an average price of $35, only the high-risk consumers would purchase the insurance. They perceive it as a great deal because they'd be willing to pay as much as $45 for the insurance. In contrast, the low-risk consumers recognize a bad deal when they see it. In fact, they'd rather face the possibility of theft than purchase insurance for $35.

If only high-risk consumers purchase insurance, the insurance company's expected costs are $40; thus, it would lose $5 on every policy it sells. Such losses would eventually drive the company out of business. This leads to the first important lesson of the chapter:

Anticipate adverse selection and protect yourself against it.

If the insurance company correctly anticipates that only high-risk consumers will buy, it will offer insurance at $45. At this price, the low-risk consumers are not served, but the insurance company earns money on the policies it does sell.

To see what happens when you don't anticipate adverse selection, let's turn to Washington D.C. In June of 1986, the D.C. government passed the "Prohibition of Discrimination in the Provision of Insurance Act," which outlawed HIV testing by health insurance companies. What do you think happened?

According to press reports at the time, the result was a "mass exodus of insurers from the city." Unable to distinguish low-risk from high-risk consumers, insurance companies faced the prospect of being able to sell only to high-risk purchasers.

When the law was repealed in 1989, the problem disappeared. Once companies were able to discriminate between consumers with HIV and those without, they were able to offer two polices based on the costs of insuring each population. When you eliminate the information asymmetry—when the company knows who is high-risk and who is low-risk—the adverse selection problem disappears.

In financial markets, adverse selection arises when owners of companies seeking to sell shares to the public know more about the prospects of the company than do potential investors. Potential investors should anticipate that companies with relatively poor prospects are the ones most likely to sell parts of their companies. For example, small Initial Public Offerings[3] (IPOs) of less than $100 million have a −50% return over five years, whereas large IPOs have "normal" returns—equal to those of comparably risky assets. Economists find it puzzling that investors don't anticipate adverse selection by reducing the price they pay for small IPOs.

Finally, we note that the winner's curse of common-value auctions is a kind of adverse selection. Unless the winning bidder anticipates that she has the most overly optimistic estimate of the item's true value, she'll end up overbidding. If bidders anticipate the winner's curse, they will bid low enough to avoid overpaying.

SCREENING

If our bicycle insurance company sells at a price of $45, the low-risk consumers can not purchase insurance, even though they would be willing to pay more than the cost of the insurance. This leads to the second point of this chapter.

The low-risk consumers are not served because it is difficult to profitably transact with them.

Adverse selection represents a potentially profitable, but unconsummated, wealth-creating transaction. Screening (the subject of this section) and signaling (the subject of the next section) are two ways to overcome the obstacles to transacting with low-risk individuals.

We saw that the adverse selection problem in Washington D.C. disappeared when the asymmetry of information disappeared. Once the insurance companies could distinguish between high- and low-risk consumers, they offered two different policies to the two groups—a low-price policy to the low-risk group and a high-price policy to the high-risk group. Obviously, one solution to the problem of adverse selection is to gather information so you can distinguish high from low risks.

But this isn't as easy as it sounds. Information gathering can be costly; moreover, privacy and anti-discrimination laws can prevent insurance companies from acquiring (and using) information that lets them sort customers into high- and low-risk categories. For example, your credit report is an excellent predictor

---

[3] An Initial Public Offering of stock describes the sale of a company by its private owners to the public who can purchase shares in the stock.

of whether you'll be involved in an auto accident. If you give an insurance company permission to look at your credit report, you can get car insurance at a low price, provided your credit is good. But two states, California and Massachusetts, prohibit car insurance companies from using credit scores. This restriction reduces the amount of information available to insurance companies and raises the cost of insurance to good drivers.

But even when it's hard to gather information about individual insurance risks directly, you can sometimes gather information indirectly. By offering consumers a menu of choices, you can sometimes get them to reveal information about the risks they face. In particular, if you offer two policies—one that appeals to each group—you'll find that the choices consumers make reveal their risk. Note the similarity to the indirect price discrimination schemes in Chapter 12, where we designed different products so they appealed to high- and low-value customers. Consumers revealed their values by the choices that they made.

Returning to our insurance example, suppose you offer two policies: full insurance for $45 and partial insurance for $15. Partial insurance would compensate the owner for just half the value of the bicycle. Typically, partial insurance involves a deductible amount[4] or a co-payment.[5]

If high-risk individuals prefer full insurance at $45 to partial insurance for $15, they will purchase the full insurance, while low-risk individuals will purchase partial insurance. At these prices, the insurance company can make money because the cost to the insurance company of offering full insurance to the high-risk group is $(0.4) \times \$100 = \$40$ and the cost of offering the partial insurance to the low-risk group is $(0.2) \times \$50 = \$10$. By offering partial insurance, the insurance company can transact (partially) with the low-risk consumers.

> *Screening* describes the efforts of the less-informed party (the insurance company) to gather information about the more-informed party (consumers). Information may be gathered indirectly by offering consumers a menu of choices, and consumers reveal information about their risks by the choices they make.

A successful screen has one critical requirement: It must *not* be profitable for high-risk consumers to mimic the choice of the low-risk consumers. In our insurance example, the high-risk group must prefer full insurance at $45 to partial insurance at $15. If high-risk individuals purchase partial insurance, the screen fails . . . and the insurance company loses money.[6]

---

[4] The customer is liable for the deductible, e.g., $50, while the insurance company pays the remainder.
[5] The customer pays the co-payment, e.g., 50%, while the insurance company pays the remainder.
[6] Every time the insurance company sells partial insurance for $15 to a high-risk individual, it loses $5 (cost is $20 = 0.4 \times \$50$).

As a consumer, you can use this information to your advantage when purchasing insurance. If you're a low-risk individual, you may be able to lower your own *expected* insurance costs by purchasing a policy with a large deductible or co-payment. This choice will identify you as a low-risk individual to the insurance company, which will then offer partial insurance for a lower price, albeit with a large deductible or co-payment. Likewise, if you purchase insurance with a small deductible or co-payment, you'll identify yourself as a high-risk consumer and pay a higher price.

Note that the software price discrimination scheme discussed in Chapter 12 is a form of screening. By offering consumers a choice between a less-expensive, disabled version of the software and a more expensive, full-featured version, the software company induced consumers to identify themselves as either high- or low-value consumers. This screen permitted the company to price discriminate. It was successful because it was too costly for the business users to mimic the behavior of home users, i.e., by purchasing the disabled version.

Let's apply these ideas to the used-car market, where adverse selection is known as the *lemons problem*. Suppose there are bad cars (lemons) worth $2,000 and good cars worth $4,000. The information asymmetry is that each seller knows whether he or she owns a lemon, but the buyer does not.

So, what happens when an uninformed buyer tries to purchase from an informed seller? If a buyer offers a price of $3,000, only lemon owners would be willing to sell, so the buyer ends up paying $3,000 for a $2,000 car. If, instead, the buyer offers to purchase at a price of $4,000, both good-car owners and lemon owners would be willing to sell, but the expected value of any purchased car will be much less than $4,000. In both cases, the buyer pays too much, on average, for what he is getting.

If the buyer anticipates adverse selection, he offers to pay just $2,000. At this price, only lemon owners will sell, but at least the buyer won't overpay for the car. Owners of good cars are analogous to low-risk consumers in the insurance market because they are unable to transact. Again, adverse selection represents an unconsummated wealth-creating transaction. Put yourself in the position of a buyer who wants to buy a good car for $4,000, and try to design a screen to solve the lemons problem.

One option is to offer $4,000 for a car, but demand a money-back guarantee. Sellers of good cars will accept the offer because they know the car won't be returned. Lemon owners will be unwilling to offer warranties like this.

Screening occurs in a wide variety of contexts beyond the insurance and auto markets. For example, the state of Louisiana allows couples to choose one of two marriage contracts: a covenant contract, under which divorce is very costly;

and a regular contract, under which divorce is relatively cheap. What is the screening function of this menu of choices?

Suppose there are two types of prospective partners: those who want only a short-term relationship and those who want to stay together until they die. Given a choice of contracts, you learn something about your intended by the choice he or she makes. A short-term partner will want the regular marriage contract. Note that this screen works only if it is too costly for short-term partners to choose a covenant contract.

Finally, as seen in our R&B story, screens can solve the adverse selection problem in hiring. Incentive pay can also have this effect. Suppose you can hire two types of salespeople—hard workers who sell 100 units in their territories, and lazy workers who sell only 50 units. Suppose hard and lazy workers alike expect to earn at least $800 for a month's work. If you offer a wage of $800 per month, you get a mix of lazy and hard workers.

To screen out the bad workers, you can offer a straight $10 commission. Hard workers will accept the offer because they know they'll earn $1,000. Lazy workers, who know they'll make only $500, will reject the offer. This is a perfect screen because the workers' own choices (accept or reject) identify them by type.

However, such an incentive compensation scheme may expose good workers to too much risk: A host of factors affect sales other than the effort of the salesperson. A screen that works just as well, but presents less risk, is a contract with a flat salary of $500 in combination with a $10 commission on sales exceeding 50. This combination guarantees each worker a base salary of $500 with no risk while adding higher compensation for the hard worker. Again, good workers will accept the offer, whereas lazy workers, who expect to earn just $500, will decline.[7]

SIGNALING

Let's recap what we've learned so far. Even when we anticipate it and protect ourselves against it, adverse selection results in unconsummated wealth-creating transactions, such as those between

- insurance companies and low-risk consumers;
- car buyers and sellers with good cars; or
- employers and hard-working employees.

Screening is a scheme by the less-informed party to consummate these transactions by getting rid of the information asymmetry. When consumers

---

[7] Under this plan, good workers expect to earn $1,000 ($500 + (100 expected sales − 50 sales base) × $10), which is $200 more than their minimum acceptable wage of $800. Lazy workers expect to earn $500 (they earn no commission because they only sell 50 units), which is $300 less than their minimum acceptable wage of $800.

identify themselves by their choices, wealth-creating transactions can be consummated.

In this section, we discuss efforts by an informed party—the low-risk consumers, the hard-working employees, and the sellers with good cars—to communicate to the less-informed party—the insurance company, the employer, and the car buyers. This is called signaling.

> **Signaling** *is an informed party's effort to communicate her type, risk, or value to less-informed parties by her actions. A successful signal is one that bad types won't mimic.*

Signaling is closely related to screening. Any successful screen that separates low-risk from high-risk consumers, good- from bad-car sellers, or lazy- from hard-working employees can also serve as a signal. To signal, the informed party could use the mechanisms just described: Low-risk consumers could offer to buy insurance with a big deductible, good employees could offer to work on commission, and sellers with good cars could include a warranty with the purchase.

The crucial element of a successful signal is that it must not be profitable for the bad-type consumers to mimic the signaling behavior of the good-type consumers.

For example, much of the value of education may derive not from what it adds to students' human capital but rather from its signaling value. Students signal to potential employers that they're hard-working, quick-learning, dedicated individuals by dropping out of the labor force and spending lots of money to pursue an education. It's not profitable for lazy, slow-learning, or undedicated individuals to pursue educations because they'll reveal their type before they can recoup the investment in their educations.

We can also consider advertising and branding as signals. By branding a product and advertising it, you signal to consumers that it is a high-quality product. Low-quality producers won't mimic this signal because, once consumers try the product, they'll learn of its low quality and avoid the brand in the future. Low-quality producers cannot sell enough to recover their advertising expenditures.

ADVERSE SELECTION ON eBAY

In 2000, Robert and Teri La Plant paid $2,950 for a 1.41-carat marquise-cut diamond on eBay. Power user MrWatch was the seller. But when the La Plants received the diamond, they noticed a visible chip and returned it. Al Bagon, who does business as MrWatch, refused to refund their money, alleging that the La Plants chipped the diamond themselves to avoid paying for it. Mr. Bagon noted that an appraisal accompanied the diamond when it was shipped. The La Plants countered by noting that the appraisal was 18 months old, and that they have collected the standard $200 insurance policy that eBay offers for all its purchases. eBay refuses to suspend MrWatch from the site, noting that he has had 1,800 positive responses from customers and only eight negative responses.[8]

Problem like this arise because eBay sellers have better information than buyers about the quality of goods being offered for sale. Buyers offer less, making sellers less willing to sell high-quality goods. Consummated transactions are more likely to leave buyers disappointed with respect to quality.

eBay tries to solve the adverse selection problem by using authentication, grading and escrow services, and insurance against fraud. Sellers can also build good reputations as customers rate each transaction with the seller. Sellers who enjoy good reputations command higher prices on eBay for the same items. An increase in a seller's rating by 10% leads to a 1.3% higher expected price.[9] eBay's ability to address the adverse selection problem has allowed them to begin selling more expensive items, such as cars, which expose uninformed buyers to bigger potential losses.

SUMMARY & HOMEWORK PROBLEMS

SUMMARY OF MAIN POINTS

- Insurance is a wealth-creating transaction that moves risk from those who don't want it to those who are willing to bear it.
- **Adverse selection** is a problem that arises from information asymmetry— anticipate it, and, if you can, figure out how to consummate the unconsummated wealth-creating transaction (e.g., between a low-risk customer and an insurance company).
- The adverse selection problem disappears if the asymmetry of information disappears.
- **Screening** is an uninformed party's effort to learn the information that the more informed party has. Successful screens have the characteristic that it is unprofitable for bad "types" to mimic the behavior of good types.
- **Signaling** is an informed party's effort to communicate her information to the less informed party. Every successful screen can also be used as a signal.
- eBay addresses the adverse selection problem with authentication and escrow services, insurance, and on-line reputations.

[8] Barbara Whitaker, "If a Transaction Goes Sour, Where Do You Turn?" *New York Times*, August 20, 2000, section 3, p. 1.
[9] www.u.arizona.edu/~dreiley/papers/PenniesFromEBay.pdf.

MULTIPLE-CHOICE QUESTIONS

1. If a life insurance company knows that smoking increases the risk of death but is unable to determine which applicants smoke, the problem of _____ refers to _____ being more likely to buy insurance.
- **a.** adverse selection, nonsmokers'
- **b.** moral hazard, nonsmokers'
- **c.** adverse selection, smokers'
- **d.** moral hazard, smokers'

2. An insurance company offers doctors malpractice insurance. Assume that settling malpractice claims against careful doctors costs $5,000 and settling malpractice claims against reckless doctors costs $30,000. Doctors themselves know whether they are reckless or careful, but the insurance company can only assume that 10% of doctors are reckless. How much do insurance companies have to charge for malpractice insurance to break even?
- **a.** $5,000
- **b.** $7,500
- **c.** $27,500
- **d.** $30,000

3. To combat the problem of adverse selection, _____ informed parties can employ _____ techniques.
- **a.** more, signaling
- **b.** less, signaling
- **c.** equally, screening
- **d.** equally, signaling

4. Which of the following is *not* an example of adverse selection?
- **a.** A business bets the proceeds of a bank loan on the over/under on the next NFL game.
- **b.** An accident-prone driver buys auto insurance.
- **c.** A patient suffering from a terminal disease buys life insurance.
- **d.** A really hungry person decides to go to the all-you-can-eat buffet for dinner.

5. To overcome the problem of adverse selection, employers can use _____ techniques, such as _____.
- **a.** signaling, monitoring employee performance
- **b.** screening, monitoring employee performance
- **c.** screening, checking employee references
- **d.** signaling, checking employee references

INDIVIDUAL PROBLEMS

16-1. Bicycle Insurance and Information Asymmetry

If bicycle owners do not know whether they are high- or low-risk consumers, is there an adverse selection problem?

16-2. IPOs and Adverse Selection

Should owners of a private company contemplating an IPO (a sale of stock to the public) release information about the company, or keep as much of it as they can to themselves?

16-3. "Soft Selling" and Adverse Selection

Soft selling occurs when a buyer is skeptical of the quality or usefulness of a product or service. For example, suppose you're trying to sell a company a new accounting system that will reduce costs by 10%. Instead of asking for a price, you offer to give them the product in exchange for 50% of their cost savings. Describe the information asymmetry, the adverse selection problem, and why soft selling is a successful signal.

16-4. Student Work Groups

You'll complete a number of your school assignments in small groups, many of which will be student selected. Assume group members are rational and select fellow group members based on their assessment of teammates' intellectual and productive capabilities. Someone you don't know invites you to join a group. Should you accept? (*Hint*: Think about the information asymmetry.)

16-5. Hiring Employees

You need to hire some new employees to staff your start-up venture. You know that potential employees are distributed throughout the population as follows, but you can't distinguish among them:

Employee Value	Probability
$50,000	.25
$60,000	.25
$70,000	.25
$80,000	.25

What is the expected value of employees you hire?

GROUP PROBLEM

G16-1. Adverse Selection

Describe an adverse selection problem your company is facing. What is the source of the asymmetric information? Who is the less-informed party? What transactions are not being consummated as a result of the information? Could you (or do you) use signaling or screening to consummate these transactions? Offer your company some sound advice, complete with computations of the attendant profit consequences.

Chapter 17

The Problem of Moral Hazard

A regional phone company, BonaComm, has installed GPS (global positioning satellite) locators on its repair trucks to track the location of each truck in its repair fleet. Every 15 minutes, the GPS sends the company the location (latitude and longitude) of each truck so that the BonaComm dispatchers can more effectively position the fleet. This information, constantly refreshed, is particularly helpful in response to emergencies, like those caused by storms or other systemwide disasters.

The system also had an unexpected side benefit. In response to complaints about a repairman's slow response times, BonaComm managers were able to plot the movement of his truck. They found that the driver made long side trips to the same house at roughly the same time each day. It turned out he was visiting a woman (with whom he'd begun an affair) when he was supposed to be repairing phones. The company fired him for violating the firm's work rules.

This story illustrates a solution to a problem that economists call **moral hazard.** The name refers not to the affair but rather to the fact that the repairman was using company time to conduct it. Closely related to the problem of adverse selection, moral hazard has similar causes and solutions. Again, these problems arise in situations characterized by information asymmetry, in which one party has more information than the other.[1]

INSURANCE

To understand moral hazard, let's return to the bicycle insurance example found in Chapter 16. Assume there is just one type of consumer, the high-risk consumer whose probability of theft is 40%. Now, however, our consumer can take certain actions that reduce the probability of theft.

Suppose that consumers can bring their bikes inside, thereby reducing the probability of theft from 40% to 30%. Suppose that the cost to the owner of doing this is $5. Without insurance, each consumer brings the bike inside because

[1] Unlike adverse selection problems, which are characterized by hidden *information*, moral hazard problems are characterized by "hidden *action*."

the *expected* benefit of doing so—the reduction in the probability of theft multiplied by the price of the bike, $(0.40 - 0.30) \times \$100 = \$10$—is greater than the $5 cost of exercising care.

Bicycle owners still face the risk of theft and are willing to pay $5 more than the cost of insurance to get rid of the risk. In this case, the expected loss is $30 (or $.3 \times \$100$), and the bicycle owner willingly pays the insurance company $35 to insure against the risk of theft.

But once consumers purchase insurance, any benefit from exercising care disappears because the insurance company reimburses the consumers for any thefts that do occur.

> *Moral hazard means that customers exercise less care once they purchase insurance because they have less incentive to do so.*

In our example, the consumer stops bringing the bicycle inside, and the probability of theft increases from 30% to 40%. The insurance company loses $5, on average, for every policy it sells. This leads to the first lesson of moral hazard:

> *Anticipate moral hazard and protect yourself against it.*

In this case, the insurance company should anticipate that the probability of theft will rise to 40% and price its policies accordingly; that is, it should price the insurance at $45 instead of $35.

What happens when an insurance company doesn't anticipate moral hazard? Consider what one of our students (who previously worked at an insurance company) had to say about antilock braking systems (ABS) and air bags:

> *People with anti-lock brakes were far more likely to get into an accident because, after buying ABS, they thought they could drive on ice or in the rain. As a result, our company was phasing out discounts for ABS with successive rate revisions, except in those states that required such a discount.*

The second point of this chapter is that, even if a firm anticipates moral hazard, the problem of consumers not exercising care may represent an opportunity to make money.

> *Moral hazard represents an unconsummated wealth-creating transaction.*

In other words, the benefits of exercising care are still higher than the costs; but because those benefits don't accrue to the consumers, they fail to exercise care.

The insurance company could easily solve the moral hazard problem if it could observe whether the customer was exercising care. In possession of such information, the insurance company could sell low-priced insurance to those taking care and higher-priced insurance to those not taking care. Alternatively, it could offer to reimburse the customer only if she took care. But since discriminating between those who take care and those who don't requires information the company doesn't have, the company can offer only a single insurance policy at $45. And customers purchase the policy because it is priced at $5 above its expected cost,[2] $40 (or 40% × $100). But they stop taking their bikes inside.

MORAL HAZARD VERSUS ADVERSE SELECTION

Although moral hazard and adverse selection are closely linked, they often offer competing explanations for the same observed behavior. Consider the fact that people who drive cars equipped with air bags are more likely to get into traffic accidents. Either adverse selection or moral hazard could explain this phenomenon (note that that buying an air bag is analogous to purchasing insurance).

The adverse selection explanation is that bad drivers are more likely to purchase cars with air bags. If you know you're likely to get into an accident, it makes sense to purchase a car with air bags.

The moral hazard explanation is that once drivers have the protection of air bags, they take more risks and get into more accidents. If you don't believe that people change behavior in this way, try running a simple experiment. Next time you drive somewhere, do not wear a seatbelt. See if you drive more carefully. (We, of course, would not recommend running this experiment in states that require seatbelt use.)

What distinguishes adverse selection from moral hazard is the kind of information that is hidden from the insurance company. Adverse selection arises from hidden *information* regarding the type of person (high- vs. low-risk) who is purchasing insurance. Moral hazard arises from hidden *actions* by the person purchasing insurance (taking care or not).

More information can solve both problems. If the insurance company can distinguish between high- and low-risk consumers, it can offer a high-price policy to the high-risk group and a low-price policy to the low-risk group, thereby solving the adverse selection problem. Similarly, if the insurer can observe whether customers are exercising appropriate levels of care after purchasing insurance, it can reward people for taking care, thereby solving the problem of moral hazard. For example, insurance investigators devote a great deal of time trying to figure out exactly what happened in accidents in

[2] Recall that consumers are willing to pay $5 more than the cost of insurance to get rid of the risk. We thank Mark Cohen for the bicycle insurance example.

order to determine whether it faces a problem of adverse selection or a problem of moral hazard.

SHIRKING AS MORAL HAZARD

Employees may be tempted into shirking, a type of moral hazard driven by the complexity or cost of monitoring their behavior *after* a firm has hired them. Consequently, rewarding workers for working hard or punishing them for shirking is very difficult. For example, only because the managers at BonaComm (our phone company) were able to observe the movement of its repair trucks were they able to detect their repairman's shirking. With the GPS information available, they were able to punish the worker by firing him—an extreme form incentive compensation, which can include using carrots or sticks to reward good behavior or to punish bad behavior.

In general, designing incentive compensation schemes often requires gathering information that is too costly to acquire. And without good information, encouraging high levels of effort becomes very costly.

Suppose, for example, a salesperson can work hard or shirk; further suppose that working hard raises the probability of making a sale from 50% to 75%. However, the increased effort "costs" the salesperson $100. How big does the sales commission have to be to induce hard work?

To answer this question, in Figure 17-1, we graph the decision tree of the salesperson who decides whether to work hard or shirk.

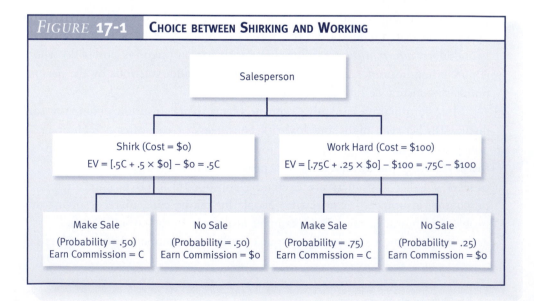

FIGURE **17-1**   **CHOICE BETWEEN SHIRKING AND WORKING**

Salesperson

Shirk (Cost = $0)
EV = [.5C + .5 × $0] − $0 = .5C

Work Hard (Cost = $100)
EV = [.75C + .25 × $0] − $100 = .75C − $100

Make Sale
(Probability = .50)
Earn Commission = C

No Sale
(Probability = .50)
Earn Commission = $0

Make Sale
(Probability = .75)
Earn Commission = C

No Sale
(Probability = .25)
Earn Commission = $0

The benefit of working harder is the increased probability of making a sale and hence earning a sales commission (C). The cost is the $100 in effort. So to induce effort, the expected profit of working harder $(0.75 \times C - \$100)$ must be at least as large as the expected profit of shirking $(0.5 \times C)$. In other words, the commission must be at least $400.[3] Rearranging this expression, you can alternatively ask whether the benefit of working harder (increase in the probability of making a sale multiplied by the commission) is greater than the marginal cost of working harder. In other words, is $.25 \times C > \$100$?

Unless the company's margin on the item is at least $400, the company cannot afford to pay a $400 commission. In other words, if the margin is less than $400, the company makes more money by letting the salesman shirk—it doesn't pay to address the moral hazard problem. "Problems" are business issues that you should work on fixing. If fixing the issue (shirking) is impossible (like when the company's margin is less than $400), the issue is no longer a "problem."

Ordinarily, it's very hard for business students to accept that some problems simply cannot be solved. They cannot understand that the solution costs more than the problem. For these students, we leave you with a simple maxim—one that's helped us make some tough decisions.

If there's no solution, there's no problem.

Note that the shirking problem the company faces arises from the same lack of information that leads to moral hazard in insurance: Only the salesperson knows how hard she is working, just as only the insurance customer knows whether he is taking care. The information that the company does possess— whether or not a sale is made—is a poor measure of effort because too frequently (50% of the time), the salesperson earns a commission for doing nothing. In other words, evaluating performance is really difficult.

One alternative is to try to find a better indicator of effort than sales. Say that, by incurring costs of $50, you could observe whether the salesperson is working hard. Would it be profitable to hire someone to monitor the salesperson's behavior?

Before you answer this question, note that you can induce hard work by spending $50 in monitoring costs, then threatening to fire salespeople who aren't working hard. The expected benefit of inducing hard work is the increased probability of making a sale (25%) multiplied by the margin. If the item's margin

[3] $.75C - \$100 > .5C$; equivalently
$.75C - .5C > \$100$; equivalently
$.25C > \$100$; equivalently
$C > \$400$

is at least $200, it pays to monitor the worker.[4] Likewise, the company would also pay $50 more for a worker who has a reputation for working hard, regardless of whether she is monitored. Having a reputation for working hard without monitoring is valuable to the company as well as the worker.

This leads directly to our last point that moral hazard injures both parties to a transaction. Consider, for example, the case of a business consulting firm paid an hourly rate. Given the rate structure and the inability of the client to monitor the consultant's actions, the client's expectations for the consultant are low. The client expects the consultant either to bill more hours than the client prefers or to spend time on projects that the consultant values but that the client does not. Clients anticipate this kind of shirking and are understandably reluctant to transact . . . unless the consulting firm can find a way to address the problem. The point is this: Both parties end up transacting less than they otherwise would if moral hazard did not exist.

The consultant can solve this moral hazard problem by establishing a good reputation, by accepting a portion of the contract on a fixed-fee basis, and by providing the client with information documenting the utility of the work being done.

MORAL HAZARD IN LENDING

As a final example, let's consider the problems that banks face when making loans to borrowers. The adverse selection problem is that borrowers who are less likely to repay loans are more likely to apply for them. The moral hazard problem is that, once the loan is made, the borrower is likely to engage in more risky behavior, which makes repayment less likely. Again, adverse selection arises from hidden *information,* while moral hazard arises from hidden *actions.*

To illustrate the moral hazard problem, suppose you're considering a $30 investment opportunity with the following payoff: $100 with a probability of .5 and $0 with a probability of .5. The bank correctly evaluates the expected value of the investment ($50) and decides to make a $30 loan at a 100% rate of interest. If the investment pays off, the bank gets $60. But if the investment returns zero, the bank gets nothing. The expected return to the bank $(.5 \times \$60 + .5 \times \$0 = \$30)$ is equal to the loan, so it breaks even, on average.

---

[4] Monitoring increases the probability of a sale's being made from .5 to .75. The respective expected values to the company under the two options are as follows: EV(monitoring) = .75 × Margin − $50 and EV(not monitoring) = .5 × Margin. To determine the point at which monitoring becomes profitable, set the two EVs equal to each other and solve for the margin:

.75 × Margin−$50 = .5 × Margin
.25 × Margin = $50
Margin = $200

The moral hazard problem arises when, after receiving the loan, the borrower discovers another, much riskier investment. The second investment has a $1,000 payoff with a probability of .05. Although the expected payoffs of the two investments are identical at $50, the payoffs for the two parties are not. Compare the expected payoffs of the borrower and the bank in Table 17-1 and Table 17-2. You can see that because the borrower receives more of the upside gain if the investment pays off, he makes more money, on average, with the riskier investment. And if the borrower does much better, the bank does much worse. The bank's share of the expected $50 payout drops from $30 to just $3.

This is an example of moral hazard—the borrower's hidden actions represent a postcontractual change in his behavior. Banks guard against moral hazard by monitoring the behavior of borrowers and by placing covenants on loans to ensure that the loans are used for their original purposes.

We can also understand moral hazard as an incentive conflict between the bank and the borrower. The bank's managers prefer the less risky investment because the bank receives its payoff before the borrower earns any money.

TABLE 17-1	PAYOFFS TO A LESS RISKY INVESTMENT ($30 LOAN AT 100% INTEREST)		
	Investment Returns $100 (p = .5)	Investment Returns $0 (p = .5)	Expected Payoff
Payoff to borrower	$40	$0	$20
Payoff to bank	$60	$0	$30

Note: p = probability.

TABLE 17-2	PAYOFFS TO A MORE RISKY INVESTMENT ($30 LOAN AT 100% INTEREST)		
	Investment Returns $1000 (p = .05)	Investment Returns $0 (p = .95)	Expected Payoff
Payoff to borrower	$940	$0	$47
Payoff to bank	$60	$0	$3

Likewise, the borrower prefers a more risky payoff because he earns money only after paying back his loan from the bank.

The incentive conflict is exacerbated when the borrower has no money of his own at risk.

When someone has nothing to lose, he's likely to take bigger risks.

In the early 1980s in Texas, a bust in the real estate market reduced the value of many savings and loan institutions (S&Ls). S&Ls are basically banks that borrow from depositors and lend to homeowners. When the real estate market collapsed, many homeowners stopped repaying their loans and forfeited their real estate to the S&L. The value of the S&Ls' assets (the real estate) fell below that of their liabilities (the money they owed depositors). With nothing to lose, these S&Ls borrowed even more money from depositors at very high interest rates and "bet" heavily on junk bonds—the most risky investment available to them. And just as in our loan example, this move decreased the expected payoff to the lender. Since deposits were insured by the U.S. government, U.S. taxpayers were stuck with the $200 billion cost of repaying depositors.

To control this kind of moral hazard, try to better align the incentives of borrowers with those of lenders by ensuring that borrowers have some of their own money at risk. If the investments don't pay off, you want to make sure that the borrower is hurt in addition to the lender. This is why banks are much more willing to lend to borrowers who have a great deal of their own money at risk. This has led many borrowers to complain that banks lend money only to those who don't need it. But if banks lend to borrowers without assets, banks have a very big moral hazard problem to solve. Otherwise, they will probably lose money.

SUMMARY & HOMEWORK PROBLEMS

SUMMARY OF MAIN POINTS

- **Moral hazard** refers to the reduced incentive to exercise care once you purchase insurance.
- Moral hazard occurs in a variety of circumstances: Anticipate it, and (if you can) figure out how to consummate the implied wealth-creating transaction (i.e., ensuring that consumers continue to take care even when the benefits of doing so exceed the costs).
- Moral hazard can look very similar to adverse selection—both arise from information asymmetry. Adverse selection arises from hidden

information about the type of individual you're dealing with; moral hazard arises from hidden actions.

- Solutions to the problem of moral hazard center on efforts to eliminate the information asymmetry (e.g., by monitoring or by changing the incentives of individuals).
- Shirking is a form of moral hazard.
- Borrowers prefer riskier investments because they get more of the upside while the lender bears more of the downside. Borrowers who have nothing to lose exacerbate this moral hazard problem.

MULTIPLE-CHOICE QUESTIONS

1. Which of the following is an example of moral hazard?
  a. Reckless drivers are the ones most likely to buy automobile insurance.
  b. Retail stores located in high-crime areas tend to buy theft insurance more often than stores located in low-crime areas.
  c. Drivers who have many accidents prefer to buy cars with air bags.
  d. After employees sign up for the company health plan that covers all doctors' visits, they start going to the doctor every time they get a cold.

2. Moral hazard means that a borrower would be more likely to use loan proceeds to invest in which of the following?
  a. A blue chip stock
  b. A mutual fund
  c. A corporate bond fund
  d. A start-up biotechnology company

3. Which of the following is *not* an example of a process designed to combat moral hazard problems?
  a. Banks include restrictive covenants in loan agreements.
  b. Universities have students complete evaluations of professor performance at the end of a class.
  c. Insurance companies require applicants to provide medical history information as part of the application process.
  d. Employers regularly monitor employee performance.

4. Due to the problems associated with _____, one would expect a doctor to spend _____ time with patients after buying malpractice insurance.
  a. moral hazard, more
  b. adverse selection, more
  c. moral hazard, less
  d. adverse selection, less

5. A moral hazard explanation would tell us that homeowners are _____ likely to lock their houses at night after buying insurance.

a. less

b. more

c. equally

d. None of the above

INDIVIDUAL PROBLEMS

17-1. Business Loan

A colleague tells you that he can get a business loan from the bank, but the rates seem very high for what your colleague considers a low-risk loan.

a. Give an adverse selection explanation for this, and offer advice to your friend on how to solve the problem.

b. Give a moral hazard explanation for this, and offer advice to your friend on how to solve the problem.

17-2. Usage-Based Insurance

With a GPS system attached to each insured vehicle, insurance companies are able to charge "usage-based insurance rates," depending on how much, when, and where the insured vehicle is driven. Autograph, a firm that was awarded a U.S. patent in 2001, was shown to save policy holders in Houston an average of 25% of what they were previously paying. Why are usage-based insurance rates lower than flat-rate insurance fees? Give two separate reasons.

17-3. AIDS Insurance

Suppose your company is considering three health insurance policies. The first policy requires no tests and covers all preexisting illnesses. The second policy requires that all covered employees test negative for the HIV virus. The third policy does not cover HIV- or AIDS-related illnesses. All insurance policies are priced at their actuarially "fair" value. All individuals are slightly risk-averse. An individual with the HIV virus requires, on average, $100,000 worth of medical care each year. An individual without the virus requires, on average, $500 worth of medical care each year.

a. Suppose that the incidence of HIV in the population is .005. Calculate the annual premium of the first policy. (*Hint*: Adverse selection.)

b. If you don't have insurance that covers HIV-related illnesses, the probability of getting HIV is 1%. If you have insurance that covers HIV-related illness, suppose that the probability of getting HIV is 2%. Calculate the premium of the second policy. Show your calculations. (*Hint*: Moral hazard.)

c. In Question 17-3b, suppose the insurance company wants to encourage low-risk behavior by individuals who have insurance. On average, it "costs" individuals $100 to engage in low-risk behavior. Assume that if people get HIV, they pay the deductible; and if they do not get HIV, they do not pay the deductible. How high must the deductible be to encourage low-risk behavior?

d. Calculate the premium of the third policy. Show your calculations.

17-4. Auto Insurance

Suppose that every driver faces a 1% probability of an automobile accident every year. An accident will, on average, cost each driver $10,000. Suppose there are two types of individuals: those with $60,000 in the bank and those with $5,000 in the bank. Assume that individuals with $5,000 in the bank declare bankruptcy if they get in an accident. In bankruptcy, creditors receive only what individuals have in the bank. What is the actuarially fair price of insurance? What price are individuals with $5,000 in the bank willing to pay for the insurance? Will those with $5,000 in the bank voluntarily purchase insurance? (*Hint*: Remember that there are state laws forcing individuals to purchase auto liability insurance.)

17-5. Moral Hazard in Bank Loans

Suppose that, as an owner of a federally insured S&L in the 1980s, the price of real estate falls, and most of your loans go into default. In fact, so many loans go into default that the net worth of the S&L is negative (−$5 million). Federal regulators haven't realized this yet, but they will shortly. As a last-ditch attempt to save the bank, you attract $1 million in new deposits with very generous interest rates to depositors. You have two possible investments you can make with the $1 million. You can invest in the stock market, which will pay $4 million with probability .5 and $2 million with probability .5. Alternatively, you can invest in junk bonds, which pay off $10 million with probability .1 and $0.5 million with probability .9.

a. Which investment has the highest expected value to an ordinary investor? Show your calculations.

b. Which investment has the highest expected value to you, the S&L owner? Show your calculations. (*Hint*: Federal deposit insurance limits an S&L's losses to zero.)

GROUP PROBLEM

G17-1. Moral Hazard

Describe a moral hazard problem your company is facing. What is the source of the asymmetric information? Who is the less informed party? Are there any wealth-creating transactions not consummated as a result of the asymmetric information? If so, could you consummate them? Compute the profit consequences of any advice.

ORGANIZATIONAL DESIGN

Chapter 18

Getting Employees to Work in the Firm's Best Interests

In the late 1990s, a large auction house, Auction Services International (ASI), employed art experts to keep track of art from various "schools"—French Impressionism, American Realism, and the like. Each expert's job was to persuade art owners to use ASI's auction services to sell art pieces. ASI earned money by charging the art owners a percentage of the final price at auction. The art expert negotiated this rate with the sellers (art owners).

The negotiated rates were supposed to vary from 10% to 30% of the auction price, depending on the art expert's assessment of the seller's willingness to pay. Instead, most of these negotiations yielded relatively low rates, much closer to 10% than 30%. Puzzled, ASI's CEO did some investigating, only to discover that the art experts were discounting rates in exchange for "gifts" from the sellers— cases of fine wine, fur coats, even luxury cars. After he found out about these kickbacks, the CEO put a stop to the kickbacks by removing the experts' discretion to negotiate the rates.

The CEO's action ended the exchange of gifts for lower rates, but it also dramatically reduced the art experts' income. The experts had become accustomed to the kickbacks, considering them an important part of their compensation package. Consequently, many of the art experts quit, leaving to set up their own independent galleries in direct competition with the auction house.

To make matters worse, the CEO was eventually convicted of conspiring with a rival auction house to fix rates at 17%. When the conspiracy was discovered, the CEO was sentenced to a year in jail, and the judge tacked on a $7.5 million fine, an amount calculated as 5% of the $150 million volume of commerce affected by the price-fixing conspiracy.

Had the CEO known how to motivate her employees to work in her firm's interest—the topic of this chapter—she wouldn't have needed to resort to price fixing to make her own firm profitable.

PRINCIPAL–AGENT RELATIONSHIPS

When we study the relationship between a firm and its employees, we use what economists call *principal–agent models*.

> A **principal** wants an **agent** to act on her behalf. But agents often have different goals and preferences than do principals.

In the ASI story, for example, the firm or the CEO is the principal, and the art expert is the agent. We adopt the linguistic convention that the principal is female and the agent male.

The problem the principal faces is that the agent's incentives differ from hers—a circumstance we call "**incentive conflict.**" In our example, ASI's CEO wanted her art experts to negotiate profitable commission rates, whereas the experts wanted to increase personal income, including "gifts" from customers. In general, incentive conflicts exist between every principal and every agent throughout the management hierarchy—for example, between shareholders and managers, between managers and subordinates, and between a firm and its various divisions.

Incentive conflict generates problems that should sound familiar:

> The principal has to decide which agent to hire (adverse selection); once she hires an agent, she has to figure out how to motivate him (moral hazard).

We know (from Chapters 16 and 17) that adverse selection and moral hazard problems are costly to control when agents are better informed than the principal. In fact, we call the costs associated with moral hazard and adverse selection "**agency costs**" because we often analyze them using principal–agent models. A well-run firm will find ways to reduce agency costs, but poorly run firms often blindly incur such costs or unwittingly make decisions that increase agency costs.

We also know that we can reduce the costs of adverse selection or moral hazard by gathering information either about the type of agent or about the agent's actions.

> A principal can reduce agency costs if she gathers information about the agent's type (adverse selection) or about the agent's actions (moral hazard).

For adverse selection, information gathering means checking the background of agents *before* they're hired; and for moral hazard, information means monitoring the agents' behavior *after* they're hired. This difference has led some to characterize adverse selection as a *pre*contractual problem and moral hazard as a *post*contractual one.

At ASI, for example, had the CEO known when agents began to exchange rate reductions for gifts, she might have devised a simple incentive compensation scheme (a reward or a punishment) to stop it. But even without this information, she should have anticipated the art experts' self-interested behavior, especially since she was paying them flat salaries—compensation unrelated to performance. Because ASI failed to compensate the art experts to set profitable rates, the art owners found it easy to bribe them to set unprofitable ones.

When the CEO decided to withdraw rate-setting discretion from the art experts, she compounded her initial mistake. This solution was costly because the CEO lacked information about what rates owners were willing to pay, information that was critical to setting profitable rates. Instead, she tried her "17% solution," the collusive rate set with her rival.

A better solution would have been to leave the rate-setting authority with the art experts but reward them with an incentive compensation scheme—for example, one that paid them a percentage of the revenue they brought to the firm. This kind of compensation scheme aligns the agents' incentives with the firm's goals. If the agents set profitable rates, they'll increase both the firm's profit and their own compensation. If you consider the art experts as salespeople, this incentive compensation scheme seems an obvious solution—a solution that also reduces the owner's need to monitor the agent's actions.

This solution does have one drawback: Like all incentive compensation schemes, it exposes the agents to risk. In this case, should the economy decline, the firm would sell fewer art pieces, and the art experts' compensation would fall through no fault of their own.

If you are the principal, imposing risk on the agent may not seem like your problem, but we know (from Chapter 9) that people, whether they are investors or employees, must be compensated for bearing risk. This raises the principal's cost of using an incentive compensation scheme.

> *Incentive compensation imposes risk on the agent for which he must be compensated.*

The risk of incentive compensation reminds us that any solution involves trade-offs. We adopt incentive compensation only if its benefits (the agent works harder) exceed its costs (the agents get higher compensation for bearing risk). We measure these costs relative to the status quo or relative to whatever other solution you might be considering.

GENERAL RULES FOR CONTROLLING INCENTIVE CONFLICT

We don't have any hard and fast rules for controlling incentive conflicts between principals and agents, but we can offer a few rules for identifying the trade-offs associated with various solutions. These rules can help you understand the basic trade-offs, allowing you to compute the costs and benefits of various solutions.

Let's start by describing an ideal organization whose agents always make decisions in the best interests of their principals.

In a well-run organization, decision makers have (1) the information necessary to make good decisions and (2) the incentive to do so.

Conversely, just two factors drive mistakes: information or incentives. To ensure that decision makers have enough information to make good decisions, we have two solutions:

Either move information to those who are making decisions or move decision-making authority to those who have information.

Typically, though not always, subordinates (who are further down in the management hierarchy), gather information. Thus, we associate the first option with *centralization* of decision-making authority and the second, with *decentralization*.

In the ASI example, the art expert had better information about what rates owners were willing to pay. Giving pricing discretion to the art expert *decentralizes* decision-making authority.

When you decentralize decision-making authority, you should also strengthen incentive compensation schemes.

The logic is clear: Once you give an agent authority to make decisions, you want to ensure that he is motivated to make choices in the firm's best interest. At ASI, the weak incentives were obvious—the art experts had rate-setting discretion, but they were given no incentive to set profitable rates. The CEO should have adopted an incentive compensation scheme to encourage profitable decision making.

It's useful to think of incentives as having two parts: Before you can reward good behavior, you have to be able to measure it. You can judge performance informally, with some kind of subjective performance evaluation, or formally, using sales or profitability as performance measures. Once you have an adequate performance measure, you create incentives by linking compensation to performance measures. Here, we speak very generally about compensation: Compensation can be pay, increased likelihood of promotion, bonuses, or anything else that the employee values. The link between performance and compensation creates the incentive for agents to act in the firm's best interest.

But decentralization, even with stronger incentive compensation, isn't always the best solution for controlling incentive conflict. Although decision makers nearer the top of the hierarchy may have less information, it's easier to motivate upper-level employees to work in the firm's overall interests. Because their decisions are more likely to affect the entire organization, you can more easily align their incentives with organizational goals just by tying their compensation to the firm's profitability. But, remember, incentives are only half the solution.

> *When you centralize decision-making authority, make sure that the decision maker has enough information to make good decisions.*

It seems likely that the CEO of ASI lacked the critical information about how much art owners were willing to pay. Without this information, it was costly to set prices centrally. By setting a uniform (albeit collusive) price, the CEO gave up the ability to price discriminate.

MARKETING VERSUS SALES

The conflict between the art experts and their employer is fairly typical of the general incentive conflict that arises in organizations with separate sales and marketing divisions. The two divisions rarely get along. For example, consider a large telecommunications equipment company, among whose customers are various government agencies that operate or regulate the telecommunications sector. In this company, the conflict manifests itself in arguments between salespeople and marketing people: Sales agents want to price aggressively to ensure that they make the sales; marketing people, however, want to restrain the sales agents' aggressive pricing to ensure that the sales are more profitable.

The incentive conflict arises because marketing managers receive stock options or profitability bonuses as compensation, while salespeople receive commissions based on revenue. They disagree about what price to charge because the marketing principal wants to maximize profitability—that is, by making sales where $MR > MC$. Meanwhile, the sales agent wants to maximize revenue by making sales where $MR > 0$. This means that the salesperson prefers more sales or, equivalently, lower prices.

If the marketing managers *know* when the salespeople are making unprofitable sales, they can easily put a stop to it. Management can use either a punishment or a reward to align the incentives of the salespeople with the marketing manager's goals. But when observing what agents should be doing is difficult or costly, incentive conflicts like this create problems.

To see why, put yourself in the place of a marketing manager who is overseeing a salesperson. He tells you that he *has* to reduce price to make a particularly tough sale. Because you don't know how much each customer is willing to pay, you can't tell whether the salesperson is really reducing price to make a particularly tough sale (which would be reasonable from the firm's perspective) or whether he's actually reducing price because he cares only about revenue, not about costs. We know from Chapter 17 that without this information, it is costly for the principal to control the agent's behavior.

It seems easy to design an incentive compensation scheme that rewards the salesperson for increasing profitability rather than for increasing revenue. With this solution, we know that the salesperson's incentives would be aligned with the profitability goals of the company.

Why, then, is this kind of incentive compensation not more widely used? Most salespeople will tell you they prefer evaluations based on revenue because revenue is what they directly control. They may also resist a change from a sales commission to a profit commission, perceiving the profit commission scheme as a sneaky way for the company to cut labor costs. Remember that profit is always lower than sales.

You should be able to persuade the sales agent to accept the change to a profit commission if you design the compensation so that it's "revenue-neutral." For example, a 20% commission on profit is equivalent to a 10% commission on revenue if the contribution margin is 50%. Agents are guaranteed to earn the same under each compensation scheme if they behave as they did. But they can earn more money if they change behavior (by pricing less aggressively), which raises their compensation—which is exactly what you want them to do.

You often see companies trying to control incentive conflicts simply by asking sales agents to change their behavior—but actions (and paychecks) speak much louder than words. The sales agents will change behavior only when they have incentives to do so.

Another common solution is to require sales agents to obtain permission to reduce price below some specific threshold. To obtain permission to reduce price, sales agents would have to provide their supervisors with evidence that the price reduction is necessary. If done well, this solution can ensure that enough information is transferred to the manager so that she can prevent sales agents' making unprofitable price reductions.

FRANCHISING

We can understand the growth of franchising in the United States over the past 50 years as a solution to a particular principal–agent incentive conflict. The principal is the parent company that owns a popular brand, like McDonald's. As the company grows, it has a choice—it can open up company-owned stores, or it can let franchisees open and run stores. The franchisees then pay the company a fee for the right to use the parent company's brand.

Suppose you are advising the owner of a fast-food restaurant chain. This chain's owner is trying to decide whether to sell one of its company-owned restaurants, currently run by a salaried manager, to a franchisee. If the chain sells the store, the franchisee will manage it and pay the owner a fixed franchise fee for every year that he operates the store. Should the owner sell the store?

Of course, the answer is "It depends." In this case, it depends on whether the restaurant is worth more to the franchisee than it is to the chain, and this depends on whether the franchise organizational form is more profitable than the company-owned organizational form. With the company-owned structure, managers don't work as hard as they would if they owned the restaurant (moral hazard), and the salaried management job may have attracted a lazy manager (adverse selection).

These agency costs disappear once a franchisee owns the firm because the agent and the principal become one and the same. The franchisee works harder than a salaried manager because he gets to keep all profit after paying off his costs—including the franchise fee—and lazy managers rarely want to run a franchised restaurant. Running a franchised store can be thought of a strong form of incentive compensation—you turn a manager into an owner (franchisee) when you give him the profit from running the store.

However, the franchisee faces more risk than does a salaried manager and, as a consequence, will demand compensation in the form of a lower franchise fee. If the franchisee demands too much for bearing risk, then the store could be more valuable to the company than it is to the franchisee.[1]

Jointly, the parties can split a larger profit pie if they can figure out how to balance these concerns. At one extreme, the company-owned store with a salaried manager leads to shirking on the part of the agent—a type of moral hazard. It also leads to adverse selection because salaried jobs are more likely to attract lazy managers. The company may also incur costs to monitor the managers' actions.

At the other extreme, the franchise organizational form is analogous to an incentive-compensation scheme because the franchisee keeps every dollar he earns after paying off his costs. But if factors other than effort affect profit, this kind of incentive compensation also imposes extra risk on the agent for which he must be compensated.

Sharing contracts fall between these two extremes. Instead of a fixed franchise fee, the franchisor might demand a percentage of the revenue or profit of the restaurant. This arrangement reduces the risk of the franchise form by reducing the amount the franchisee pays to the franchisor when the store does poorly. However,

---

[1] The variability of franchisee profit represents risk, and the franchisee must be compensated for bearing this risk. Note also that the franchisor needs to be aware of the incentive conflict regarding quality. Franchisses have an incentive to free ride on the brand name of the franchisor by, for example, not cleaning bathrooms.

sharing contracts may also encourage some shirking because the franchisee no longer keeps every dollar he earns. The franchisee's marginal compensation diminishes, and he responds to the weakened incentive by shirking.

A FRAMEWORK FOR DIAGNOSING AND SOLVING PROBLEMS

Understanding the trade-offs between information and incentives is useful, but it still doesn't tell you how to identify and fix specific problems within an organization. For that you need to be able to find the source of the incentive conflict and come up with specific alternatives to reduce the associated agency costs. Then choose the alternative that gives you the highest profit.

To analyze principal–agent problems, begin with the bad decision that is causing the problem; then ask three questions:

1. Who is making the (bad) decision?
2. Did the employee have enough information to make a good decision?
3. Did he have the incentive to do so—that is, how is the employee evaluated and compensated?

The first question serves to identify where the problem occurred, while the second and third examine the employee's information and incentives. Remember that incentives have two parts: The performance evaluation scheme measures whether the individual is doing a good job; the compensation scheme ties rewards to performance.

Let's answer the three questions for the ASI example:

1. *Who is making the bad decision?* The art experts. They were negotiating rates that were too low.
2. *Did the decision makers have enough information to make good decisions?* Yes, they did have enough information to set profitable rates.
3. *Did the decision makers have the incentive to make good decisions?* No. The art experts received a flat salary, making it relatively easy for art owners to bribe them with gifts.

In general, answers to the three questions will suggest alternatives for reducing agency costs in three general ways: by (1) changing decision rights, (2) transferring information, and/or (3) changing incentives. In this case, we have two obvious solutions: Leave rate-setting authority with the art experts, but adopt stronger incentive compensation; or transfer rate-setting authority to a marketing executive, and then transfer crucial information to her. The first is a *decentralization* solution, and the second is a *centralization* solution.

To see how well you understand how to use the framework, imagine that you are called in as a consultant to a large retail chain of "general stores" that target low-income customers in cities having fewer than 50,000 people. As the company has grown, the CEO and the stock analysts who follow the company have noticed that newly opened stores are not meeting sales projections. The CEO wants you to find out what's causing the problem and fix it.

In the course of your investigation, you learn that the company uses "development" agents to find new store locations and negotiate leases with property owners. The company rewards these agents with generous stock options, provided they open 50 new stores in a single year. Although agents are supposed to open new stores only if the sales potential is at least $1 million per year, this is obviously not happening. Recently opened stores earn just half that much.

STOP. *Before continuing, try to identify the problem.*

Begin your analysis by asking the three questions.

1. *Who is making the bad decision?* The development agents. They were opening unprofitable stores.
2. *Did they have enough information to make a good decision?* Yes. The development agents had good information about whether the new stores would be profitable.
3. *Did they have the incentive to do so?* No. The agents got stock options for opening 50 stores each year, regardless of the new stores' profitability.

The problem is not with information but rather with the incentives of the agent, who's rewarded for opening stores regardless of profitability. Before you continue, suggest at least two solutions to the problem and choose the best one.

STOP. *Before continuing, try to fix the problem.*

You have at least two obvious solutions:

1. The company could change the incentives of the development agents by rewarding them for opening only *profitable* stores.
2. Or, the company could withdraw the authority to open stores from agents and then gather its own information about the potential profitability of new store sites.

The first choice would let the company continue to rely on the agents' specialized knowledge about promising locations for new stores. But this choice would be very unpopular with the agents, who would have to wait for a year of store operation before receiving their bonuses. In addition, this solution exposes the agents to risk beyond their control—their compensation would depend on the behavior of the store manager, as well as on the state of the national economy. The agent would have to be compensated for bearing this risk in the form of higher compensation, which is the usual trade-off between incentive compensation and risk.

In fact, the general store chain chose the second option. It developed a forecasting model to predict the profitability of new stores based on local demographic information and the locations of rival stores. Agents could open new store locations only if the model predicted sales exceeding $1 million.

If the model is good at predicting which stores are likely to be profitable, this solution will work well. But if the model cannot identify profitable locations, it will be a poor substitute for the agents' specialized knowledge or intuition about which new store locations are likely to be profitable. In this case, the model predicted well, and the problem disappeared.

SUMMARY & HOMEWORK PROBLEMS

SUMMARY OF MAIN POINTS

- **Principals** want **agents** to work in their (the principals') best interests, but agents typically have different goals than do principals. This is called **incentive conflict.**
- Incentive conflict leads to moral hazard and adverse selection problems when agents have better information than principals do.
- Three approaches to controlling incentive conflicts are
  - fixed payment and monitoring (shirking, adverse selection, and monitoring costs),
  - incentive pay and no monitoring (must compensate agents for bearing risk), or
  - sharing contract and some monitoring (some shirking and some risk compensation).
- In a well-run organization, decision makers have (1) the information necessary to make good decisions and (2) the incentive to do so.
- If you decentralize decision-making authority, you should strengthen incentive compensation schemes.
- If you centralize decision-making authority, you should make sure to transfer needed information to the decision makers.

- To analyze principal–agent conflicts, focus on three questions:
  - ○ Who is making the (bad) decisions?
  - ○ Does the employee have enough information to make good decisions?
  - ○ Does the employee have the incentive to make good decisions?
- Alternatives for controlling principal–agent conflicts center on one of the following:
  - ○ Reassigning decision rights
  - ○ Transferring information
  - ○ Changing incentives

MULTIPLE-CHOICE QUESTIONS

1. Your notebook computer's hard drive recently crashed, and you decide to take it to a local repair technician to have it fixed. In this relationship,
- **a.** you are the agent.
- **b.** the technician is the principal.
- **c.** the technician is the agent.
- **d.** no principal–agent relationship exists.

2. Principal–agent relationships
- **a.** reduce monitoring costs.
- **b.** occur because managers have good information about employees.
- **c.** are not related to asymmetric information.
- **d.** are subject to moral hazard problems.

3. Principal–agent problems
- **a.** occur when firm managers have more incentive to maximize profit than shareholders do.
- **b.** help explain why equity investments are an important financing source for firms.
- **c.** would not arise if firm owners had complete information about the actions of the firm's managers.
- **d.** All of the above.

4. Decentralization of decision-making authority is supported by which of the following?
- **a.** A trend of stronger, more active CEOs
- **b.** Shrinking costs of computing bandwidth, which allows information to be inexpensively aggregated from geographically diverse business units
- **c.** Development of microcomputing resources at the corporate, division, and employee level
- **d.** Reduction in the use of incentive compensation

5. You own a retail establishment run by a store manager who receives a flat salary of $80,000. If you set up another store as a franchise with incentive compensation to the franchisee, what would be a reasonable total compensation range that the franchisee could earn?

   a. $80,000
   b. $40,000–$80,000
   c. $60,000–$100,000
   d. $80,000–$100,000

INDIVIDUAL PROBLEMS

18-1. Real Estate Agents
When real estate agents sell their own, rather than clients', houses, they leave the houses on the market for a longer time (10 days longer on average) and wind up with better prices (2% higher on average). Why?

18-2. Incentive Compensation
Firm X is a small environmental consulting firm. The firm pays employees according to how much time they bill on projects. Because they are out in the field, in close contact with clients, employees also have opportunities to recognize client demands for new projects and to "sell" more projects to the clients. However, none of the employees makes the effort to do so. How would you change the organizational architecture of the firm to raise profitability?

18-3. Incentive Conflicts
Which of the following are characteristic of *principal–agent conflicts* that often exist in a firm? (*Note:* The entire statement must be true in order to be a correct answer.)

   a. Managers do not always operate in the best interest of owners because owners are generally more risk-averse than managers.
   b. Managers generally have a shorter time horizon than owners; thus, managers do not fully take into account the future long-run profitability of the firm.
   c. Managers do not always operate in the best interest of owners because managers care about the noncash benefits of their jobs.
   d. Firms can usually find solutions that reduce agency costs without increasing monitoring or bonding costs.

18-4. British Physicians
The British government offered physicians incentive pay to offer better customer (patient) service, such as managing appointments better. In particular, physicians can score "points" by seeing a patient within 48 hours after making an appointment. This year, each point brings £75; next year, it will be £120. Do you think this is a good incentive payment scheme?

18-5. Venture Capital

Venture capital (VC) firms are pools of private capital that typically invest in small, fast-growing companies, which usually can't raise funds through other means. In exchange for this financing, the VCs receive a share of the company's equity while the founders of the firm typically stay on and continue to manage the company.

a. Describe the nature of the incentive conflict between VCs and the managers, identifying the principal and the agent. VC investments have two typical components: (1) Managers maintain some ownership in the company and often earn additional equity if the company performs well; (2) VCs demand seats on the company's board.

b. Discuss how these two components help address the incentive conflict.

GROUP PROBLEMS

G18-1. Incentive Conflict

Describe an incentive conflict in your company. What is the source of the conflict, and how is it being controlled? Could you control it in a less costly way?

G18-2. Incentive Pay

Describe a job compensated with incentive pay in your company. What performance evaluation metric is used, and how is it tied to compensation? Does this compensation scheme align the incentives of the employee with the goals of the company? Estimate the agency costs of the scheme relative to the next best alternative.

G18-3. Centralization versus Decentralization

Describe a decision that is centralized (or decentralized) in your company. How could you decentralize (or centralize) the decision? What would happen if it were decentralized (or centralized)?

Chapter 19

Getting Divisions to Work in the Firm's Best Interests

In 1997, the managers of Acme Company's Paper Division were trying to decide what to do with black liquor soap, a by-product of paper manufacturing. The Paper Division normally sold the soap to the Resins Division using a transfer price—the price the buying division pays to the selling division. The Resins Division converted the soap into crude tall oil, which is required to manufacture certain resins. Obviously, a lower transfer price raises the buying (Resins) division's profit while simultaneously reducing the selling (Paper) division's profit, so each division's managers devoted considerable time and effort trying to persuade senior management that *their* preferred price was the appropriate transfer price.

Corporate headquarters favored the Resins Division with a low transfer price of $100 per unit.[1] This price was so low that the Paper Division decided to burn the soap for fuel instead of transferring it to the Resins Division because its value as a fuel to the Paper Division was $110. Although the Paper Division's profit increased due to lower fuel costs, the Resins Division's profit decreased because buying the black liquor soap on the open market at a price of $125 was more costly. On net, burning the soap decreased company-wide profit because black liquor soap was less valuable as fuel than it was as an input to resin manufacturing. To make matters worse, the Paper Division's burners, not designed to handle black-liquor soap, were in danger of exploding. When I heard this story in the fall of 1998, I can't say that I was hoping for an explosion. But it would have added a certain weight to my lectures—bad economics can kill, or something along those lines. Fortunately, however, corporate headquarters recognized the danger. Their "solution" was to construct a special furnace at a cost of $5 million to burn the soap.

The moral of this story is that incentive conflicts between divisions can reduce the parent company's profit. In this case, a low transfer price prevented the movement of an asset (black liquor soap) to a higher-valued use (resin manufacturing). Remember the one lesson of business: Find an asset in a

---

[1] The prices of black liquor soap are completely fictitious and are provided for illustration purposes only.

lower-valued use, and try to figure out a way to profitably move it to a higher-valued use. In this case, the incentive conflict between divisions of the same parent company destroyed wealth by sending the black liquor soap to a lower-valued use (burned as a fuel instead of as a valuable input into resin manufacturing). Here, we apply the lessons from Chapter 18 to show you how to control the incentive conflict between the various divisions of the same company.

INCENTIVE CONFLICT BETWEEN DIVISIONS

Incentive conflicts need not reduce a parent company's profit. In fact, these kinds of conflicts inevitably arise while doing business. Without much extra work, we can apply the framework set up in Chapter 18 for diagnosing and solving principal–agent problems to diagnose and solve problems between parent companies and their various subdivisions. The only difference is that we "personify" the divisions and think of them as rational, self-interested agents. We begin by asking the same three questions:

1. Which division is making the bad decision?
2. Does the division have enough information to make a good decision?
3. Does the division have the incentive to do so?

We asked these same questions about employers (principals) and employees (agents) in the last chapter; now, however, we're focused on the parent company (principal) and the division (agent). The idea of a division's making decisions and responding to incentives requires some explanation. Division managers make decisions for the division, and, typically, the division manager's compensation is tied to the division's performance. So, to understand divisions' incentives, we have to understand how the parent company evaluates the division and how the division's compensation is tied to its performance evaluation metric.

The incentive conflict between the Resins Division and Paper Division arose because the transfer price raised the profit of one division while simultaneously reducing the other's profit. In other words, because profit was the source of the incentive conflict, we can infer that the company evaluated division managers based on division profit. Otherwise, the transfer price would not have been a source of conflict.

> A **profit center** is a division whose parent company evaluates it on the basis of the profit it earns.

The virtue of a profit center is that it largely runs by itself. The parent company looks at division revenue, subtracts division costs, and evaluates division management based on the difference. Because the parent company has a good performance evaluation metric, it's relatively easy to tie pay to performance. Ordinarily, the parent company gives division managers extraordinary discretion because the parent knows that the managers' incentives (division profit) closely align with company goals—company-wide profit. Such incentive compensation allows the principal (parent company) to avoid the costs of monitoring its agents (division managers).

But as our paper company illustrates, problems can arise between separate profit centers. Let's see how well our framework does in analyzing problems between divisions:

1. *Who is making the bad decision?* The Paper Division made the bad decision to burn the soap for fuel instead of transferring it to the Resins Division.[2]

2. *Did they have enough information to make a good decision?* The Paper Division had enough information to know that the soap's value as fuel was below its value as an input to resin manufacturing.

3. *Did they have the incentive to make a good decision?* The Paper Division received a reward for increasing its own profit, not the profit of the Resin Division.

The three answers clearly show that Paper profited from burning the soap, but the parent company lost profit because the transfer price was below the soap's value as a fuel.

Once you understand the problem, you can employ the familiar solutions—changing decision rights, moving information, or altering incentives. One obvious solution is simply to raise the transfer price of black liquor soap. But the problem with this solution is information. Does senior management at the parent company have enough information to set a good transfer price? If senior management has to rely on the divisions for information about the correct transfer price, they almost invite competition between the two divisions.[3]

Another possible solution is to change the incentives of the Paper Division so that it is evaluated based on parent company profit. This would eliminate their incentive to do things that reduce company profit, but it might also create a free riding problem. Division managers might exert less effort because their compensation is less closely linked to division profit.[4]

Another solution would be to give the Paper Division the right to sell black liquor soap to the external market if its managers couldn't negotiate

---

[2] The decision is "bad" from the perspective of the parent company because it results in lower overall profit. From the perspective of the Paper Division, the decision to burn the fuel was reasonable.

[3] Using this solution would also require that you make sure senior management has the correct incentive to set a good transfer price.

[4] This solution would also expose the managers to additional risk, likely requiring additional compensation.

favorable terms with Resins. With this simple organizational change, the Paper Division's incentives align more closely with those of the parent company. Under these terms, the Paper Division would burn the by-product only if its value as a fuel exceeds the price of black liquor soap on the open market—which is exactly the decision that increases parent company profit. Additionally, this organizational change means that senior management need not spend time resolving disputes between divisions about the magnitude of the transfer price.

Choosing the best solution depends on the magnitude of all the costs and benefits of the various solutions. In this case, the last solution appears to be the best, but only because no downside effects are readily apparent.

This story has a happy ending (and no explosions). Soon after the company had the burners redesigned to handle black liquor soap, an increase in the price of energy raised the soap's value as a fuel, making it profitable to burn. So the company's initial mistake became profitable owing to an unforeseen increase in energy prices. In other words, the company got lucky. It's still important to redesign the organization because the problem will reappear when the price of energy falls. Allowing the Paper Division's managers to do what they want with the soap would ensure that they'd quit burning the soap if energy prices were to fall and sell it to the Resins Division instead.

TRANSFER PRICING

The story of the black liquor soap is all too common. Transfer pricing is a contentious issue for almost any company that forces one division to buy from another at fixed transfer prices. Together with corporate budgeting (a topic we'll cover later in this chapter), transfer pricing causes more conflict among divisions than almost any other issue. To illustrate another, perhaps more typical, transfer pricing conflict, let's stick with our paper company and examine the transfer of paper from the upstream Paper Division to the downstream Cardboard Box Division. Paper is the most costly input to cardboard box fabrication.

When two profit centers negotiate a transfer price, sometimes the divisions bargain so hard that they reach an impasse. In this case, the downstream Box Division might purchase from an external supplier, even though the parent company would find it more profitable for the Box Division to purchase from the Paper Division. And even if the divisions reach agreement, the cost of interdivision haggling may exceed any benefit the company derives from the product transfer.

To reduce such costs, the paper company set the transfer price high enough to guarantee a 25% contribution margin[5] on paper sales. Although this decision ensured that the Paper Division transferred the paper to the Box Division, the transfer price also raised the costs of the downstream Box Division, making the boxes difficult to sell.

To understand the effects of a high transfer price we have to examine how it affects the downstream Box Division, as shown in Figure 19-1. If the Paper Division produces paper at a marginal cost of $100, it transfers the paper to the Box Division at a price of $125; this price includes a markup over marginal cost of 25%. The downstream Box Division counts the transfer price as part of its costs and makes all sales where MR > MC + $25. Again, the $25 represents the markup that Paper Division builds into the transfer price, and MC is the true marginal cost of boxes without the markup. This is a higher threshold for making sales than the profit-maximizing threshold, MR > MC. In other words, under this pricing scheme, the Box Division makes fewer sales, and charges higher prices, than would maximize parent profit. As a result, the Box Division loses a lot of sales to its main rival. The reduced sales of the Box Division also lead to reduced demand for paper, with

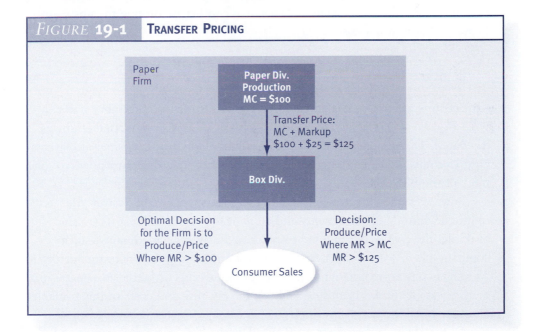

FIGURE **19-1**   **TRANSFER PRICING**

Paper Firm

Paper Div. Production MC = $100

Transfer Price: MC + Markup $100 + $25 = $125

Box Div.

Optimal Decision for the Firm is to Produce/Price Where MR > $100

Decision: Produce/Price Where MR > MC MR > $125

Consumer Sales

[5] Computed as (price − MC)/MC.

the result that both the Paper Division and the Box Division operate well below capacity.

Note that this problem is the opposite of the one faced by a marketing division in Chapter 18. Recall that its sales agents made more sales and charged lower prices than they would have had they been maximizing company-wide profit. In this case, the downstream division made fewer sales and charged a higher price than they would have if they were maximizing profit—all because of an inflated resource transfer price.

To identify the source of the problem, we ask our three questions:

1. *Who is making the bad decision?* The Paper Division is charging too much for paper. This raises the cost of the downstream boxes, reducing downstream sales and profit.
2. *Did the division have enough information to make a good decision?* Both divisions are familiar enough with the other's operations to have enough information to know better.
3. *Did the division have the incentive to do so?* The divisions are run as separate profit centers, so they will work to increase profit of their own divisions.

The analysis makes clear that the conflict arises because two profit centers are each trying to extract profit from a single product. One way of solving this problem would be to eliminate the incentive conflict by turning the upstream Paper Division into a cost center.

A **cost center** *receives rewards for reducing the cost of producing a specified output.*

Cost centers are not evaluated based on the profit they earn, so they don't care what the transfer price is. Specifically, if the Paper Division became (and was evaluated as) a cost center, its managers would gladly transfer paper at marginal cost. And this would cause the downstream division to reduce box prices to their most profitable level.

But cost centers have problems, too. As always, the right answer "depends" on the magnitude of the benefits and costs of the relevant alternatives. For example, the cost center may try to reduce cost by reducing quality, so the company may have to add a quality control and testing facility to the factory. As long as this kind of monitoring is not prohibitively costly, the cost center may be the best solution. But this depends on the benefits and costs of the available alternatives.

As we might expect, once our Paper Division became a cost center and began transferring paper at marginal cost, the Box Division began winning more jobs from its rivals. Ironically, though, the Box Division's success set off a price war[6] in the industry, lowering profit for everyone. It took the industry five years to recover.

FUNCTIONAL SILOS VERSUS PROCESS TEAMS

Many firms are organized into functional divisions. Adam Smith's pin factory and Henry Ford's automobile assembly line are classic examples of production processes that divide tasks into narrow functional steps.

> A *functionally organized firm* is one in which various divisions perform separate tasks, such as production and sales.

Functional organization offers firms the advantage that workers develop functional expertise and can easily share information within their division. Functional divisions also make it easy to tie pay to performance because performance is narrowly defined and thus relatively easy to measure. *Piece-rate pay*—compensation based on the number of units a worker produces—is an example of such a simple measurement scheme.

In a functionally organized firm, the company's success depends on each division coordinating its particular task with other divisions. Without strong management oversight to ensure that divisions are working toward a common goal, problems can arise. Consider the efforts of a functionally divided company to design and build a new turbine jet engine. The Engineering Division designs the engine, the Production Division manufactures it, and the Finance Division decides how much to charge for it. The engineers came up with a radical new design incorporating hollow fan blades. The award-winning design required less fuel than conventional engines, but the hollow fan blades were very difficult to build. When the Finance Division finally computed the cost of the engine, it discovered that the new engines were much more expensive than rival engines, even after accounting for the expected fuel savings. The lack of coordination between the divisions resulted in a product whose cost was higher than its value.

A similar coordination problem arose at a midsized regional bank divided into a Loan Origination Division (LOD) and a Loan Servicing Division (LSD). The LOD identifies potential borrowers, lends money to them, and then hands them over to the LSD. The LSD collects interest on the loan and makes sure that borrowers repay the loans as payments come due. However, the bank had a problem—an unusually high number of defaults.

---

[6] Mikhail Shor, "Double Marginalization as a Collusive Device," Vanderbilt working paper, September 1, 2002.

Again, let's ask our three questions to diagnose the problem:

1. *Who is making the bad decision?* The Loan Origination Division was making risky loans.
2. *Did the LOD have enough information to make a good decision?* The LOD could have verified the credit status of the borrowers easily.
3. *Did the LOD have the incentive to do so?* The parent bank evaluated the LOD managers on the amount of money they were able to lend. They had no incentive to verify credit status.

The analysis makes the source of the conflict clear: The Loan Origination Division was paid to make loans, regardless of profitability.

We could change the incentives of the LOD so that its managers are rewarded for making profitable loans only. But this kind of change is difficult to implement because unprofitable loans become obvious only when the borrowers don't repay the loans, often after a period of many years.

We could adopt a solution similar to the one used by the General Store whose development agents were opening unprofitable stores. If we could design a good predictor of whether the loan would be profitable, we could let the LOD make loans only when the model predicts a good chance of repayment.

Another solution, one that banks commonly use, is to put the origination and servicing personnel in the same division, essentially reorganizing the bank into an M-form company:

> An **M-form firm** *is one whose divisions perform all the tasks necessary to serve customers of a particular product or in a particular geographic area.*

In a bank, an M-form reorganization might consist of two divisions, one focused on both originating and servicing residential loans and the other focused on commercial loans. In each division, the profit of the loans originated and served would determine the managers' evaluation and subsequent rewards.

In fact, our bank decided to do just that—reorganize as an M-form. Not only did the number of bad loans decrease, but the speed of decision making increased. The M-form organization made it relatively easy for the divisions to respond to the changing demands in local markets because its managers no longer had to coordinate with a sister division who shared responsibility for the customer. The bank also found it easier to develop long-term customer relationships because borrowers always dealt with the same person, whose responsibility included origination and servicing.

BUDGET GAMES: PAYING PEOPLE TO LIE[7]

Corporate budgets can provide a valuable mechanism for transferring information among divisions that need to coordinate with one another. Consider a toy company in which the sales division's managers submit a budget that includes a forecast of the number and types of toys they expect to sell in the upcoming holiday season. The manufacturing division's managers use the sales forecast to plan production for the coming year. An accurate sales forecast means that the company will produce the right amount and types of goods in time for the holiday demand. At least, that's how the process is supposed to work.

In reality, a very different exercise usually occurs. It begins with the stock analysts who follow the company and set profit and sales expectations for the coming year. If the company doesn't meet their expectations, the stock analysts change their recommendation to investors from a "buy" to a "hold" or, worse, to a "sell" rating. This low rating reduces demand for the stock and causes its price to fall, often precipitously.

The CEO and top management understand this process and do everything they can to meet the analysts' expectations because the executives' evaluations often depend on how well the stock price performs. Their compensation may even include stock options, the value of which reflects the stock price. But even in cases without explicit incentive compensation, top management labors under an implied threat that the board of directors will fire them if the stock does poorly.

To meet stock analysts' expectations, senior managers adopt the analysts' aggregate earnings (profit) forecast as their budget for the coming year. To make sure that all division managers do their part in meeting company-wide profit goals, senior managers assign responsibility for meeting profit goals to each division. To motivate lower-level managers to meet division budgets, they promise big bonuses if these managers meet or exceed profit goals. So, in essence, stock market analysts drive budget goals, pushing them down to senior managers to lower-level managers.

To see how this process might cause problems, put yourself in the place of a division manager who has good information about how much her division can earn. If the budget goal is above what she thinks she can earn, she complains to senior managers that her goal is unreachable. Even if the goal is below what she thinks she can earn, she still complains because she doesn't want the goal to be revised upward. In fact, she always has an incentive to try to reduce the targets to make them easier to reach. As a consequence, the budget process fails in its

---

[7] This section was inspired by the ideas of Michael Jensen, "Paying People to Lie: The Truth about the Budgeting Process," HBS Working Paper 01-072, September 2001. An executive summary of this paper entitled "Corporate Budgeting Is Broken, Let's Fix It" was published in the *Harvard Business Review* (November 2001).

most basic function—transferring information from those who have it to those who need it.

When budgets are used to coordinate activities among the various divisions of a firm, this lack of information can cause problems. For example, if the Marketing Division of the toy manufacturer argues successfully for a low budgeted sales goal for its product in order to make it easier to qualify for the bonus, the Manufacturing Division may produce too little of a popular item just as the holiday season begins.

And the problems do not end there. Bonuses are tied to reaching specific budget goals. Once the goal is set, a division may accelerate sales or delay costs to make sure that it can meet the goal. For example, a division's managers may ship products to retail outlets near the end of the year and record these shipments as "sales," just so they can reach their budget. They do this despite knowing that the items will be returned later.

Alternatively, division managers who have already met their goals—or those who know they have no chance of meeting their goals—will delay sales or accelerate costs to make it easier to meet next year's goals. And these practices can generate real losses for the parent company. If, for example, a division tries to persuade a customer to delay purchasing a new piece of equipment, that customer might purchase from a rival instead of waiting to place the order with the division's firm.

Fortunately, these problems have a relatively simple solution. Instead of using a pay-for-performance scheme that rewards managers only if they reach a specific goal, use a linear compensation scheme that doesn't have sharp kinks in it. A linear compensation scheme always rewards managers for increasing sales, regardless of how many they have already sold. In other words, it removes the incentive to shirk once the goal is reached, or if the manager has no chance of meeting the goal.

Consider the difference between two compensation schemes illustrated in Figure 19-2 and Figure 19-3 (adapted from Michael Jensen's very interesting article called "Paying People to Lie: The Truth about the Budgeting Process"). Figure 19-2 is a fairly typical compensation scheme that pays division managers a bonus when they reach a minimum profit goal (e.g., a $20,000 bonus for reaching $4 million in profit). Note the kink in the compensation scheme. This kink gives division managers an incentive to lie—to convince the parent company to set the goal low, to make it easier to reach, and thus earn a bonus. If division managers have better information than the parent company, this kind of scheme encourages managers to lie about the information they have.

Figure 19-3 shows the solution to the budget-gaming problem: Remove all kinks from the compensation schedule. Straight-line pay-for-performance

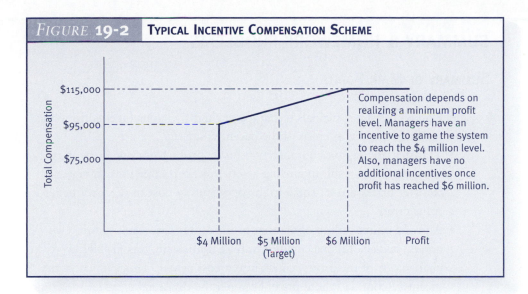

FIGURE **19-2**   **TYPICAL INCENTIVE COMPENSATION SCHEME**

Compensation depends on realizing a minimum profit level. Managers have an incentive to game the system to reach the $4 million level. Also, managers have no additional incentives once profit has reached $6 million.

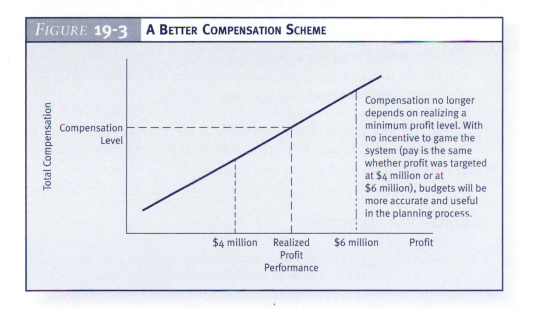

FIGURE **19-3**   **A BETTER COMPENSATION SCHEME**

Compensation no longer depends on realizing a minimum profit level. With no incentive to game the system (pay is the same whether profit was targeted at $4 million or at $6 million), budgets will be more accurate and useful in the planning process.

functions eliminate division managers' incentives to lie about the budget because compensation does not depend on meeting a particular budget goal. Managers get rewards for doing more and punished for doing less, no matter where they are relative to the budget target. This compensation scheme keeps pressure on managers to meet and exceed goals, no matter how big the goals are and eliminates the perverse incentive to hide information.

SUMMARY & HOMEWORK PROBLEMS

SUMMARY OF MAIN POINTS

- Companies are principals trying to get their divisions (agents) to work profitably in the interests of the parent company.
- Transfer pricing does not merely transfer profit from one division to another; it can result in moving assets to lower-value uses. Efficient transfer prices are set equal to the opportunity cost of the asset being transferred.
- A **profit center** on top of another profit center can result in too few goods' being sold; one common way of addressing this problem is to change one of the profit centers into a **cost center.** This eliminates the incentive conflict (about price) between the divisions.
- Companies with functional divisions share functional expertise within a division and can more easily evaluate and reward division employees. However, change is costly, and senior management must coordinate the activities of the various divisions.
- Process teams are built around a multifunction task and are evaluated based on the success of the project on which they are working.
- When divisions are rewarded for reaching a budget threshold, they have an incentive to lie to make the threshold as low as possible, thus ensuring they get their bonuses. In addition, they will often pull sales into the present, and push costs into the future, to make sure they reach the threshold level.

MULTIPLE-CHOICE QUESTIONS

1. A computer manufacturer has two divisions, one serving residential customers and one serving business customers. If an incentive conflict arises between the two divisions, how will overall company profits be affected?
  a. Profits will fall.
  b. Profits will rise.
  c. Profits may either rise or fall.
  d. The conflict has no potential to affect overall profit.

2. Joe runs the Service Division for a car dealership. The overall dealership has profits of $10 million on sales of $100 million and costs of $90 million. Joe's division contributed

$9 million in sales and $7 million in costs. If the Service Division is evaluated as a profit center, what dollar amount is most relevant to Joe?

   a. $2 million
   b. $7 million
   c. $9 million
   d. $10 million

3. As the CEO of a large multidivisional company, it falls to you to set a transfer price between your Materials Division and your Production Division. Which cost is most relevant in making your decision?

   a. Average cost
   b. Average avoidable cost
   c. Direct cost
   d. Opportunity cost

4. Which of the following organizational forms requires the strongest management oversight?

   a. Profit centers
   b. Functional organizations
   c. M-form organizations
   d. Functional and M-form organizations likely require similar oversight.

5. Which of the following actions is consistent with a manager whose compensation reflects a specific budget goal and who does not believe he can make that goal?

   a. Asking a vendor to preship and invoice materials for the following year
   b. Discovering a "problem" in the order-taking process, thereby forcibly pushing sales into the ensuing year
   c. Increasing accounting reserve estimates, leading to higher recognized expenses
   d. All of the above

INDIVIDUAL PROBLEMS

19-1. Divisional Profit Measure
Discuss the advantages and disadvantages of using divisional profit as the basis of incentive compensation for division managers compared to using company profit as the basis.

19-2. Furniture Forecasting
Futura Furniture Products manufactures upscale office furniture for the "Office of the Future." In addition to a manufacturing division, the company includes a sales division comprised of regionally based sales offices. Sales representatives, who report to regional sales managers, conduct direct sales efforts with firms in their own regions. As part of the sales process, representatives gather information about likely future orders and convey that information back to the regional sales managers. Sales managers use that information to create sales forecasts, which are used as the basis for manufacturing schedules.

Sales representatives are compensated on a salary plus commission (percentage of revenue as pricing is centrally controlled), and sales managers are compensated based on salary plus commission. Sales manager commission is calculated based on regional sales that exceed the forecasted budget.

One of Futura's key products is the DeskPod. Corporate managers are concerned that the DeskPod forecasts are always very inaccurate for this very important item, causing extreme havoc in the manufacturing process. How are the forecasts likely to be inaccurate? What do you think is driving this inaccuracy? How might this problem be solved?

19-3. Jet Turbine Design

This problem is mentioned in the text (see the section on "Functional Silos versus Process Teams"). Your task is to propose an organizational solution. To briefly recap, a manufacturer is trying to design the next generation of turbine engines for jet airplanes. The company is divided along functional lines. Engineering designs the engine, production manufactures it, and finance figures out how much to charge for it. The engineers invented a radical new design that used hollow fan blades. The award-winning design used less fuel than conventional engines, but the hollow fan blades were very difficult to build. When the Finance Division computed the marginal cost of an engine, it discovered that the new engines were much more expensive than rival engines, even accounting for the expected fuel savings. No one purchased the engine. How would you make sure that this problem does not recur?

19-4. Bank Transfer Pricing

Banks earn money by borrowing from depositors at low interest rates and lending to individuals and businesses at high interest rates. As banks grow, they split into functional divisions that either generate deposits or make loans. To measure the profitability of each division, banks use transfer pricing. For example, if a deposit costs 5%, a loan earns 8%, and the transfer price is 6%, then the deposit division earns 1% times the size of the deposit, and the loan division earns 2% times the size of the loan. Normally, loans and deposits of shorter maturities (less than one year) earn and pay lower interest rates, while those of longer maturities (more than one year) pay higher interest rates. This is illustrated in the following table, which shows four types of customers: those who want one- and five-year loans, and those who want one- and five-year deposits. Assume equal numbers of each consumer type, and each wants to borrow or deposit $100,000.

	One-year Rates	**Five-year Rates**
Deposits	2%	5%
Loans	4%	7%

a. If the bank sets a single transfer price between the deposit and the loan divisions, what is the profit-maximizing transfer price or range of prices and what is the bank's maximum profit? (*Hint*: The amount of total deposits must equal the amount of total loans.)

b. Do you see any problem with this kind of performance evaluation scheme? (*Hint*: What happens to bank profit if one-year rates rise?) How can the bank solve the problems by changing its performance evaluation scheme?

19-5. Transfer Pricing

Suppose that a paper mill "feeds" a downstream box mill. For the downstream mill, the *marginal profitability* of producing boxes declines with volume. For example, the first unit of boxes increases earnings by $10, the second $9, the third, $7, and so on, until the tenth unit increases profit by just $1. The cost the upstream mill incurs for producing enough paper to make one unit of boxes is $3.50.

a. If the two companies are separate profit centers, and the upstream paper mill sets a single transfer price (the price the box company pays the paper mill), what price will it set, and how much money will the company make?

b. If the paper mill were forced to transfer at marginal cost, how much money would the company make?

GROUP PROBLEMS

G19-1. Transfer Pricing

Does your company use transfer pricing to "charge" divisions for the cost of the products they consume? Are these prices set equal to the opportunity cost of the product? Why or why not? Can you think of a better organizational architecture? Compute the profit consequences of changing the organizational architecture.

G19-2. Divisional Evaluation

Discuss a division or subunit of your organization and how it is evaluated (revenue center, profit center, cost center, etc.). How does the evaluation scheme affect performance? If it is optimal, explain why. Otherwise, explain why you think it is suboptimal, and recommend what you would do if you were free to change it.

G19-3. Budget Games

Does your company tie compensation to meeting a budget? If so, what kind of problems does this practice cause? What can you do to fix these problems? Compute the profit consequences of changing the process.

G19-4. Functional Silos versus Process Teams

Is your company organized around functional divisions? If so, what kind of problems does this cause? What can you do to fix these problems? Compute the profit consequences of fixing the problem.

Chapter 20

Managing Vertical Relationships

Consider a large regulated power company, United Consolidated (UC) Power and Light. UC's managers want to purchase the mine that supplies the company with coal. If you were hired as an investment banker to advise the company, would you recommend the acquisition?

The first question to ask is "Is this a potentially profitable transaction?" The answer depends on whether the assets are moving to a higher-valued use.

> *Unless the assets are worth more to the buyer than they are to the seller, there's no reason to transact.*

In this case, UC has a clever plan to make money. After purchasing the coal mine, they'd form a multidivisional company with a parent company directing the Coal Division to raise the price of coal sold to its own Power Division. Ordinarily, increasing the price of coal would raise the Coal Division's profit while simultaneously reducing the Power Division's profit. But in this case, the move allows the merged company to evade the regulation that limits its profit.

Here's how it works. Government regulations allow UC to charge its power customers prices just high enough to earn a 9% return on its invested capital. With $1 billion invested in capital equipment, the Power Division can earn $90 million each year, computed as the margin (price minus marginal cost) multiplied by the amount of electricity sold. When the price of coal increases, its costs go up, and the Power Division's profit falls below $90 million. Under the regulation, the company is allowed to raise the price of electricity until its profit goes back up to $90 million. The net effect of the higher coal price is that the Coal Division earns more, while the Power Division profit doesn't change. Because the power company can use the acquisition to evade this regulation, the coal mine is worth more to the power company than it is to its current owners.

Many regulations are worth evading, especially those erected to protect incumbent firms from the forces of competition. Sales-below-cost laws that prevent new competitors, like Wal-Mart, from selling gasoline at low prices fall into this category. State legislators typically pass these laws at the request of incumbent gas stations to make it difficult for new competitors to enter a market and reduce price. But other regulations are ostensibly designed to protect consumers in cases where competition doesn't work as well as we would like. Despite their mixed record (see Chapter 2 for stories of well-intentioned regulations that do more harm than good), these regulatory restraints are designed to help consumers. In this chapter, we do not take a view of whether evading regulation is good or bad for consumers. Instead, we focus on the effects of regulatory evasion on firm profit because it offers one of the simplest and most readily understood reasons for vertical integration. It is obvious why the vertically integrated firm is more profitable than two independently run firms who buy from, or sell to, each other. In addition, regulatory evasion is not uncommon and should be anticipated—especially if you're a customer of a regulated industry.

In this chapter, we examine acquisitions and other kinds of contractual relationships between firms located at adjacent stages along the vertical supply chain, running from raw materials down to finished goods. We examine the means and motives for vertical relationships, as well as the laws governing such relationships. Vertical relationships can increase profit by giving firms a way to evade regulation, eliminate the double-markup problem, better align the incentives of manufacturers and retailers, and price discriminate.

DO *NOT* BUY A CUSTOMER OR SUPPLIER SIMPLY BECAUSE THEY ARE PROFITABLE

Before we turn to the reasons that make vertical acquisitions profitable, let's begin with a warning—one that most of you will forget when you face the opportunity to buy a profitable customer or supplier.

> *Purchasing a profitable upstream supplier or downstream customer will not necessarily increase your profit.*

Rather, it depends on what you pay. The current owners will likely value the company properly through a discounted cash flow analysis, so you'll be paying a price exactly equal to the value of the company's profit stream. If the profit of the acquired firm is high, the purchase price will be high, and vice versa. The current owners will also likely have better information than potential buyers about the size of this profit stream, so adverse selection is a problem (current owners tend to sell only when the buyers pay too much).

> *Without some kind of synergy that makes the assets more valuable to the buyer than they are to current owners, the acquisition will not be profitable.*

Based on the stock price reactions following acquisition announcements, about three-quarters of all acquisitions are unprofitable. The acquired firms gain slightly, but this gain is more than offset by the acquiring firm's loss.

But even if acquisitions turn out to be unprofitable, this doesn't necessarily mean that acquiring the company was the wrong thing to do at the time. In 1999, for example, AT&T purchased the cable assets of Tele-Communications, Inc. (TCI), for $97 billion, anticipating that the acquisition would allow them to offer local telephone service through TCI's cable lines. Three years later, the technology failed to develop as expected, so AT&T sold the old TCI cable assets to Comcast for just $60 billion.

AT&T purchased the company because it anticipated a synergy. After that synergy failed to materialize, it sold the assets and moved on. A lesser firm might have held onto the assets to avoid the embarrassment of publicizing a $37 billion mistake—a version of the sunk-cost fallacy.

More typically, purchasing firms underestimate the costs of integrating newly acquired assets into the firm. An acquisition creates a more complex organization, raising the costs of running the organization. As Chapter 19 has illustrated, these costs may be considerable. For example, acquisitions often require redesigning the entire company by changing some divisions from profit centers to cost centers, and these changes can cost more than the value of the synergies created.

EVADING REGULATION

Not only does regulatory evasion offer one of the simplest and most understandable reasons for vertical integration, but it also illustrates how a variety of related strategies can accomplish the same thing.

> *If unrealized profit exists at one stage of the vertical supply chain—as often happens when regulations limit profit—a firm can capture some of the unrealized profit by integrating vertically, by tying, by bundling, or by excluding competitors.*

Let's return to the simple example of rent control. Suppose a rent-controlled apartment has a price ceiling of $1,000, meaning that city regulations require that the apartment rent for less than $1,000 per month. If a renter is willing to pay $1,500 per month, the landlord has an incentive to evade the price regulation by "bundling" the apartment, say, with furniture or by tying the apartment rental to furniture rental. In the first case (**bundling**), the landlord offers a "furnished apartment" for $1,500; in the latter (**tying**), the landlord requires the renter to rent furniture from the landlord for an additional $500.

Preventing rival furniture sellers from selling to the tenant—**exclusion**—could accomplish the same thing. If a building owner can make it costly or difficult for rival furniture sellers to sell to the tenant, the tenant can purchase furniture only from the landlord, so the landlord can capture the unrealized profit through overpriced furniture sales.

Regulators usually anticipate these strategies, often requiring unbundled pricing, or they make it illegal to tie the sale of a regulated good to the sale of an unregulated one. To thwart exclusionary tactics, the regulators mandate access for rival sellers. For example, local phone companies that also sell long-distance service have to allow rival long distance firms to sell long-distance service to the local phone company's customers. This prevents the local phone company from evading rate regulation by excluding rival long-distance companies.

Vertically integrated multinational companies use similar schemes to evade national corporate profit taxes. A company manufacturing shirts in Mexico, for example, can transfer the shirts at a low price to a sister division located in the Cayman Islands. This sister division then ships the shirts, at a high price, to the United States where they're sold to final consumers. The company reduces its tax burden by choosing to realize most of their profit in the Cayman Islands, which has lower taxes than Mexico.

Regulators in Mexico anticipate this strategy and force goods to be sold for at least a 5% markup over cost before they are transferred out of the country. This forces the company to realize at least some of its profit in Mexico.

ELIMINATE THE DOUBLE MARKUP

Gasoline refiners, like ExxonMobil, sell branded gasoline both to independently owned gas stations and to company-owned stations. Gas stations receive gasoline by truck at a delivered price, called the *dealer tank wagon* (DTW) price, or pick it up themselves at the "rack" with their own trucks and pay what is known as a *rack* or *wholesale price*. A refiner makes money by selling wholesale gasoline, to independently owned stations at a price above marginal cost.

Since the refiner marks up rack prices, the gas sold by independently-owned gas stations has a double markup, one imposed by the refiner and the other, by the retailer. So the price is higher than the price that maximizes profit for both firms. This problem should sound familiar, as it is analogous to the pricing of commonly owned complementary products (see Chapter 10); it is also analogous to the problem of transfer pricing above marginal cost (see Chapter 19). The gasoline refiner can solve the problem by purchasing the retail outlet and setting the optimal retail price.

We can analyze this problem more generally as a prisoners' dilemma faced by any two firms in the same vertical supply chain or by any two firms selling complementary goods. We often think of vertically related goods as complementary because consumers demand both together, not one or the other. In this case, consumers want the gas, and they want the retail outlet to dispense it.

TABLE 20-1	VERTICAL PRICING DILEMMA		
		Refiner	
		Price High	Price Low
Gas Station Price High		0, 0	4, −2
Price Low		−2, 4	2, 2

We diagram the game in Table 20-1. The only Nash equilibrium is the upper left cell of the table. Both firms try to capture a bigger piece of the profit pie by pricing high; but when both price high, they collectively reduce profit. Just as in the horizontal dilemma, firms end up hurting themselves by following their self-interests.

When firms producing complementary products compete with each other, they price too high.

The firms could increase their profit by coordinating to reduce price (which would take them to the lower right cell); fortunately, such coordination is both legal and common, at least in the United States.[1] Unlike the horizontal pricing dilemma in Chapter 13, where price rose following coordinated pricing among substitute products, here price falls following pricing coordination. The difference is that the firms are eliminating competition among complementary, not substitute, products.

Vertical integration offers a means of coordination that solves the double-markup problem. In fact, vertical integration is common in the gasoline industry: Manufacturers (refiners) purchase retail outlets (gas stations) for this reason. Some states, however, have laws preventing refineries from purchasing gas stations. In these states, gas prices average three cents per gallon higher than those in states that permit vertical integration. This differential translates into hundreds of millions of extra dollars that consumers who live in regulated states must pay each year.[2] The Federal Trade Commission spends time pointing out the perverse consequences of these laws to state legislators, which sometimes shames them into not passing them. If you live in Hawaii, Connecticut, Delaware, Maryland, Nevada, Virginia, or the District of Columbia, you may want to complain to your state legislator about higher gas prices caused by your state's *vertical divorcement* laws.

---

[1] In Europe, the antitrust authorities are only beginning to treat such vertical constraints with tolerance. See http://europa.eu.int/rapid/start/cgi/guesten.ksh?p_action.gettxt=gt&doc=IP/99/286|0|RAPID&lg=EN.

[2] Michael G. Vita, "Regulatory Restrictions on Vertical Integration and Control: The Competitive Impact of Gasoline Divorcement Policies," *Journal of Regulatory Economics* 18, no. 3 (November 2000): 217–233.

ALIGNING RETAILER INCENTIVES WITH THE GOALS OF MANUFACTURERS[3]

When a manufacturer and a retailer have differing incentives to provide effort to generate additional sales, a manufacturer may put limits on competition between its own retailers to guarantee them a higher profit. This higher profit increases the incentive of retailers to provide demand-enhancing services that generate additional sales.

Restrictions on intrabrand competition can enhance interbrand competition.

Eliminating competition among retailers selling the same brands can make the brands more attractive. Consider the plight of a manufacturer of high-end electronic equipment, such as cameras or computers, whose potential customers require expert assistance to select the proper product. Without such assistance from retailers, consumers frequently choose not to purchase. The manufacturer's problem is how to design incentives for retailers to invest in training for its sales people. Then, once the retailer has trained its salespeople, the manufacturer must find ways to motivate those same sales people to provide high-level in-store assistance for the manufacturer's products.

The incentive conflict arises because retailers have less incentive to engage in sales generation efforts than does the manufacturer. For example, when a manufacturer's profit margin is large relative to the retailer's (as is often the case for branded products), the retailer provides a lower level of promotion than is optimal from the manufacturer's point of view.[4]

A similar incentive conflict arises over the costs of maintaining product quality. Because retailers do not reap all of the benefit from a manufacturer's reputation, they have less incentive to incur the costs necessary to maintain the brand reputation.[5] The classic example is McDonald's reputation for clean bathrooms. The reputation encourages travelers to stop at McDonald's to use the bathrooms, and they often purchase food during their stop as well.

To encourage the retailers to clean the bathrooms, the manufacturer could enter into a contract that spells out the services that a retailer must perform. But

---

[3] Adapted from the writings of Michael Vita.

[4] For example, one study reports that apparel manufacturers' average gross profit margin is 46% compared with just 9% for "multiple apparel retailers." The authors note that this disparity in compensation for marginal sales "will limit the incentive of retailers to invest in developing and promoting their Web sites unless there is some form of co-op funding or restructured pricing." Robert Gertner and Robert Stillman, "Vertical Integration and Internet Strategies in the Apparel Industry," *Journal of Industrial Economics* 49 (2002): 415, 427.

[5] This phenomenon may be likely to arise in a franchise context. For example, although a restaurant franchisee using low-quality ingredients would lose repeat sales at its outlet, it may also cause fewer patrons to visit other franchisees' outlets as well. The low-quality franchisee does not internalize the full costs of actions that depreciate the brand-name capital of the franchisor. See Benjamin Klein, "The Economics of Franchise Contracts," *Journal of Corporate Finance* 2 (1995): 9; Paul H. Rubin, "The Theory of the Firm and the Structure of the Franchise Contract," *Journal of Law and Economics* 21 (1978): 223.

because retail service provisions like this can be complex and difficult to measure, a manufacturer often finds it impractical to write contracts that induce the "right" level of service. A brewer, for instance, may insist that a retailer store its beer in a certain way to preserve its quality. Unless the beer is properly stored, *total* demand for the manufacturer's beer (not merely demand at the offending retail location) would fall because consumers associate the poor quality not with the retailer's inadequate storage but with the manufacturer's brewing ability.[6]

To solve this problem, a manufacturer may utilize distribution policies that insulate retailers from intrabrand competition. By reducing intrabrand competition, a manufacturer can provide its retailers with sufficient profit to create incentives to supply the desired retail service.[7] It can do this by granting exclusive territories, thereby preventing competition among retailers for customers. Or they can fix a minimum retail price; however, that kind of price fixing is illegal in certain states and countries. By protecting retailers from intrabrand competition, both of these policies guarantee the retailers a higher profit on each sale, raising the incentive to provide demand-increasing services.

Limited distribution policies also can also prevent discounters from free-riding on a full-service retailer's efforts to increase demand.[8] Without exclusive territories, for example, a consumer may come to the full-service retailer to learn about the product from a knowledgeable and attentive sales staff, and then purchase from a discounter that offers lower prices. The discounter is able to offer lower prices because it doesn't incur the costs of providing service. Without protection from discounters, full-service retailers couldn't provide the level of service the manufacturer wants.[9]

Many practices that limit distribution are illegal under antitrust laws, especially if undertaken by a firm with a dominant share of the market. For example, European authorities have prohibited Coke from purchasing refrigerators for retail outlets (a demand-enhancing investment) because the practice

---

[6] See, e.g., *Adolph Coors Co. v. FTC*, 497 F.2d 1178 (10th Cir. 1974).

[7] See Benjamin Klein and Kevin M. Murphy, "Vertical Restraints as Contract Enforcement Mechanisms," *Journal of Law and Economics* 31 (1988): 265.

[8] See Lester G. Telser, "Why Should Manufacturers Want Fair Trade?," *Journal of Law and Economics* 3 (1960): 86. See also *Isaksen v. Vermont Castings, Inc.*, 825 F.2d 1158, 1161–62 (7th Cir.) (Posner, J.) (describing how minimum resale price maintenance can also be used to ensure dealers provide the proper level of service by preventing discounters from free-riding).

[9] Empirical studies of on-line marketing strategies find that manufacturers have tended to pursue Internet retailing in a way that preserves incentives to provide retail service. For example, one study finds that high-end fragrance producers that have restrictive distribution practices in the brick-and-mortar world are more likely to practice similarly restrictive distribution strategies on-line, such as offering their product only through their own Web site at an equal or higher price than is available elsewhere. See Judith Chevalier and Dennis Carlton, "Free Riding and Sales Strategies for the Internet," *Journal of Industrial Economics* 49 (December 2001): 441; see also Robert Gertner and Robert Stillman, "Vertical Integration and Internet Strategies in the Apparel Industry," *Journal of Industrial Economics* 49 (2002): 415. More generally, the empirical literature tends to show that vertical integration and restraints like resale price maintenance and exclusive dealing/exclusive territories typically tend to reduce price and/or induce demand-increasing investments. See James C. Cooper et al., "Vertical Antitrust Policy as a Problem of Inference," *International Journal of Industrial Organization* 23 (2005): 639.

may unfairly exclude rival soft drink manufacturers from retail outlets. In the United States, Dentsply has been convicted of excluding rival teeth manufacturers from its dealer distribution network. Similarly, 3M has been convicted of unfairly using discounts that encourage retailers to carry a full line of 3M products. This is called *abuse of dominance* in Europe and *monopolization* or *exclusion* in the United States. To avoid running afoul of these laws, we offer the following advice:

> *If you have significant market power, you should consider the effect any planned action will have on competitors.*

If your planned action is likely to hurt your competitors badly, be sure that such harm is a by-product of actions that have a sound business justification. These laws are in a state of flux right now, so be sure to seek counsel if your firm is dominant in your market and you are considering adopting contracts or practices that would disadvantage your competitors. Ironically, these laws, which were designed to protect competition, often end up protecting competitors—and hurting consumers.

PRICE DISCRIMINATION

Vertical integration into downstream sales of a product may allow a manufacturer to price discriminate. If there are two separate consumer groups who use the product differently, then integrating downstream can allow discrimination that would otherwise be defeated by arbitrage.

Suppose that a firm sells an herbicide to two groups, home gardeners and farmers. Home gardeners are willing to pay $5 for a one-liter spray bottle ($5 per liter), while the farmers are willing to pay $600 for a 200-liter barrel ($3 per liter).

An unintegrated herbicide manufacturer setting a single price per liter faces the usual price–quantity trade-off: She can sell only to retailers who serve home gardeners for $5 per liter, or she can sell to retailers serving both home gardeners and farmers for $3 per liter.

A vertically integrated herbicide manufacturer can do better by selling directly to consumers at different prices. If the manufacturer vertically integrates into the retail sector, it could produce and sell two different bottles at two different prices: $5 for the spray bottle and $600 for the 200-liter barrel.

Vertical integration is necessary for discrimination because it is often the only way to prevent arbitrage at the wholesale level. For example, if our manufacturer were to sell the herbicide to two separate downstream producers ($5 per liter to home retailers and $3 per liter to farm retailers), the farm retailer would find it profitable to compete for the higher-value home business by buying herbicide in 200-liter barrels and putting it in small spray bottles. This kind of arbitrage would defeat the price discrimination scheme. By vertically integrating, the manufacturer can prevent the farm retailer from competing for the home retail business.

Another reason vertical integration is necessary for sellers to be able to price discriminate is that some countries, like the United States, deem it illegal to give or receive a price discount at the wholesale level. The Robinson–Patman Act applies only to goods, not services; moreover, price discounts are acceptable if they are cost justified or done to match a competitor's price. But wholesale price discrimination in goods is otherwise illegal. This law means a retailer that doesn't receive the discount can sue you. Economists dislike the Robinson–Patman law because it can discourage discounting by manufacturers. Offering a discount to one retailer but not to another may violate the law, unless the discount is justified by the lower costs.

OUTSOURCING

No discussion of vertical integration would be complete without examining its opposite—*outsourcing*. The decision to outsource follows a logic that is exactly opposite to the logic of deciding to integrate vertically:

> *Outsource an activity to an upstream supplier or downstream customer if they can do it more profitably.*

Outsourcing is often a way to take advantage of a diseconomy of vertical integration. You should outsource if suppliers or customers can take advantage of economies of scale or scope that are not available to you, or if they can better align the retailers' incentives to manufacturers' goals than you can.

But outsourcing leaves you with less control than you might otherwise have over your upstream manufacturing process or your downstream distributors and retailers. If you outsource, you may create a double-markup problem; you may find it difficult to motivate your downstream customers or upstream suppliers to invest in activities that benefit you; and you may find it more difficult to price discriminate.

SUMMARY & HOMEWORK PROBLEMS

SUMMARY OF MAIN POINTS

- Do not purchase a customer or supplier merely because that customer or supplier is profitable. There must be a synergy that makes them more valuable to you than they are to their current owners. And do *not* overpay.
- If unrealized profit exists at one stage of the vertical supply chain—as often happens when regulations limit profit—a firm can capture some of the unrealized profit by integrating vertically, by **tying,** by **bundling,** or by **excluding** competitors.
- The double-markup problem occurs when complementary products compete with one another. Setting prices jointly eliminates the double-markup problem and is often a motive for vertical integration or maximum price contracts between a manufacturer and retailer.
- Restrictions on intrabrand competition like minimum resale price maintenance or exclusive territories provide retailers with higher profit, giving them incentives to provide demand-enhancing services to customers.
- If a product has two retail uses, a manufacturer may find it profitable to integrate downstream so that the firm can capture the profit through price discrimination. Vertical integration stops arbitrage between the two products, which allows price discrimination.
- Outsource an activity if the outsourcer can perform the activity better than you can.

MULTIPLE-CHOICE QUESTIONS

1. Alpha Industries is considering acquiring Foxtrot Flooring. Foxtrot is worth $20 million to its current owners under its existing operational methods. Due to some opportunities for synergies between the two companies, Alpha believes that Foxtrot is worth $25 million as part of Alpha Industries. What do you predict for a sale price of Foxtrot?
   a. Less than $20 million or Alpha will not buy
   b. More than $25 million or Foxtrot will not sell
   c. Something between $20 and $25 million
   d. The different valuations make a sale very unlikely.

2. Which of the following is an example of vertical integration?
- **a.** A custom software company purchasing a competing software firm
- **b.** A soft drink producer buying one of its bottling plants
- **c.** A coal manufacturer purchasing a nuclear power plant
- **d.** A gourmet cheese company purchasing a wine maker

3. In which of the following instances would an acquisition make the most sense?
- **a.** The acquiree is a very profitable company.
- **b.** Synergies exist between the acquirer and the acquiree.
- **c.** Integration costs are low between the two.
- **d.** Synergy benefits outweigh the costs of integration.

4. Giganto Grocery Chain wishes to sell Boldo detergent. Boldo's manufacturer, CPG Industries, will not supply Giganto unless Giganto agrees to carry all of CPG's other detergents. This is an example of
- **a.** exclusion.
- **b.** tying.
- **c.** territory restriction.
- **d.** bundling.

5. In which of the following cases might you expect to find a manufacturer granting exclusive territories?
- **a.** A pet supply chain that requires heavy local advertising to drive sales
- **b.** Custom computer sales that require a good deal of consultation
- **c.** A submarine sandwich chain that relies on its nationwide brand reputation
- **d.** All of the above

INDIVIDUAL PROBLEMS

20-1. Local Phone Companies
State utility commissions typically regulate local phone companies, but local phone companies also offer long-distance service to their customers. Rival long-distance carriers also connect to local phone lines to provide long-distance service to customers. Recently, the rival long-distance carriers have complained that the local phone company repair persons have put peanut butter on rival long-distance carrier's phone lines to encourage rats to eat through the lines. If true, is this a profitable strategy?

20-2. Tape Manufacturer
A transparent adhesive tape manufacturer produces a wide array of products, including sticky notes, as well as branded and unbranded adhesive tape of different sizes and shapes. Large office supply retailers, like Office Depot and Staples, carry only the most popular

SKUs (shopkeeping units—a unique product with its own bar code). The manufacturer's managers are convinced that they could make more sales if they could convince the retailers to carry a full line of its products. How could the manufacturer induce its retailer to carry a fuller line of products?

20-3. Artificial Tooth Manufacturer

An artificial tooth manufacturer sells teeth to distributors through a dealer network. The dealers sell to dental labs, which construct dentures for consumers. The manufacturer has spent a great deal of money advertising its teeth, and it has become the most popular brand of artificial teeth. It is now a dominant firm in the industry. But recently, it has discovered that its rivals are offering very attractive sales incentives for dealers to steer customers toward rival brands. How should the manufacturer respond to this competitive threat? Suggest at least two alternatives.

20-4. Copier Service

Suppose a copy machine manufacturer uses independent service operators (ISOs) to service its copiers. Recently, its machines have become more complex and difficult to service, and the manufacturer is concerned that the ISOs lack the necessary expertise to service the machines correctly. The manufacturer is especially concerned that customers who receive lousy service will blame the manufacturer if the machine breaks down, not the ISOs. How should the manufacturer address this problem?

20-5. Herbicide Integration

Suppose the herbicide manufacturer mentioned in the chapter can vertically integrate into just one of the downstream retail businesses, either home gardening or farming, but not both. Which one would allow the manufacturer to price discriminate?

GROUP PROBLEMS

G20-1. Managing Vertical Relationships

Identify a vertical relationship in your company and determine whether it could be managed more profitably by tying, bundling, exclusion, or vertical integration. Clearly identify the source of the profitability (regulatory evasion, elimination of double markup, goal alignment, or price discrimination), and describe how to exploit it. Estimate the gain in profit from the change.

G20-2. Undoing Vertical Relationships

Identify a vertical relationship in your company, and determine whether it could be managed more profitably by untying, unbundling, inclusion of rivals, or vertical disintegration. Clearly identify the source of the profitability (regulatory evasion, elimination of double markup, goal alignment, or price discrimination), and describe how to exploit it. Estimate the gain in profit from the change.

WRAPPING UP

Chapter 21   You Be the Consultant

Chapter 21

You Be the Consultant

The preceding chapters have given you the analytical tools to solve business problems on your own. In this chapter, we give you an opportunity to use these tools. Here, you can test yourself to see whether you have absorbed the material by working through more problems from real companies. We'll give you a brief description of a problem, after which you'll see a break in the text. At that point, take a couple of minutes to identify the source of the problem. Then propose a solution.

It is important to begin by breaking the problems down into two pieces: First figure out what's wrong, and then devise a solution. In a company, problem solving usually means identifying profitable decisions and then making sure the organization makes them. Avoid the trap of identifying a problem as simply a failure to implement a specific solution. This is a mistake because it locks you into a specific solution. Instead, identify a problem as an asset in a lower-valued use, not as a specific solution that hasn't been followed. For example, in "Getting Divisions to Work in the Firm's Best Interests" (Chapter 19), the problem facing the paper company was not that the transfer price was set too low; rather, it was that the Paper Division burned black liquor soap for fuel instead of using it for resin manufacturing. Beginning with the former characterization of the problem locks you into the specific solution of raising the transfer price. This may cause you to overlook other, better solutions—like turning the Paper Division into a cost center and setting a transfer price at marginal cost.

EXCESS INVENTORY OF PROSTHETIC HEART VALVES

Heart valve size is as varied as body size. So when a surgeon operates to replace a diseased valve, no one knows exactly what size replacement valve the patient will need. To ensure that the right size is available, medical device companies must keep an entire set of different-sized heart valves at a hospital.

The Heart Plus medical device company employs salespeople to place and maintain valve inventories at hospitals in each region. After a valve is used, Heart Plus bills the patient's insurance company and credits the salesperson with a sale.

Each salesperson earns a commission based on a percentage of revenue of the sales in her territory.

Because Heart Plus doesn't get paid until it sells its valves, it must bear the cost of holding inventory, calculated as the cost of capital (12%) multiplied by the wholesale cost of the valves placed at hospitals. The problem: Heart Plus faces a cost of holding inventory that's higher than its competitors' inventory costs. Heart Plus calls you in as a consultant to figure out what's wrong and to fix it.

Before Continuing, Try to Diagnose and Solve the Problem

Answer: Start by asking and answering our three questions.

1. *Who is making the bad decision?* The salesperson, who decides whether to put valves on inventory at a hospital, appears to be overstocking hospitals, raising inventory costs.

2. *Does she have enough information to make a good decision?* Through her continuing interactions with the hospitals and her specific sales experience, the salesperson knows whether it is profitable to keep valves on inventory at the hospital.

3. *And the incentive to do so?* However, the salesperson doesn't care about inventory costs because her evaluation and compensation depend only on the revenue she generates from sales.

The problem should now be clear. The only way a salesperson can make sales is to place valves at a hospital and wait for them to be used. She has an incentive to place as much inventory in hospitals as she can, regardless of whether the expected revenue covers the inventory holding costs. As a consequence, the salesperson places inventory at hospitals, even when the probability that the valve will be used is very small. Note that this problem is similar to the problems created by incentive conflict between marketing and sales discussed in Chapter 18. Our salesperson's rewards depend on maximizing revenue, so she ends up placing inventory at every hospital where MR > 0. To maximize profit, she should place inventory at hospitals only if Heart Plus expects to earn enough to cover the inventory holding costs—that is, only where MR > MC. In essence, salespeople behave as if making sales involves no costs.

To fix the problem, change the sales incentives so that the salesperson faces both the costs and the benefits of making sales. Evaluate her based on net revenue—revenue above the costs of carrying inventory. Rewarding the salesperson for increasing net revenue better aligns her incentives with the goals of the company. The salesperson will place heart valves only at hospitals where the expected revenue is above the costs of carrying inventory.

You can expect the salesperson to make fewer sales after the change, but this is exactly what you want because she stops making unprofitable sales. Also remember that fewer sales will translate into lower income for the salesperson. If you don't want to reduce her compensation, pay the salesperson a larger commission on net revenue—revenue minus the inventory carrying cost. Otherwise, sales compensation will fall, and the salesperson may quit. And due to adverse selection, the best salespeople are the ones who are more likely to quit.

HIGH TRANSPORTATION COSTS AT A COAL-BURNING UTILITY

A large coal-burning electric power plant is located on a river, and every week, a dozen barges arrive loaded with coal to feed the power plant. The Transportation Division of the parent company, which is responsible for transporting coal to the Power Plant Division, pays a barge company to make these deliveries.

Once the barge arrives at the docks, the Power Plant Division is responsible for unloading the barge. The Power Plant Division is very slow to unload barges, especially if more than one barge must be unloaded simultaneously, or if a barge arrives on a weekend. The Power Plant Division has just one crew of dockworkers, who rarely work overtime or on weekends. If the company ties up the barges for more than the usual three-day period, the barge companies charge the Transportation Division a fee (demurrage) for all time above and beyond the customary three-day unloading period. And because very few barges are unloaded within three days, the Transportation Division faces unusually high transportation costs. You are brought in to fix the problem.

Before Continuing, Try to Diagnose and Solve the Problem

Answer: Start by asking and answering our three questions:
1. *Who is making the bad decision?* The Power Plant Division is unloading the barges too slowly, raising costs for the Transportation Division.
2. *Does the Power Plant Division have enough information to make a good decision?* The Power Plant Division knows that leaving barges at the dock beyond three days penalizes the Transportation Division and knows the customary demurrage rates.
3. *And the incentive to do so?* Promptly unloading the barges would require overtime work from the dockworkers. Since dockworkers' overtime wages are twice the normal wages, the Power Plant Division saves money by waiting until the barges can be unloaded by workers during normal work hours.

The problem should now be obvious. The Power Plant Division decides when to unload the barges but doesn't face the profit consequences of its decision—the Transportation Division bears the costs of leaving full barges at the dock. Unloading more quickly requires overtime pay, so the Power Plant Division increases its own *division* profit by keeping the barges at the dock until they can be unloaded during regular work hours, requiring no overtime pay.

The simplest way to solve the problem is to compel the Power Plant Division to pay the barge company for late unloading. If the costs of paying overtime are less than the demurrage costs, the Power Plant will unload the barges within three days. If not, it won't. Either way, this solution aligns the incentives of the Power Plant Division with the profitability goals of the parent company.

OVERPAYING FOR ACQUIRED HOSPITALS

A health care management (HMO) company purchases orthopedic surgical hospitals and makes money by running them more efficiently. But of the 12 acquisitions the HMO made in 2002, 4 were unprofitable (not worth the purchase price).

Typically, the parties involved negotiate the purchase price using some multiple of operating cash flow, typically five to six times EBITDA.[1] When the development team (those in charge of making acquisitions) paid too much, the HMO found that the team typically overestimated EBITDA by a significant amount. One particularly egregious error involved the purchase of a Jackson, Wyoming, orthopedic hospital; they paid five times EBITDA based on six months of winter data. To compute annual EBITDA, the development team simply multiplied winter earnings by two. Since the hospital earned the bulk of its profit during ski season, the EBITDA estimates turned out to be 40% too high, translating into a purchase price $8 million too high.

Not only did the development team pay too much for the hospital, but its high budget estimates made it very difficult for the Operations Division to meet its profitability goals, which were based on the team's EBITDA estimate. Given the Operations Division staff's extensive experience, Operations had the expertise to forecast EBITDA accurately for new hospitals, but the development team performed this task as part of the acquisition evaluation process. The Operations Division's compensation was based on the percentage difference between actual EBITDA and budgeted EBITDA. However, the budget was set by the development team's purchase price, so Operations earned *no* bonus

---

[1] EBITDA—earnings before interest, taxes, depreciation, and amortization.

because budgeted EBIDTA exceeded actual EBITDA. Meanwhile, team members earned large bonuses based on the budgeted EBITDA of the acquired hospitals.

Before Continuing, Try to Diagnose and Solve the Problem

Answer: Start by asking and answering our three questions:

1. *Who made the bad decision?* The development team overestimated the EBITDA of acquired hospitals, leading to overpayment for the acquired hospitals.

2. *Did the development team have enough information to make a good decision?* Team members did not have enough information to estimate EBITDA; they lacked the expertise necessary to evaluate the earnings potential of acquired hospitals.

3. *Did the development team have the incentive to make a good decision?* Development team members earn compensation based on how much they pay for the hospitals, which is, in turn, based on budgeted EBITDA. And since they can manipulate EBITDA, they actually have an incentive to overpay for the acquired hospitals.

Asking and answering the three questions should make the problem obvious to all. The development team has neither the information nor the incentive to estimate future EBITDA accurately. The necessary expertise resides in Operations, not Development.

These circumstances immediately suggest two possible solutions: (1) Move the decision rights to acquire hospitals (now with Development) to those having the necessary information (Operations), or (2) move the necessary information to those who have the decision rights. The former option is probably not feasible. The skills necessary to purchase a company at a good price include much more than simply being able to forecast earnings accurately. Moreover, these skills are significantly different from those necessary to run the company.

The latter option would mean that Operations would be given a *ratification* role in estimating the target hospital's EBITDA. Operations must OK or ratify the purchase price of each acquired hospital. Because Operations has an obvious incentive to make sure the budgets are right, its compensation scheme may not need much adjustment.

Recall that we encountered a similar problem in Chapter 18, with the low profitability of newly opened general stores. In that case, the development executives deliberately overestimated profitability just to earn bonuses based on the number of stores they opened. Our solution there was to allow development executives to open only profitable stores, where profit was forecast using a statistical model based on area demographics. Here our solution is similar—require

Operations to estimate the EBITDA on which purchase price is based, but leave the negotiations with the development team.

LARGE E&O CLAIMS AT AN INSURANCE COMPANY

An insurance brokerage firm has more than 40 retail offices, each run as an independent profit center. The profit centers earn money by selling insurance to clients on behalf of several insurance carriers. The insurance company pays the brokerage 15% of the revenue it earns on insurance. In the case of an accident that is covered by the insurance policy, the insurance carrier pays for the resulting loss. The brokerage firm acts only as an intermediary between the insurance carrier and the client. At least, that's how it's supposed to work.

Too often, however, disputes arise over exactly what the policy covers. For example, a small business owner whose store has burned down may claim *replacement value,* the amount of money it would take to replace the store and the merchandise. The insurance company, however, may offer *book value,* what the owner originally paid for the store and merchandise. Unsurprisingly, replacement value is usually much higher than book value. The brokerage that sold the policy then finds itself in the middle of a dispute between the small business owner and the insurance carrier.

If a client's insurance carrier fails to pay a claim for loss and the client attributes that failure to misrepresentation[2] by the broker who sold the policy, the client files an errors & omission (E&O) claim against the brokerage that employs the broker. The brokerage must either litigate the case in court or settle with the client. If the brokerage decides to settle, the local retail office whose brokers sold the policy pays the first $250,000 of the claim and the parent company assumes responsibility for losses above that limit. The broker who actually sold the policy pays no part of the settlement.

The local retail offices have broad authority to negotiate settlements below $250,000, and they often hire local attorneys to represent them in these matters. For matters above $250,000, the local offices are supposed to refer the case to headquarters. Typically, however, they make this report very late in the process, long after the local brokers have made damaging statements that could harm the company in court.

Compared with similar insurance companies, our particular insurance brokerage seems to suffer a disproportionately high number of E&O losses. After

---

[2] Failing to procure appropriate coverage or failing to inform client properly.

several seven-figure jury verdicts, the brokerage hires you to reduce their E&O losses. What do you recommend?

Before Continuing, Try to Diagnose and Solve the Problem

Answer: Start by asking and answering our three questions:

1. *Who is making the bad decision?* Local brokers are settling too many E&O small claims in favor of the client. Also, the admissions they make to small clients open them up to larger losses when they litigate large cases. Brokerage employees appear more sympathetic to the client than to the brokerage that employs them.

2. *Do the local brokers have enough information to make a good decision?* The local brokers know whether the E&O claims are valid, but they're slow in passing this information along to the parent company.

3. *Do the local brokers have the incentive to make a good decision?* The revenue they earn on sales of insurance determines the brokers' evaluation and compensation. Consequently, they have no incentive to reduce E&O losses. In fact, they have an incentive to please the client, regardless of the merits of the claim, in order to preserve the sales commissions they earn on future business.

The problem should now appear obvious. The brokerage wants their employees to do two things—sell insurance *and* resolve disputes over E&O claims—but the brokerage rewards brokers for doing only one of these tasks. It's no surprise that the brokers devote most of their effort to selling and developing relationships with their clients. So, when disputes threaten those relationships with clients, they side with the clients.

You might suggest two obvious solutions to this problem. First, you could make the brokers bear the costs of resolving E&O claims in favor of their clients, say by subtracting the cost of E&O claims from the broker's commission. But sometimes E&O claims are not the broker's fault, and the size of just one claim could easily exceed the broker's entire income. In general, it's very difficult to balance incentive payments to motivate employees to perform two separate, but conflicting, tasks. One management tool, the *balanced scorecard,* promises to show you how to do this; the trouble is that it seems to confuse employees as often as it encourages them to give both tasks appropriate attention.

The second obvious solution is to split the tasks—let the brokers sell, and let the attorneys handle E&O disputes. In 1995, the company decided to give its legal department responsibility for all claims, both large and small. To make sure that the attorneys had enough information to know whether to settle or litigate the claims, the brokerage firm's managers created processes to transfer information about cases to the legal department as quickly as possible. They also performed regular audits to ensure that the local offices were not trying to settle claims on their own.

The early reporting of claims gave the legal department an opportunity to investigate matters at an early stage—before anyone could make damaging admissions or offers to resolve the client's loss. The early reporting also preserved critical documentary evidence that raised the probability of success at trial. In the first two years following the change, E&O losses decreased by more than 60%—a savings of more than $5 million. This figure includes neither the costs of transferring the information to the legal department nor the cost of periodic audits, so it probably overstates the savings.

Note that this solution involved taking decision rights away from those with the best information. While this authority transfer increased the costs of transmitting specific information to centralized decision-makers, it also reduced the incentive costs of settling bogus claims just to keep clients happy.

WHAT YOU SHOULD HAVE LEARNED

If you've read and understood this book, you should know how to

1. use the rational-actor paradigm to predict behavior,
2. use benefit–cost analysis to evaluate decisions,
3. use marginal analysis to make extent (how much) decisions,
4. compute break-even quantities to make investment decisions,
5. compute break-even price to make shutdown and pricing decisions,
6. set optimal prices and price discriminate,
7. predict industry-level changes using demand–supply analysis,
8. develop long-run strategies to increase firm value,
9. predict how your own actions will influence others' actions,
10. bargain effectively,
11. make decisions in uncertain environments,
12. solve the problems caused by moral hazard and adverse selection,
13. motivate employees to work in the firm's best interests,
14. motivate divisions to work in the best interests of the parent company, and
15. manage vertical relationships with upstream suppliers or downstream customers.

Now go forth and find unconsummated wealth-creating transactions, and devise ways to profitably consummate them.

Epilogue

Out of the Classroom, into the Fire—What I Learned as a Manager
by Luke Froeb

I finished this book while managing 110 employees in the Bureau of Economics at the Federal Trade Commission. The experience taught me much about management that isn't in this book.

The government has no well-defined goals, few metrics to measure performance, and no sticks or carrots to align employees' incentives with organizational goals. In addition, most federal employees are lifetime civil servants, with better information and strong ideas about what the agency should be doing. They can easily outlast the political appointees who come for just a few years.

The rational-actor paradigm predicts that government employees would shirk, or follow objectives of their own choosing. And while this is true of some, the majority work hard and take considerable pride in their work. If you want to accomplish anything during a short government stint, you have to identify these employees and motivate them to work toward a common goal.

But before you can work toward a common goal, you must have one. Set realistic goals during annual or semi-annual meetings that review past accomplishments, and outline what you hope to accomplish in the future. Be as specific as possible with time tables and measurable benchmarks.

Constantly monitor progress toward those goals. Otherwise, subordinates will infer that your priorities have changed and, as a consequence, stop working toward your goals. To guard against this, require weekly reports from your subordinates; ask questions during weekly meetings to assure them that you still care about what they're doing and to motivate them to keep making progress. Refine and re-adjust your goals as new information becomes available. If you discover that a goal has become too costly to reach, drop it and replace it with another.

If the organizational structure is broken, fix it. Otherwise, respect the organizational structure you have. This means letting your subordinates manage their own people. If you jump over them to become directly involved in specific matters, you're implicitly telling them that you don't think they're capable of doing their assigned jobs. Every time I did this, I ended up creating more work for subordinates with no better outcome.

Finally, manage yourself. Do not let your "In" box run your life. Put yourself on a schedule where you do the routine tasks at the same time every day. Exercise daily. Answer e-mail *only* once each day—otherwise, you'll soon find yourself glued to your computer, putting out fires rather than making progress toward your goals. Figure out what you can do that no one else in the organization is capable of doing, and then do it. If you find yourself doing something that your subordinates can do, stop. If you continue to do work that others could do, you're leaving undone those things that you ought to be doing, like working on a strategy to match the resources and capabilities of your organization to its external competitive environment.

A

Accounting costs—costs that appear on the financial statements of a company.

Accounting profit—profits as shown on a company's financial statements. Accounting profit does not necessarily correspond to real or economic profit.

Adverse selection—refers to the fact that "bad types" are likely to be selected in transactions where one party is better informed than the other. Examples include higher-risk individuals being more likely to purchase insurance, more low-quality cars (lemons) being offered for sale, or lazy workers being more likely to accept job offers. Adverse selection is a precontractual problem that arises from hidden information about risks, quality, or character.

Agency costs—costs associated with moral hazard and adverse selection problems.

Agent—a person who acts on behalf of another individual, a principal. Principal–agent problems are created by the incentive conflict between principals and agents.

Aggregate demand curve—describes the buying behavior of a group of consumers: We add up all the individual demand curves to get an aggregate demand curve (the relationship between the price and the number of purchases made by a group of consumers).

Average cost—the total cost of production divided by the number of units produced.

Avoidable costs—costs that you get back if you shut down operations.

B

Break-even price—the price that you must charge to at least break even (make zero profit). It is equal to average avoidable cost per unit.

Break-even quantity—the amount you need to sell to at least break even (make zero profit). The formula (assuming that you can sell all you want at price and with constant marginal cost) is $Q = F/(P - MC)$, where F is fixed costs, P is price, and MC is marginal cost.

Bundling—the practice of offering multiple goods for sale as one combined product.

Buyer surplus—the difference between the buyer's value (what he is willing to pay) and the price (what he has to pay).

C

Common-value auction—in a common-value auction, the value is the same for each bidder, but no one knows what it is. Each bidder has only an estimate of the unknown value, and the value is the same for everyone. In common-value auctions, bidders have to bid below their values in order to avoid the winner's curse.

Compensating wage differentials—in equilibrium, differences in wages that reflect differences in the *inherent* attractiveness of various professions or jobs.

Competitive industry—competitive industries are characterized by these three factors: (1) firms produce a product or service with very close substitutes so they have very elastic demand, (2) firms have many rivals and no cost advantage over those rivals, and (3) the industry has no barriers to entry or exit.

Complement—a good whose demand increases when the price of another good decreases. Examples include a parking lot and shopping mall or a hamburger and a hamburger bun.

Constant returns to scale—when average costs are constant with respect to output level.

Consumer surplus—see **Buyer surplus.**

Contribution margin—the amount that one unit contributes to profit. It is defined as Price – Marginal Cost.

D

Controllable factor—something that affects demand that a company can change. Examples include price, advertising, warranties, and product quality.

Cost center—a division whose parent company rewards it for reducing the cost of producing a specified output.

Cross-price elasticity of demand—the cross-price elasticity of demand for Good A with respect to the price of Good B measures the percentage change in demand of Good A caused by a percentage change in the price of Good B.

D

Decreasing returns to scale—see **Diseconomies of scale.**

Demand curves—describe buyer behavior and tell you how much consumers will buy at a given price.

Direct price discrimination scheme—a price discrimination scheme in which we can identify members of the low-value group, charge them a lower price, and prevent them from reselling their lower-priced goods to the higher-value group.

Discount rate—the interest rate used to discount future cash flows. It converts future dollars into present value by the formula $C_0 = C_t/(1 + r)^t$, where r is the discount rate, C_t measures cash "t" periods in the future, and C_0 measures cash in the present.

Diseconomies of scale—diseconomies of scale exist when average costs rise with output.

Diseconomies of scope—diseconomies of scope exist when the cost of producing two products jointly is more than the cost of producing those two products separately.

E

Economic profit—a measure of profit that includes recognition of implicit costs (like the cost of equity capital). Economic profit measures the true profitability of decisions.

Economies of scale—economies of scale exist when average costs fall as output increases.

Economies of scope—economies of scope exist when the cost of producing two products jointly is less than the cost of producing those two products separately.

Efficient—an economy is efficient if all assets are employed in their highest-valued uses.

Elastic—a demand curve on which percentage quantity changes more than percentage price is said to be elastic, or sensitive to price. If $|e| > 1$, demand is elastic, where e is the price elasticity of demand.

English auction—see **Oral auction**.

Exclusion—the practice of blocking competitors from participating in a market.

Extent decision—a decision regarding how much or how many of a product to produce.

F

First Law of Demand—consumers demand (purchase) more as price falls, assuming other factors are held constant (i.e., demand curves slope downward).

Fixed costs—costs that do not vary with output.

Fixed-cost fallacy—consideration of costs that do not vary with the consequences of your decision (also known as the sunk-cost fallacy).

Functionally organized firm—a firm in which various divisions perform separate tasks, such as production and sales.

H

Hidden-cost fallacy—occurs when you ignore relevant costs, those costs that do vary with the consequences of your decision.

I

Implicit costs—additional costs that do not appear on the financial statements of a company. These costs include items like the opportunity cost of capital.

Incentive conflict—the fact that principals and agents often have different goals.

Income elasticity of demand—income elasticity of demand measures the percentage change in demand arising from a percentage change in income.

Increasing returns to scale—see Economies of scale.

Indifference principle—if an asset is mobile, then in long-run equilibrium, the asset will be indifferent about where it is used; that is, it will make the same profit no matter where it goes.

Indirect price discrimination scheme—a price discrimination scheme in which a seller cannot directly identify low- and high-value consumers or cannot prevent arbitrage between two groups. The seller can still practice indirect price discrimination, by designing products or services that appeal to groups with different price elasticities of demand.

Inelastic—a demand curve on which percentage change in quantity is smaller than percentage change in price is said to be inelastic, or insensitive to price. If $|e| < 1$, demand is price-inelastic.

Inferior goods—for inferior goods, demand decreases as income increases.

L

Law of diminishing marginal returns—as you try to expand output, your marginal productivity (the extra output associated with extra inputs) eventually declines.

Learning curves—when current production lowers future costs.

Long-run equilibrium—when firms are in long-run equilibrium, economic profit is zero (including the opportunity cost of capital), firms break even, and price equals average cost (i.e., no one wants to enter or leave the industry).

M

Marginal cost (MC)—the additional cost incurred by producing and selling one more unit.

Marginal profit—the extra profit from producing and selling one more unit (MR – MC).

Marginal revenue (MR)—the additional revenue gained from selling one more unit.

Market equilibrium—the price at which quantity supplied equals quantity demanded.

Mean reversion—suggests that performance eventually moves back toward the mean or average.

M-form firm—a company whose divisions perform all the tasks necessary to serve customers of a particular product or in a particular geographic area.

Monopoly—a firm that is the single seller in its market. Monopolies have market power because they produce a product or service with no close substitutes, they have no rivals, and barriers to entry prevent other firms from entering the industry.

Moral hazard—postcontractual increases in risky or negative behavior. Examples include reduced incentive to exercise care once you purchase insurance and reduced incentives to work hard once you have been hired. Moral hazard is similar to adverse selection in that it is caused by information asymmetry; it differs in that it is caused by hidden actions rather than hidden types.

Movement along the demand curve—change in quantity demanded in response to change in price.

N

Nash equilibrium—a pair of strategies, one for each player, in which each strategy is a best response against the other.

Nonstrategic view of bargaining—a view that does not focus on the explicit rules of the game to understand the likely outcome of the bargaining. This view says that the likely outcome of bargaining is determined by each players gains to agreement relative to alternatives to agreement.

Normal goods—for normal goods, demand increases as income increases.

NPV rule—if the present value of the net cash flows is larger than zero, the project is profitable (i.e., earns more than the opportunity cost of capital).

O

Opportunity cost—the opportunity cost of an alternative is the profit you give up to pursue it.

Oral auction—in this auction type, bidders submit increasing bids until only one bidder remains. The item is awarded to the last remaining bidder.

P

Postinvestment hold-up—an attempt by a trading partner to renegotiate the terms of trade after one party has made a sunk cost investment or investment specific to the relationship.

Price ceilings—a type of price control that outlaws trade at prices above the ceiling.

Price discrimination—the practice of charging different people or groups of people different prices that are not cost-justified.

Price elasticity of demand (e)—a measure of how responsive quantity demanded is to changes in price. Formula: (% change in quantity demanded) ÷ (% change in price).

Price floors—a type of price control that outlaws trade at prices below the floor.

Principal—an individual who hires another (an agent) to act on his or her behalf.

Prisoners' dilemma—a game in which conflict and cooperation are in tension; self-interest leads the players to outcomes that no one likes. It is in each player's individual interest to not cooperate regardless of what the other does. Thus, both players end up not cooperating. Their joint interest would be better served, however, if they could find a way to cooperate.

Profit center—a division whose parent company evaluates it on the basis of the profit it earns.

R

Random variable—a variable whose values (outcomes) are random and therefore unknown. The distribution of possible outcomes, however, is known. Random variables are used to explicitly take account of uncertainty.

Rational-actor paradigm—this paradigm says that people act rationally, optimally, and self-interestedly.

Relevant benefits—all benefits that vary with the consequence of a decision.

Relevant costs—all costs that vary with the consequence of a decision.

Risk premium—higher expected rates of return that compensate investors in risky assets. In equilibrium, differences in the rate of return reflect differences in the riskiness of an investment.

Risk-averse—a risk-averse individual values a lottery at *less* than its expected value.

Risk-neutral—a risk-neutral individual values a lottery *at* its expected value.

Robinson–Patman Act—part of a group of laws collectively called the *antitrust laws* governing competition in the United States. Under the Robinson–Patman Act, it's illegal to give or receive a price discount on a good sold to another business. This law does not cover services and sales to final consumers.

S

Screening—a solution to the problem of adverse selection that describes the efforts of a less informed party to gather information about the more informed party. Information may be gathered indirectly by offering consumers a menu of choices, and consumers reveal information about their type by the choices they make. A successful screen means that it is unprofitable for bad types to mimic the behavior of good types. Any successful screen can also be used as a signal.

Sealed-bid first-price auction—a sealed bid auction in which the highest bidder gets the item at a price equal to his bid.

Second-price auction—see **Vickrey auction.**

Seller surplus—the difference between price (what the seller is able to sell for) and the seller's value (what she is willing to sell for).

Sequential-move games—in these games, players take turns, and each player observes what his or her rival did before having to move.

Shift of the demand curve—a change in demand caused by any variable except price. If demand increases (shifts up), consumers demand larger quantities of the good at the same price. If demand decreases (shifts down), consumers demand lower quantities of the good at the same price. Shifts are caused by factors like advertising, changes in consumer tastes, and product quality changes.

Signaling—a solution to the problem of adverse selection that describes an informed party's effort to communicate her type, risk, or value to less informed parties by her actions. A successful signal is one that bad types won't mimic. Any successful signal can also be used as a screen.

Simultaneous-move games—in these games, players move at the same time.

Specific investments—investments that lack value outside of a particular relationship. They are similar to sunk costs in that the costs are "sunk" in the relationship.

Stay-even analysis—analysis that allows you to determine the volume required to offset a change in cost, price, or other revenue factor.

Strategic view of bargaining—a view that focuses on how the outcome of bargaining games depends on the specific rules of the game, such as who moves first, who can commit to a bargaining position, or whether the other player can make a counteroffer.

Substitute—a good whose demand increases when price of another good increases. Two brands of cola soft drinks are substitutes.

Sunk costs—costs that cannot be recovered. They are unavoidable even in the long run.

Sunk-cost fallacy—see **Fixed-cost fallacy.**

Supply curves—describe the behavior of sellers and tell you how much will be offered for sale at a given price.

T

Tying—the practice of making the sale of one good conditional on the purchase of an additional, separate good.

U

Uncontrollable factor—something that affects demand that a company cannot control. Examples include consumer income, weather, and interest rates.

Unit elastic—If $|e| = 1$, demand is unit price elastic, where e is the price elasticity of demand.

V

Value—an individual's value for a good or service is the amount of money he or she is willing to pay for it.

Variable costs—costs that change as output levels change.

Vertical integration—refers to the common ownership of two firms in separate stages of the vertical supply chain that connects raw materials to finished goods.

Vickrey auction—a sealed-bid auction in which the item is awarded to the highest bidder, but the winner pays only the second-highest bid.

W

Winner's curse—the winner's curse arises in common value auctions and refers to the fact that the "winner" of the auction is usually the bidder with the highest estimate of the item's value. To avoid bidding too aggressively, bidders should bid as if their estimate is the most optimistic and reduce their estimate accordingly.

INDEX